T0400115

THE CITY AROUSED

THE WILLIAM & BETTYE NOWLIN SERIES
in Art, History, and Culture of the Western Hemisphere

THE CITY AROUSED

Queer Places and Urban Redevelopment in Postwar San Francisco

Damon Scott

University of Texas Press *Austin*

Requests for permission to reproduce material from this work should be sent to:
    Permissions
    University of Texas Press
    P.O. Box 7819
    Austin, TX 78713-7819
    utpress.utexas.edu

♾ The paper used in this book meets the minimum requirements of ANSI/NISO
Z39.48-1992 (R1997) (Permanence of Paper).

Library of Congress Cataloging-in-Publication Data

Names: Scott, Damon, author.
Title: The city aroused : queer places and urban redevelopment in postwar San Francisco
    / Damon Scott.
Description: First edition. | Austin : University of Texas Press, 2024. | Includes bibli-
    ographical references and index.
Identifiers: LCCN 2023009360 (print) | LCCN 2023009361 (ebook)
    ISBN 978-1-4773-2834-7 (hardcover)
    ISBN 978-1-4773-2835-4 (pdf)
    ISBN 978-1-4773-2836-1 (epub)
Subjects: LCSH: Gay bars—California—San Francisco—History. | Gay bars—Political
    aspects—California—San Francisco—History. | Sexual minority community—
    Political activity—California—San Francisco—History. | Sexual minority
    community—California—San Francisco—History. | City planning—Political
    aspects—California—San Francisco—History. | Urban renewal—Political aspects—
    California—San Francisco—History.
Classification: LCC HQ76.3.U62 S368 2024 (print) | LCC HQ76.3.U62 (ebook) |
    DDC 306.7609794/61—dc23/eng/20230518
LC record available at https://lccn.loc.gov/2023009360
LC ebook record available at https://lccn.loc.gov/2023009361

doi:10.7560/328347

CONTENTS

ACKNOWLEDGMENTS

This project began many years ago when I was a graduate student in a sun-filled living room in the Haight-Ashbury neighborhood of San Francisco. As a summer intern at the Gay, Lesbian, Bisexual, and Transgender Historical Society of Northern California, I had volunteered to create a map of queer sites of historical significance in the city. In his apartment crammed with memorabilia, the Society's archivist, Willie Walker, shared with me his annotated list of gay bars, bathhouses, bookstores, restaurants, cruising spots, and other places. He and several of his predecessors had culled the names and addresses of these sites from newspapers, organizational records, and oral histories beginning in the 1980s. With deep gratitude, I dedicate the following pages to Walker and a generation of gay community historians, archivists, and preservationists in and out of academia who have endeavored to document and interpret San Francisco's queer past.

The maps I created that summer drew my attention to a handful of long-gone waterfront bars with addresses that no longer existed. Like much of the surrounding area, these once-popular queer nightlife spots of the 1940s and 1950s had been razed and rebuilt in the 1960s. When I moved to the city in the early 1990s, I knew this area firsthand as a great place to meet up with friends during our lunch break. Most of us were recent college graduates who had moved to the city together and supported ourselves with temporary office jobs. With jackhammers removing remnants of the earthquake-damaged Embarcadero Freeway as a backdrop, Justin Herman Plaza was our preferred place to sit on a bench or stairstep while we ate the sandwiches we had brought from home. We had no inkling of the queer history of the area nor the details of its demise under Herman's tenure as head of the San Francisco Redevelopment Agency. I wish Jim Smith—a dear friend and my first lunch companion—were still here to read these lines. He would be delighted.

In graduate school at the University of Texas at Austin, the Social Science Research Council's Sexuality Fellowship program supported my preliminary research based on Walker's "queer sites" lists. During this early stage of the project, Steven Hoelscher and Susan Stryker were instrumental in helping me conceptualize past queer places as bound up with the social and material transformation of urban landscapes. My early efforts to map queer sites in San Francisco led to a collaboration with the Friends of 1800, a pioneering LGBTQ preservation group. They hired me to draft a context statement outlining the rationale for creating the country's first LGBTQ historic district. It was these early attempts to interpret sites of historical significance, as well as the limitations of primary sources about past queer places, that sparked my foray into the city's urban planning and redevelopment archives—which became the basis of this book.

Numerous archivists and librarians helped me access sources to piece together the social history and legacy of the queer waterfront. I am indebted to the staff of the GLBT Historical Society, the San Francisco History Center, the San Francisco Public Library, the California State Archives, the California State Law Library, the Special Collections at the University of California, Santa Cruz, and the Special Collections at the California State University, Northridge. I am especially grateful for the diligence, foresight, and generosity of contributors to the GLBT Historical Society's oral history collection, including Allan Bérubé, Paul Gabriel, Jim Duggins, Martin Meeker, Nan Boyd, Len Evans, Terence Kissack, Jim Breeden, Susan Stryker, Everett Erlandson, and Willie Walker.

Staffs at several other archives and repositories provided invaluable assistance in uncovering the history and fate of gay bars on the waterfront. Carmen Mohr at the Central Records Division of the Office of Community Investment and Infrastructure, the successor agency of the San Francisco Redevelopment Agency, was particularly helpful in providing access to newspaper clippings, administrative records, and property management records related to the Golden Gateway urban renewal project. San Francisco Public Library reference librarians assisted with tracking down and providing access to its rich holdings of government documents and serial publications, many of which were fortuitously available online at archives.org. San Francisco History Center staff shared their expertise in helping me locate relevant manuscript collections, reproduce historical photographs, track down property records, and build a pre–urban renewal base map of the waterfront. Finally, the Environmental Design Archives staff provided access to sources on the area's interrelated histories of freeway development, park planning, and urban renewal.

In developing the arguments and structure of this book, I benefited from feedback from scholars and students in several forums. At several meetings of the Society for American City and Regional Planning Historians (SACRPH), Alison Isenberg provided invaluable input and suggestions on the project. I thank her also for inviting me to share an earlier draft with her graduate student seminar. In addition, the Miami University Humanities Center has been a productive venue for stimulating deeper thinking about the meaning and significance of the queer archive of postwar urban redevelopment that I have assembled. My thanks go to Tim Melley, Luis "Iñaki" Pradanos-Garcia, and Cathy Wagner. Finally, I am also grateful for the assistance of Lana Pochiro, who, as an undergraduate research apprentice, helped me map the queer world of the pre–urban renewal waterfront.

At the University of Texas Press, I thank my editor, Robert Devens, for skillfully shepherding this project through the publishing process from proposal to finished book. The two external readers selected by the press also deserve special recognition for carefully reviewing several drafts and providing invaluable comments. Thanks also to Adrienne Gilg, Robert S. Kimzey, and Danni Bens for their roles at the press in producing this book and putting it out into the world. Several people deserve credit for helping me clarify, refine, and polish the text, including Kelly Waldrop, Beth Sherouse, and Carolyn Elerding. I also thank Ursula Roma and Alex Cox for their assistance and patience in producing multiple illustrations based on my preliminary sketches.

I benefited from the support of many family members and friends who spurred me to bring this book to the light of day. I thank my parents, John and Sunny Scott, for telling me they are proud of me—seemingly always when I need to hear it the most. I also express my deep appreciation for the friends and colleagues who sustained me when my home institution valued me as a teacher, not a scholar. In addition, I owe a debt of gratitude to Jim Smith, Kelly Quinn, Nishani Frazier, Marguerite Shaffer, Andrew Busch, Elena Albarrán, Juan Carlos Albarrán, Roxanne Ornelas, Ana María Díaz Burgos, Sergio Gutiérrez Negrón, and Susan Vallade. Finally, I reserve my most heartfelt appreciation for my partner, José Amador, who has stood by me through the many seasons of this project. It is because we have been able to build a home and a livelihood together that this book was ever even possible. His wisdom, words, and spirit infuse the pages of this book. Te quiero mucho, amorcito!

THE CITY AROUSED

INTRODUCTION
Exodus on the Eve of Destruction

On the evening of April 18, 1962, George Bauman, a gay bar operator evicted to make way for construction on the Embarcadero Freeway, proclaimed: "Jack's Waterfront will close its doors at midnight at 111 Embarcadero and will open its doors at 12:01 [A.M.] at 226 Embarcadero." Determined not to leave behind any half-empty bottles as they prepared to vacate the premises, the bartenders poured stiff drinks to the large crowd of regulars and well-wishers. Half an hour before midnight, patrons began stripping the interior furnishings from the bar, removing the wall décor, the bamboo drapes, the ashtrays, and a sign above the door that read, "If you are molested here, tell the management." Taller patrons pulled the star decals off the ceiling. Then at midnight, they all left the original Jack's and walked the quarter-mile distance along the Embarcadero to the bar's new, larger waterfront quarters in the former Seaboard Hotel—which they renamed the "Edgewater Hotel." In the new location, Bauman reopened Jack's in a space just off the ground-floor lobby and soon began renting out the refurbished hotel rooms upstairs to both permanent and transient guests.

Jack's had the unenviable honor of being the first of a network of waterfront gay bars to be razed as a part of San Francisco's ambitious urban redevelopment program (see figure 0.1). As part of a national wave of downtown expansion projects designed to replace blighted districts with urban freeways, modern housing, and gleaming office towers, city authorities opted to fast-track a plan devised by corporate leaders to secure federal urban renewal funds to redevelop much of the Embarcadero waterfront and the adjacent wholesaling district. Jack's demolition would make way for a set of new highway ramps that linked the Embarcadero Freeway to a massive new parking garage topped by a new office tower on the site of the city's

FIGURE 0.1 Jack's Waterfront Hangout (ca. 1958), located across from the Ferry Building, became a popular gay nightclub when George Bauman took over management in the fall of 1957. (San Francisco Redevelopment Agency Records, San Francisco History Center, San Francisco Public Library.)

former produce market. In less than a decade, these ramps and the new urban spaces taking shape adjacent to them transformed the historic core of the city's port operations into a modern, automobile-oriented "Golden Gateway" composed of office blocks, luxury apartment buildings, and parks. Placing blame for the bar's destruction on the mayor, gay-newspaper publisher Guy Strait equated the decision to tear down Jack's with paving over relics from classical antiquity (figure 0.2).[1]

Local law enforcement and patrons alike were aware of the relocation of Jack's well in advance. The moving party had been advertised for weeks in a bar rag published by and for gay patrons. Strait, publisher of the *Citizen's*

"But this is the way that Christopher did it in San Francisco"

FIGURE 0.2 The city's first gay newspaper, the *LCE News*, criticized Greek American mayor George Christopher's disregard for Jack's Waterfront Hangout by equating the gay bar with the cultural and civic landmarks of ancient Athens. The text below the cartoon proclaims, "But this is the way that Christopher did it in San Francisco." (*LCE News*, April 30, 1962, 3, microfilm, San Francisco Public Library.)

News, San Francisco's first newspaper "of particular interest" to gay bar patrons, characterized the closure of Jack's as a cataclysmic loss for the city by making a series of historical parallels. He referred to the day of the move as "D-Day," which coincided with the anniversary of the 1906 earthquake and fire that destroyed much of the city. He speculated that if the survivors of that calamity who laid a commemorative wreath that morning could have seen the parade of men clad in black leather motorcycle jackets leaving Jack's at the end of the day, they would have died of shock.[2] He called the procession of patrons laden with furnishings from the bar an "Exodus."[3] The crowd, however, did not protest the eviction, nor did the police enforce it. Instead, the bar patrons threw a party to mark the occasion. These hijinks played out not behind closed doors but publicly on the streets of San Francisco, with the police nowhere in sight.

Jack's moving party in 1962 marked the end of a relatively permissive period of queer nightlife on the waterfront. State and city officials had been directly involved in the continuing operation of Jack's Waterfront, *as a gay bar*, for nearly five years. Bauman, a popular gay bartender from north of the city, took over Jack's in the fall of 1957. At the time, the building was owned by state officials responsible for managing the port. They, along with local law enforcement and state liquor agents, were on board with the new operation. Over several years, police officers extorted $2,900 in protection money from Bauman.[4] One sergeant brought his wife in for a drink and showed her the paintings of unclothed men hanging on the wall. When rumors circulated about an imminent crackdown, a local patrolman reassured Bauman that Jack's would be spared. In 1959, the port officials sold the building to the State Division of Highways.[5] In the transaction, one state agency transferred Bauman's lease to another, which continued collecting commercial rent from the gay bar.[6] By the time highway officials evicted the Jack's crowd from a building to prepare the site for two new freeway ramps, the state agency had been the bar's landlord for several years. Remarkably, Bauman was able to take over Jack's, turn it into a gay bar, and keep it open for years with the support of state and local officials.

The tacit support Jack's received grew out of shifting policing tactics and urban redevelopment objectives of local leaders during the 1950s. In the early 1950s, San Francisco's seamen's haunts on the waterfront became a vibrant gay cruising strip as an unintended consequence of the systematic expulsion of homosexuals from the merchant marines and naval forces up and down the West Coast. Business leaders and city officials responded by cracking down on those bars frequented by merchant marines that had growing crowds of homosexuals. After bar raids, street sweeps, and liquor license suspensions proved ineffective, local law enforcement and state liquor agents treated the waterfront as a queer containment zone, a place set aside to isolate the homosexual threat within the heteronormative metropolis.[7] Turning the waterfront into a marginal vice district reserved for queer nightlife primed the area for redevelopment. Exposés of so-called hangouts for homosexuals helped make a case for declaring the waterfront blighted while also driving down the cost of a federally backed urban redevelopment proposal to raze and rebuild much of the area.

Rooted in the dialectics of society and space, *The City Aroused* argues that significant change in the understanding and valorization of categories of sexual difference emerged in the early 1960s in San Francisco as a response to critical changes in the urban built environment. State actors had a hand in the creation and destruction of a circuit of gay bars on the San Francisco waterfront from the late 1940s to the early 1960s. The drinking publics within these bars mounted one of the most historically significant, sustained, collective responses to multiple forms of antigay discrimination in the twentieth century. Queer waterfront hangouts, which supported a racially diverse public of gay patrons, leather men, drag performers, and transgender people, became an explicit target of urban renewal when San Francisco's pro-growth coalition sought to replace queer land uses with heteronormative, desexualized land uses that served larger postwar urban development objectives. Urban redevelopment, however, not only physically reshaped the social and sexual terrain of the city, it brought queer San Franciscans into a collective struggle *to act as a community*, first to defend and then reconstitute their gathering places ahead of the bulldozer.

In looking at the historical roots of these transformations, *The City Aroused* interrogates how the former hangouts of working-class men in the maritime trades on the San Francisco waterfront became sites where queer drinking publics coalesced and challenged the heteronormative state in the postwar era. In the early 1950s, the transformation of these seamen's hangouts into a circuit of gay bars was an unintended consequence of an intensive federal initiative to identify and isolate homosexuals from Pacific ports, shipping lanes, and naval facilities up and down the West Coast. By the decade's end, these hangouts no longer functioned as informal social hubs for the city's maritime labor force but had become a strip of gay bars and nightclubs controlled by local law enforcement and state liquor agents. To clean up other areas and put a lid on the city's growing gay population, government officials attempted to contain queer nightlife to a margin of the city slated for urban renewal. By the early 1960s, a new network of patrons, staff, and operators of these gathering places organized collectively to challenge an onslaught of liquor licensing revocations, police crackdowns, and commercial evictions as physical destruction loomed large. Despite collective actions against persecution, the wrecking ball and bulldozer ultimately razed five gay bars to clear the ground for the Golden Gateway project and Embarcadero Freeway. Other urban rehabilitation and rebuilding projects in the immediate vicinity shuttered or destroyed related land uses, including residential hotels, bars, and restaurants, that were also part of the queer world of the waterfront.

PLANNING AND STATE POWER

The City Aroused argues that gay community-organizing developed on the San Francisco waterfront in the early 1960s as a collective response to urban redevelopment. The following chapters trace how the waterfront became a national epicenter of queer containment during the Lavender Scare and how gay bar operators and patrons responded when city leaders acted on plans to raze and rebuild the area. Following the expulsion of suspected homosexuals from the maritime labor force, state and local officials treated the San Francisco waterfront as a vice containment area reserved for the city's growing queer nightlife crowds. By deploying targeted bar raids and vagrancy arrests, local law enforcement and state liquor control agents prioritized driving gay men out of the parks and established nightlife strips adjacent to the downtown shopping and business districts, namely Union Square, the Tenderloin, and North Beach.[8] At the same time, seamen's haunts on the waterfront grew increasingly queer in their patronage under a payola system involving police, state liquor agents, and bar operators. In the mid-1960s, queer containment on the waterfront unraveled when urban renewal officials dismantled property relations and demolished buildings in the area. During the planning phase of urban renewal, queer containment to the blocks slated for redevelopment both depressed property values and created an opening for queer drinking crowds to grow. Once land acquisition began, queer displacements became a catalyst for organized, collective resistance among members of a new queer counterpublic of bar operators, staff, and patrons.

Building on critiques of heteronormative government policies and programs, *The City Aroused* locates the workings of state-led heterosexism at the municipal level in anxieties about San Francisco's economic future during the 1950s.[9] Federal bureaucracies took aggressive steps during and after World War II to build what Margot Canady calls the "straight state" by codifying a homosexual/heterosexual binary in immigration, military, and social welfare policy.[10] In the late 1940s and early 1950s, anti-communist ideologues rationalized the systematic identification and exclusion of homosexuals from positions of public trust as a national defense measure. During the Lavender Scare, the Truman and Eisenhower administrations purged thousands of so-called sexual perverts from naval forces and the maritime trades on the West Coast, declaring them national security risks vulnerable to communist influence and blackmail.[11] The incorporation of homosexuals as an explicitly stigmatized category in administrative codes, statutes, and legal findings was a means of both marginalizing sex and gender "deviates" and privileging heteronormative social reproduction. By the 1950s, a heteronormative ideology of "domestic containment" framed the suburban home as a privileged sphere of sexual citizenship insulated from a perceived internal threat from racialized, queer subversives.[12]

During the 1950s and 1960s, urban renewal and freeway building became powerful tools championed by pro-growth coalitions in many cities to reverse declines in central city land values and tax revenues. They pushed through aggressive programs to redevelop the least desirable sections of cities across the country with large-scale land clearance and rebuilding initiatives.[13] Federal urban renewal assistance enabled localities to acquire, raze, and dispose of large swaths of "blighted" urban land by underwriting the expense of land assembly and empowering local authorities to compel property owners to sell their holdings.[14] To qualify for federal aid under the 1954 Housing Act, cities adopted comprehensive plans that specified the interdependence and location of proposed urban renewal projects and new urban freeway networks. Siting redevelopment schemes to facilitate direct freeway access to the central city became a common, blunt instrument for land use planning. From the perspective of pro-growth advocates, freeways helped clear blighted blocks, partition the city into community areas, segregate different land uses, and incentivize redevelopment in adjacent properties.

In delineating and prioritizing urban renewal and freeway projects, pro-growth proponents in government and the private sector often slated communities of color and residential hotel districts for destruction.[15] They did this by explicitly using race as an index for tagging blocks for land clearance and rebuilding.[16] As a result, postwar urban renewal and highway-building projects, along with racially discriminatory real estate practices, zoning codes, deed restrictions, homeowner associations, and education policies, systematically advantaged suburbanizing white families at the expense of urban communities of color.[17]

Heterosexism also shaped the postwar vision and planning interventions for modernizing and revitalizing cities.[18] As the Cold War came to dominate every aspect of American culture and society, suburban housing policies and built environments reinforced white, heteronormative cultural values.[19] From coast to coast, city planners often deployed discourses of social order/disorder, instituted prescriptive assumptions about family and household relations, and imposed legal geographies of private and public rights over land uses, all to the detriment of queer people.[20] In the case of Northern California, for instance, historian Clayton Howard shows how federal housing policies and programs fueled an exodus of heterosexual families to the suburbs. Anxious about the growing queer segment of the population, redevelopment officials and police responded by trying to clean up or demolish residential hotels and nightlife districts in an effort to lure families back to the city.[21] This fits a broader pattern of sexual- and gender-transgressive people and places serving as evidence of urban decline and a pretext for redevelopment.[22]

As these and other scholars have shown, declension narratives about sex in the city were powerful in formulating and advancing urban renewal proposals during the 1950s.[23] City leaders used discourses of social disorder, physical dilapidation, functional obsolescence, economic decline, poor sanitation, negligent care, and "tax-eating" economic dependency to designate particular areas as "blighted," a legal classification that could unlock urban renewal assistance.[24] In San Francisco, pro-growth advocates drew on tropes of sexual danger near the foot of Market Street to focus public attention on their proposals to turn this area into a "beauty spot attractive to private investment" that would become the "birthplace of modern San Francisco."[25] Public exposure of queer happenings on the waterfront often coincided with drives by project boosters to secure funds or approval for urban renewal or freeway construction in the area.

What more do queer nightspots on the waterfront have to tell us about this intense period of demolition and disruption? Only recently has same-sex desire—and the transactions and exchanges it arouses—been credited as a factor in shaping trajectories of postwar urban development.[26] Urban redevelopment has had a particularly devastating impact by replacing queer, multiracial leisure spaces with heteronormative or desexualized land uses.[27] This book adds a circuit of emergent gay bars on the San Francisco waterfront in the 1950s and 1960s to the roster of places and people displaced by postwar urban renewal.

SAN FRANCISCO'S ROUGH ROAD TO URBAN RENEWAL

The City Aroused examines the intersections of urban redevelopment and sexual politics in San Francisco, from the first stirring of waterfront revitalization to the razing of the area for a federal urban renewal project in the mid-1960s.[28] Like most American cities during this period, San Francisco followed a "treacherous course toward the seemingly elusive goal of urban renaissance."[29] Unlike other cities, however, the growing number of gay men on the waterfront provoked local leaders to carry out an aggressive urban renewal program. Neither the availability of federal urban renewal assistance, nor an embrace of modern environmental design, nor declining urban land values alone adequately explains why San Francisco embarked on an ambitious plan to raze and repurpose its central waterfront in the 1950s. Anxieties over the influx of queer merchant marines and naval personnel during the Lavender Scare convinced a new pro-growth coalition of corporate executives and bank officers to seek federal urban renewal assistance to raze and rebuild the central Embarcadero waterfront.

The 1939 opening of the San Francisco–Oakland Bay Bridge—the first trans-bay transit and traffic connection to the peninsular city—had profound implications for maritime-oriented land uses near the city's central waterfront. With the start of automobile traffic on the upper deck and commuter train service on the bridge's lower deck, the principal point of entry into the city shifted from the Ferry Building at the foot of Market Street to a new transit terminal six blocks away that was built near the bridge's off-ramps.[30] Overnight, the lower Market Street area lost its status for daily commuters and out-of-town visitors as the principal gateway to the city. The loss of a steady flow of foot traffic due to a steep drop in ferryboat service sapped economic activity from the coffee shops, diners, hotels, lodging houses, taverns, liquor stores, cigar stores, and newsstands in the area. For the same reason, the area lost its underlying advantages as the gateway for goods arriving in the city. Before the bridge's inauguration, fruit and vegetable wholesalers were well situated to receive waterborne cargo shuttled by railcar from the piers to their warehouses. Now idling trucks laden with fruits, vegetables, and other foodstuffs jockeyed for spots to sell their goods to wholesale produce merchants. This new flood of trucks snarled the narrow streets of lower Washington Street between the Ferry Building and the central business district.

In the 1940s and 1950s, an "ethic of city rebuilding" swept across the country as real estate interests, urban reformers, and planning proponents tried to reverse the impact on American cities of years of economic stagnation, deferred maintenance, and decentralization.[31] Postwar suburbanization escalated these festering problems into a crisis of confidence in the future of the city. White middle-class families fled, property values fell, tax revenues shrank, private investment dried up, and the social order of stable neighborhoods unraveled. The prescription for ailing cities offered by a new generation of architect-planners was to erase the older urban fabric and redevelop the cleared land into high-rise office towers, better housing, parking garages, and modern retail facilities.[32] The premise of this remedy was that the sections of the city most directly implicated in fueling the crisis could be completely redesigned from the ground up to restore order, value, and vitality to city centers. An emboldened professional class of real estate specialists, planning consultants, design experts, and land-use economists sprang into action, drafting expansive redevelopment proposals that would return profits and people to the city.[33] Large-scale, comprehensively planned rebuilding projects supplanted code enforcement, rehabilitation, and spot clearance as a culture of clearance equated demolition with progress in postwar America.[34] Local elected officials, business leaders, and planning agencies ironed out the administrative, legal, and funding challenges of assembling land for redevelopment in partnership with federal urban renewal administrators.[35]

San Francisco leaders initially embraced urban redevelopment as a tool to reverse the impact of the wartime mobilization. In the 1940s, the San Francisco Chamber of Commerce spearheaded two separate redevelopment initiatives with support from Sacramento. The first initiative focused on race-based slum clearance and public investment in housing, parks, and industrial facilities under the 1945 California Community Redevelopment Act.[36] The city's new Redevelopment Agency focused its energies on four projects: razing a neighborhood of African American "temporary" wartime workers that was formerly home to Japanese American internees, building a modern housing complex on an underdeveloped hilltop, finishing a stalled park project, and expanding an industrial district south of Market Street.[37] The second initiative aimed to replace the downtown produce market with a Rockefeller Center–style maritime office and convention complex under the auspices of the World Trade Center (WTC) Authority.[38] Its backers hoped a new global trade center in San Francisco would be the West Coast counterpart to commercial complexes under development in New York City and New Orleans. The four Redevelopment Agency projects and the WTC proposal were the principal components of the city's postwar agenda for turning back the clock on what local leaders viewed as the negative consequences of the war. During the late 1940s and early 1950s, city officials and business leaders were principally preoccupied with the growing African American population, dilapidated or insufficient housing, stalled public works projects, and the loss of maritime commerce to naval operations.[39]

In the mid-1950s, the city's urban redevelopment priorities dramatically changed when Congress broadened the definition and scope of urban redevelopment by amending the 1949 Housing Act—ushering in a new emphasis on revitalizing the urban core.[40] The turning point came in 1954 when federal housing officials unleashed a new era of urban renewal with an infusion of funds, greater local latitude in defining blighted districts, looser requirements for new housing construction, and a broader interpretation of state power over property rights. The new guidelines also incentivized localities to partner with federal agencies to secure funds for planning studies, grant and loan applications, and, most importantly, land acquisitions. To access the funds, federal urban renewal administrators required cities to revise their zoning ordinances and building codes, complete comprehensive community plans and neighborhood studies, and expand their administrative capacity to execute redevelopment projects.[41] In San Francisco, a growing coalition of business leaders leaned on elected officials and city planners to use this expanded urban renewal authority to replace the city's maritime-oriented land uses near the central waterfront with an expanded central business district. In particular, this coalition underwrote and championed expansive plans to raze and rebuild a waterfront strip of seamen's hotels, bars, and nightclubs along with the adjacent produce wholesaling district.

During the second half of the 1950s, a Chamber of Commerce–sponsored working group of city officials, design consultants, property owners, technical staff, and architecture firms met regularly to jumpstart the city's flagging urban redevelopment program.[42] Out of these work sessions, a group of corporate executives and bankers calling themselves the Blyth-Zellerbach Committee (BZC) quickly emerged as an incredibly effective advocate for reordering the city's urban redevelopment priorities.[43] The BZC prepared and eventually won approval for a proposal to transform San Francisco's central waterfront into the financial and administrative center of the Bay Area. In a series of blows to rival business groups and competing initiatives, the BZC and its allies privately vetted and publicly championed different aspects of what came to be known as the Golden Gateway project. In particular, they advanced sweeping plans to turn the produce market and Ferry Building area into an automobile gateway into the central business district, lined with new office towers, modern residential buildings, and a waterfront park. As they made headway, they sidelined the World Trade Center project and leapfrogged the Golden Gateway proposal over several other slum clearance projects to be first in line for federal urban renewal funds. By 1960, they had marshaled the political commitment, administrative capacity, and financial resources to buy properties within the urban renewal project area, demolish buildings, and prepare the cleared site for resale to private developers for rebuilding.[44]

The City Aroused argues that this pro-growth coalition grew out of a series of failed efforts to initiate urban redevelopment at the foot of Market

Street.[45] The first priority of the redevelopment booster club—and the cause that initially brought them together—was a proposal to raze and rebuild the waterfront blocks across from the Ferry Building. Over five years, their involvement in urban affairs deepened. They reordered the city's urban renewal agenda to prioritize the waterfront redevelopment, extended the blight declaration for the produce market to encompass all maritime-oriented land uses, sidelined rival proposals for the area, took control of the planning and design process, and tried to rally the public to fund a series of waterfront park and plaza proposals. As the following chapters make clear, the expanding queer nightlife circuits at the foot of Market Street aroused the interest and deepened the involvement of leading corporate and banking firms in setting up and executing an aggressive urban redevelopment program.

CORE CONCERNS ABOUT VALUE

In 1956, Marybeth Branaman, an analyst from the Real Estate Research Program at the University of California, attended a series of closed-door meetings organized by the San Francisco Chamber of Commerce's Redevelopment Coordinating Committee.[46] She was the leading local expert on metropolitan land economics and the only woman in the group. She was included in the discussions because she was preparing a comprehensive study of changing patterns of land use and property values throughout the San Francisco Bay area. At the time, a new "sprawling metropolitan form" was taking shape, with rapid population and industrial growth in the East Bay.[47] Combing through the data, Branaman concluded that San Francisco might lose its status as the region's core of business activity and cultural life. She wrote, "No ready formula for increasing or even maintaining land values in the central cores is available, and it is debatable whether the encouragement of high land values in the central core is a proper objective." She added, "Factors contributing to the maintenance of a strong central core . . . [like] scenic beauty, climate, the strategic geographic position of the area, and the cultural advantages . . . will probably not offset the more important and continued shift in functions from the center to the outlying area."[48] The "shift in functions" she recognized included three trends that undercut land values in San Francisco's urban core: the suburbanization of housing, the decentralization of industrial development, and—most importantly for the waterfront—the containerization of shipping.

Like many American cities, San Francisco began to lose residents in the 1950s as surrounding suburban counties drew families—disproportionately middle-class white families—away from the urban core. Although some families relocated to newly developed areas of the western and southern districts of the city, a significant number left the city altogether for the neighboring counties of Marin, Alameda, Contra Costa, San Mateo, and Solano.[49] Over that decade, San Francisco's population shrank—from over 775,000 in 1950 to nearly 740,000. City officials demanded a recount of the census numbers in the spring of 1960 after the figures showed a greater population loss than had been expected.[50] Preoccupied with the loss of political clout and tax receipts, Mayor Christopher ordered his secretary to gather information about the school population, telephone installations, and new utility connections for the previous ten years. In the end, however, the population had fallen by nearly 35,000—much greater than the anticipated 10,000. The loss of population was a concern among city officials and residents alike. However, the composition of the remaining population was most concerning to officials: the city was becoming more racially diverse and increasingly the domain of unmarried individuals.[51]

Shifting manufacturing patterns also added to the dim prospects of San Francisco's continuing primacy in the region. The relative availability of large tracts of land, patterns of public investment, and even racial preferences fueled the decentralization of industrial activity toward outlying areas around the Bay. For example, south of San Francisco, fruit orchards in the Santa Clara Valley gave way to the growing electronics and defense industries. University-based research projects at Stanford and the University of California—funded through government defense contracts—fueled development to the south and east of the traditional urban core.[52] Auto production plants moved from the multiracial cities of Richmond and Oakland further south to smaller, predominantly white Fremont. Ultimately, the suburbanization of industry dramatically affected the employment opportunities for San Francisco's blue-collar workforce. In the early 1960s, the city was on the brink of profound changes in the underlying economic base. Initially, white-collar workers joined existing blue-collar workers in an expanding job market. Between 1958 and 1962, total manufacturing employment remained stagnant, while finance, insurance, real estate, and other nonmanufacturing employment grew by twenty thousand new jobs.[53] Soon the city's manufacturing sector began to shrink as the business services sector grew dramatically. Through the 1960s and 1970s, the engines of job creation were the real estate, insurance, retail trade, and business services sectors.[54]

Finally, changes in the shipping industry loomed that would have dev-astating effects on the city's port and warehousing facilities. The peacetime drawdown of troop and matériel movement and the subsequent revival of Pacific trade prompted fundamental shifts in the manner and location in which goods flowed through San Francisco Bay. Oakland had room to perfect innovative containerized shipping technologies capable of moving goods more efficiently.[55] Shipping companies abandoned San Francisco's system of piers, rail lines, and warehouses dependent on large teams of long-shoremen and warehousemen. As an alternative, they invested in developing new technologies and infrastructure to transship cargo through mechanized port facilities located across the Bay. The new terminal had physical and logistical advantages over San Francisco's system of wharves and finger piers, in addition to being less labor-intensive and isolated from the threat of work stoppages and labor strikes. A similar anti-labor logic justified the decentralization of manufacturing. For example, postwar planners noted that managers of smaller plants in peripheral areas "testify that their employees are more loyal, more cooperative, more productive workers than those they have had in the big cities."[56] Financiers echoed the same sentiments. They rationalized the dispersion of manufacturing plants on "less happy relations with management" and "outside disrupting influences" among the urban working class.[57]

PLACING SAN FRANCISCO'S QUEER PAST

Urbanization and industrialization were deeply implicated in the historical geography of where and when urban sexual subcultures flourished in the United States during the late nineteenth and early twentieth centuries. Rapidly industrializing cities afforded growing numbers of wage laborers the anonymity and opportunities that came with living in a world of strangers.[58] In addition, a significant number of new arrivals living away from the social and moral expectations of their families of origin generated new opportuni-ties for sexual encounters and social belonging. In larger cities, they created or co-opted a diversity of settings to meet one another, act on their desires, and organize their lives and livelihoods around one another. On a grand scale, New York's sexual subcultures made a gay "world" that residents and visitors could come out in—or be brought into—that encompassed hotel and rooming-house districts; bars and clubs; cafeterias, bathhouses, and cruising spots in theater balconies; shopping promenades; city parks; public restrooms; and transit terminals.[59] Cities across the country, and up and down the urban hierarchy, had an array of similar places—to the degree to which they attracted a sufficient number of residents, patrons, and visitors.

Before World War II, queer subcultures developed with particular shared sensibilities, behavioral codes, and racial configurations.[60] Many cities had queer nightlife spots, often located within larger bar and entertainment districts. In major cities, queer nightlife circuits were extensive enough to define cruising zones and racially and sexually transgressive slumming districts. For example, the Great Migration of Black southerners to the North in the early twentieth century fueled the growth of new sexually permissive racial mixing zones in Chicago and New York.[61] In Miami, place marketing, transnational migrations, and sexual tourism converged to create a "fairyland" hub for pleasure seekers.[62] In small towns and even rural areas, men "like that" found ways to co-opt everyday places to meet one another.[63]

During World War II, the massive mobilization of 16 million Americans in the armed forces—and the ramping up of industrial production—fueled a growing self-awareness and sense of social belonging among gays and lesbians who met in barracks, on ships, in factories, and throughout the queer nightlife circuits of war-boom cities.[64] When many of these soldiers and naval personnel returned to civilian life at the end of World War II, they sought out and cultivated wider social and sexual networks in bars and nightclubs. Thriving queer venues usually occupied corners of predominantly heterosexual nighttime entertainment districts, including Scollay Square in Boston, the Block in Baltimore, Calumet City south of Chicago, the French Quarter in New Orleans, and Miami Beach and Colored Town in Miami.[65] In addition, some cities had cruising strips with a circuit of gay bars centered around a large park or square that facilitated casual pickups, such as the environs of Dupont Circle in Washington, DC, Bughouse Square in Chicago, Rittenhouse Square in Philadelphia, the Brooklyn Navy Yard and Times Square in New York, and Pershing Square in Los Angeles.[66]

A backlash soon followed. Between the late 1940s and early 1950s, a nationwide campaign against urban vice districts ended the relative openness that enabled queer nightlife to flourish in the United States during the war. The 1950–1951 Kefauver Committee heard public testimony about organized criminal networks in fourteen cities, fueling raids on brothels, dance halls, gaming parlors, and nightclubs across the country. The military police and local law enforcement joined the crime-fighting campaign with crackdowns on queer bars flagged as out-of-bounds to servicemembers. For example, in Boston, liquor licensing authorities outlawed drag performers and singing waiters at the College Inn when the nightclub operator attempted to move into much larger quarters to accommodate the growing crowds.[67] In Miami, local officials reversed a decades-long liberal attitude toward queer nightlife and shut down the Club Jewel Box nightclub and Mother Kelly's bar and restaurant.[68] Similarly, law enforcement shuttered queer venues in New Orleans's French Quarter and Chicago's nearby Calumet City.[69] In San Francisco, anti-vice efforts focused on shutting down narcotics rings, gambling operations, houses of prostitution, and abortion providers, while also reining in juvenile delinquency and the politically powerful state liquor industry.[70]

While the anti-vice crusade cracked down on nightlife districts, the Lavender Scare damaged the lives and livelihoods of tens of thousands of so-called sexual perverts by systematically removing them from government employment, the armed forces, and sensitive defense-related jobs.[71] Throughout all departments and agencies, federal officials authorized antigay purges that had a chilling impact on the federal government workforce, particularly in Washington, DC.[72] However, some of the most intense state efforts to identify and contain the threat of homosexuals unfolded in West Coast ports. In the early 1950s, undercover FBI agents surveilled leaders and attended meetings of homophile organizations in Los Angeles and San Francisco to try to ferret out connections between homosexuality and Communism.[73] With the onset of the Cold War in East Asia, federal officials acted swiftly to exclude suspected subversives from working aboard ships, on wharves, and in warehouses up and down the Pacific Coast.[74] They fired or discharged men from the merchant marines and naval forces who refused to sign a loyalty oath, had connections to leftist political organizations, including the Communist Party, or had an arrest record related to sexual perversion.

The City Aroused is indebted to the work of historians of queer subcultures who have underscored the importance of San Francisco as a site for gay and lesbian community formation in the post–World War II era.[75] A key question among these scholars has been the relative importance of the city's homophile organizations and gay bar publics in the earliest articulations of a movement to secure sexual minority civil rights. By the mid-1950s, San Francisco was the national headquarters for two of the three major homophile organizations. As the 1960s began, an emerging social and political consciousness among gay bar patrons, staff, and operators grabbed the public's attention during a 1959 antigay smear political campaign, a 1960 police corruption scandal, and a 1961 run for public office by a well-known, openly gay drag performer.[76] As historian John D'Emilio has argued, these events signaled the popularization of the emancipatory project of a relatively insular homophile membership organization into a broader social movement.[77] Foregrounding a longer history of queer culture, historian Nan Boyd traced the roots of the city's lesbian and gay community to its sexually permissive and gender-transgressive bar cultures during Prohibition. She persuasively showed that a particularly repressive period of crackdowns by local police and liquor agents during the 1950s pushed these bar subcultures "into the limelight" and created "a space for lesbian and gay community development."[78] Historian Martin Meeker has emphasized the widening interpersonal networks that bars enabled. He convincingly shows that homophile leaders and bar operators actively promoted San Francisco as a gay capital in nationally circulating media outlets beginning in the early 1960s.[79] This historical scholarship on the emergence of queer communities and social networks has largely overlooked the spatial dynamics of San Francisco's changing political economy from the country's principal Pacific port into the financial and administrative hub of an expanding metropolitan region. This transformation unfolded in the middle decades of the last century and reshaped the contours and spatial logic of the city's sexual culture and queer geography. The following chapters reconstruct how state programs and policies affecting maritime operations in the city from the 1940s to the early 1960s had profound, lasting effects on the lives, livelihoods, and social identities of the operators and patrons of an emerging circuit of waterfront gay bars.

At the height of the Red and Lavender Scares in the early 1950s, San Francisco stands out—not only among the Pacific ports but nationally—for the intense efforts of the state to expel homosexuals from oceangoing ships and port facilities. An unintended consequence of these purges was the development of a distinctive network of gay bars in former maritime labor hangouts on the central waterfront. As subsequent chapters will show, these bars constituted the everyday spaces where queer subjects worked out ways to challenge the straight state in the early 1960s. This queer nightlife circuit coalesced into a countercultural public sphere—or an "independent realm in which criticism of state authorities became possible"—among patrons, staff, and operators.[80] In other words, these bars cultivated a "counterpublic" whose members were conscious of their subordinate political status and, in queer theorist Michael Warner's formulation, willing to "work to elaborate new worlds of culture and social relations in which gender and sexuality can be lived."[81] In a series of queer world-making actions in the early 1960s, waterfront gay bar operators, employees, and patrons worked together on many fronts. They challenged racketeering by law enforcement, formed a political action group, published a regular newsletter, held voter registration drives, raised legal defense funds, pooled investments for new businesses, and united around an emancipatory call for equal treatment under the law.

The queer bar culture that developed on the waterfront reflected the racial hierarchies, working-class sensibilities, and gendered division of labor of the maritime labor force. The beer halls, private clubs, and nightlife venues frequented by seamen and dockworkers served as hangouts for different organized-labor crowds according to occupational trade. The social character of each drinking establishment was shaped by the system of labor contracting on the waterfront. After the 1934 Waterfront Strike, maritime unions won the right to set up their own hiring halls, where they dispatched work gangs of their members to the piers, wharves, and warehouses in the area. Before World War II, men of color in the maritime trades were largely limited to working as cooks, messmen, and cabin stewards. When ashore, they found lodging at a cluster of rundown seamen's hotels on lower Jackson Street near the railyard. By the last years of World War II, the maritime labor force of merchant marines and dockworkers was both more racially mixed and integrated. The scarcity of available labor loosened the hold of previously predominantly white labor unions. In the marine cook and steward's union, African Americans, as well as queens from different racial and ethnic backgrounds, were in leadership positions. In the postwar period, internal ideological struggles, anti-homosexual purges, and the assertion of white privilege in hiring halls reversed many hard-won gains by racially and sexually marginalized laborers.[82] Primarily frequented by men, queer nightlife spots on the waterfront in the 1950s were places of sexual boundary-crossing across race and class.[83] Steeped in the lore of the area's receding maritime past, former seamen's hangouts attracted both "rough trade" working-class men and "trade queens" of all backgrounds. Out of this social context, queer drinking publics—led by some of the most marginalized queer people of color on the scene—organized collectively to push back against discriminatory practices by state actors. As was the case at the Stonewall Inn riots that occurred nearly a decade after the waterfront was razed, the first calls to resist displacement and demand redress for discrimination came from queer and gender outlaws—including many of color—who had been most vulnerable to state violence.[84] No less important, it also occurred within— and as a struggle over—places that had been at the center of labor activism and cross-racial solidarity among working-class men in the maritime trades going back to the 1930s.[85]

MAPPING THE QUEER PAST

Drawing from feminist and queer historical geography, this book grounds the emergence of a new collective politics of sexual citizenship in the transformation of queer social spaces in mid-twentieth-century San Francisco.[86] This project takes seriously how societal shifts are both reflected in and reinforced by changing spatial relations.[87] The spaces and places at the heart of this work are bars where sexual- and gender-transgressive subjects cultivated social relations and sought sexual pleasure. While these bars catered to a queer, racially diverse, and working-class crowd, the most consequential, world-making episodes were led by men of color and trans people who frequented and, in several cases, ran these places. These bars were simultaneously commercial operations subject to regulatory control, business enterprises serving a growing clientele, places of social engagement and lived experience, and physical spaces that constrained and enabled queer desire. The following chapters recount the planned destruction of these bars and assess the historical significance of these places in generating new sexual subjectivities and political identities. They show that the variety, character, and social significance of sexually coded spaces changed in concert with the city's physical transformation.[88]

The City Aroused employs a historical geographic framework to uncover the impact of state-directed urban development on the shifting sexual terrain of postwar San Francisco. At the heart of this story is the "creative destruction" of queer land uses on the waterfront.[89] In this context, I define *queer land uses* as patterns of commercial activity that accommodated non-normative sexual desires, provoked anxieties about urban decline, undermined land values, and fueled postwar urban revitalization projects.[90] Much of the physical remnants of the city's maritime economy adjacent to the central business district fit this definition. In the 1950s and early 1960s, a constellation of sexual- and gender-transgressive nighttime entertainment venues flourished in the moribund sailortown sections of the city that once served the portside labor, residential, and commercial interests of seamen and dockworkers.[91]

Critical to understanding how these past places reflected and reinforced emergent activisms around sexual minority rights has been reconstructing how marginalized sexual subjects created, adapted, defended, and reconstituted queer land uses in the face of large-scale urban landscape destruction.[92] Central to this project has been triangulating among social memories of past queer places, contemporaneous accounts of stigmatized land uses, and records of changing property relations in bygone landscapes.[93] Planning reports, meeting minutes, and redevelopment proposals are largely silent about the sexual character of the places and people that showed up in their maps of urban blight. Without direct references to gay bars, queer happenings, sexual solicitations, or even policing problems, these silences in the planning archive can only be filled by registering the recollections of queer subjects who transited these places alongside contemporaneous, sensationalized exposés of urban vice conditions. Oral histories housed in the GLBT Historical Society of Northern California include a recurring pattern of details about the sexual geography of mid-twentieth-century San Francisco.[94] A portrait of the shifting social and spatial characteristics of these places comes into focus by cross-referencing oral histories with business directories, property records, Sanborn maps, legal proceedings, and newspaper clippings.[95] This portrait came into better focus after October 1961 with the publication of the first gay bar rag, which contained print advertisements, nightlife columns, editorials, and feature stories.[96] The *LCE News* publisher frequently promoted a handful of waterfront gay bars in his biweekly coverage of queer nightlife in the city through the early 1960s.

The historical subjects and places at the center of this project are often difficult to index without using terms that flatten how they saw themselves or how others saw them in the past. This work is heavily indebted to the field of queer studies, which takes seriously the terms and meanings associated with gender and sexual transgressors as historically contingent and mutable. For historical subjects, "queer" is a useful term to connote sexual- and gender-transgressive subjectivities that preceded and persisted along with self-identified "gay" subjects in postwar San Francisco.[97] In contrast, I reserve the modifier "gay" for instances when historical actors used the term themselves to either identify with others who organized their lives around same-sex social and sexual relations or to characterize places that enabled the pursuit of those relations. For example, the first reference to a "gay bar" in the San Francisco press appeared in 1953 as part of the quoted testimony by a Tenderloin bartender in an extortion trial against a Hollywood gossip-magazine publisher.[98] The generic toponym circulated along with coded references to "unique places," "interesting places," and "places of particular interest" to identify sites with an openness to sexual nonconformity in an era of increasing state scrutiny and discrimination against same-sex desire.[99] By the early 1960s, "gay bars" proliferated in San Francisco as a growing commercial nightlife economy developed and businesses openly advertised to gay locals, tourists, and migrants through print media.[100] Gay bars became popularly recognized—and likely more common—as a specialized commercial enterprise with the commodification of same-sex desire and the self-segregation of bar crowds by sexual orientation.

Furthermore, throughout the book, I use "queer" without the same precision or attention to historical sourcing, as a way to situate people, places, and events on the margins of prevailing sexual and gender norms.[101] Queer subjects of the past, like those in the present, foster and act upon stigmatized sexual desires and, in some instances, also embody or perform extraordinarily gendered lives in private, in public, or on the stage. Similarly, I characterize as queer those provisional spaces of sexual possibility for marginal subjects. In contrast, I reserve "gay" to signify particular identitarian places claimed by and for the gay community. By distinguishing between queer subjectivities and gay identities, gay serves as both a category of analysis and a particular, historically contingent social formation. Sexual- and gender-based subjectivities are not necessarily reducible to identities. This approach inserts socially engaged, self-identified gay subjects into what queer theorists Lauren Berlant and Michael Warner call a "queer project" to "support forms of affective, erotic, and personal living that are public in the sense of accessible, available to memory and sustained through collective activity."[102]

The geographic scope of *The City Aroused* covers a roughly triangular area bounded by the Embarcadero waterfront, the Broadway nightlife corridor in the North Beach neighborhood, and the financial district. Often referred to as the Wholesale Produce Market, the Commission District, or Lower Market, this area developed on reclaimed land that was once a shallow cove dotted with sailing vessels anchored offshore. First built up with sunken ships and long wharves during the Gold Rush, the shoreline was fixed by a seawall by the late 1800s, built by state harbor commissioners. A roadbed and a handsome string of piers topped the seawall. This publicly funded port facility, the Embarcadero, served as the core of maritime shipping and wholesale trade activity for much of the early twentieth century. In the mid-1950s, this area became one of the city's highest-priority urban renewal projects when the San Francisco Redevelopment Agency (SFRA) declared the roughly twenty-eight-block jumble of warehouses, seamen's hotels, small factories, printing firms, and modest office buildings blighted. The SFRA designated the condemned area the "Embarcadero–Lower Market Urban Renewal Area, E" (figure 0.3).

Before the SFRA acquired and razed most of Area E, it encompassed most of the places discussed in the following chapters. During the 1950s, a queer nightlight circuit developed in the sailor bars and seamen's hotels clustered around union hiring halls. The two southernmost waterfront

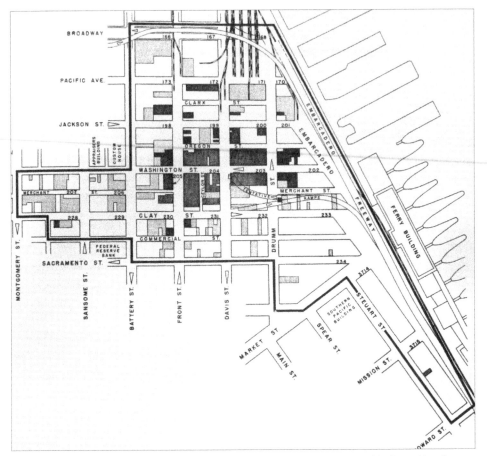

FIGURE 0.3 The geographic scope of this book encompasses a multi-block jumble of maritime-oriented land uses slated for redevelopment by the city in 1955. Area E, or the Embarcadero–Lower Market Urban Renewal Area, centered on the city's wholesale produce market (shaded parcels above) and anticipated the construction of the Embarcadero Freeway. (Excerpted from San Francisco Planning Department, "Wholesale Produce Market Area Proposed Redevelopment Area," map, 1954, Golden Gateway folder, box PLN-00778, Planning Division Records, SFAR.)

blocks, known as "The Front," anchored this circuit. There were also several queer hangouts—including Jack's—in the jagged blocks opposite the Ferry Building. Finally, within and just to the north of the westernmost block of Area E was another cluster of queer hangouts. In terms of both patrons and operators, one of these (the Black Cat) had ties to the waterfront as well as the bohemian scene in North Beach, the neighborhood adjacent to Area E to the north. Bordering Area E to the west and south, the city's downtown financial district was packed with handsome skyscrapers. For the most part built in the early twentieth century, they rose on solid ground that had once delimited the city's shoreline. In contrast, Area E overlapped closely with the city's first shallow harbor and consisted primarily of low-rise buildings filled with maritime-oriented land uses.

MOVING FORWARD

The following chapters are organized roughly chronologically, from the 1940s to the early 1960s, around the transformation of particular geographies of queer desire on the San Francisco waterfront. The places foregrounded in each chapter include the lower Market Street maritime quarter, the circuit of queer nightlife along the Embarcadero waterfront, individual bars with changing drinking publics and operational histories, and the mix of properties targeted by and ultimately razed by urban redevelopment officials.

Chapter 1 reconstructs how the reorganization of West Coast port operations during the height of the Red and Lavender Scares generated an influx of queer merchant marines and naval personnel on the San Francisco waterfront. In the late 1940s and early 1950s, the spread of Communism in Asia fueled growing anxieties about the possible infiltration of domestic sympathizers in sensitive, defense-related positions. As a national security measure, Coast Guard officers systematically expelled suspected subversives from working out of Pacific ports and military facilities, specifically singling out a racially integrated, left-wing, queer-friendly labor union headquartered in San Francisco. In addition to barring homosexuals from the maritime trades, this federal program fomented internal race- and gay-baiting purges within the ranks of union halls up and down the West Coast. As a local consequence of these anti-homosexual shake-ups in the shipping industry, the social character and significance of waterfront bars began to change. By the mid-1950s, former merchant marines and navy men who organized their lives around social and sexual relations with other men transformed former seamen's hangouts into gay bars, which state and city leaders pejoratively tagged as hangouts for deviates and homosexuals.[103]

Chapter 2 argues that the expansion of queer nightlife along the Embarcadero during the early 1950s soon fueled an imperative to expand and fast-track waterfront redevelopment over other languishing postwar rebuilding projects. In the mid-1950s, local elites formed a powerful pro-growth coalition by using the queer cruising strip in front of the Ferry Building as a pretext for declaring the entire lower Market Street area blighted. After incorporating these waterfront blocks into an expansive urban renewal project, this group of corporate executives and banking leaders tacitly encouraged the further concentration and containment of queer nightlife in the bars and nightclubs along this strip to bolster their plans for area-wide redevelopment. By the decade's end, they had marshaled the political will, administrative capacity, federal resources, and legal authority to raze and rebuild the area, ushering in a new era of large-scale rebuilding projects in San Francisco.

In reconstructing the spatial and operational history of one of the most notorious queer waterfront hangouts, chapter 3 underscores the ways local and state officials purposely treated the environs of the Ferry Building as a queer nightlife containment zone while also drafting proposals to raze and rebuild the area. In the mid-1950s, redevelopment proponents repeatedly used the Ensign Café to illustrate blight conditions on the waterfront and to prime the area for a federally subsidized urban renewal project. At the same time, however, local law enforcement and state liquor agents enabled and defended the Ensign operator's business practices. The Ensign Café is best understood not as a gay bar but as a holdover from an older era of queer nightlife operations. Its internal, physical configuration resembled a Prohibition-era speakeasy set up to obscure illicit commercial exchanges inside and shield the identity of patrons and managers. While the Ensign was the oldest, queerest, and longest-lasting nightlife spot on the waterfront, it remained a managed vice operation until the end, never joining the network of gay bars in the area that organized for equal rights in the early 1960s.

Chapter 4 reframes the historiography of pre-Stonewall political mobilization in San Francisco as a story of local resistance to urban development pressures. The key moments that fueled bar-based political activism in the late 1950s and early 1960s are well known; however, they have largely been understood from the perspective of homophile organizations and framed as part of an emerging, affirming discourse about (middle-class, white) homosexuality in popular media. The imminent closure of a handful of waterfront gay bars for the Golden Gateway urban renewal project played a crucial role in arousing the social consciousness and political engagement of the city's gay nightlife crowds. When land acquisition and clearance activities began, bar managers at 90 Market Street and Jack's Waterfront Hangout exposed the payola system and spearheaded new forms of collective organizing in a failed effort to stave off eviction. With a better understanding of the urban conditions and places that sparked bar-based activism in the city, the subsequent turn toward creating and defending spaces of gay sociality comes into sharper relief.

The final chapter reconstructs the last days of the queer world of the waterfront, when commercial evictions, real estate transactions, and building demolitions destroyed this circuit of gay bars to clear the ground for the Golden Gateway urban renewal project. Administrative records of property transfers reveal that the operators of the most socially organized and politically engaged of these bars fared much worse than those who operated within the system of queer containment and exploitation under the auspices of local law enforcement and state liquor agents. These closures capped off a decade-long exercise of state power to devalue and destroy queer land uses on the San Francisco waterfront. The bartender's last call at these queer hangouts immediately preceded the growth of gay commercial strips in outlying sections of the city.

1

THE CHANGING SEXUAL
GEOGRAPHY OF THE WATERFRONT

In a 1976 column in a San Francisco gay newspaper, Robert looked back to the once-thriving landscape of gay bars on the waterfront that flourished decades earlier. "My friends tell me that in the 40s and 50s that San Francisco was even wilder than it is now," he wrote. "Times were different then," he added. "The Embarcadero, or 'The Waterfront' as it was called in those budding days, hosted many a gay bar, the likes of which you will probably never be seen again."[1] Passages like this make it easy to imagine that the move to San Francisco was an arrival at the epicenter of gay life for men like Robert. While Robert's account can be read more as a nostalgic homage to "those budding days," contemporaneous sources and recollections confirm that many bars in the Embarcadero were wildly popular with gay men during World War II and the Cold War. Nightlife guides from the time included numerous veiled references to queer happenings in seamen's haunts on the waterfront. Coverage of bar raids and street sweeps aimed at rounding up homosexuals characterized a handful of drinking establishments in the same area as "homosexual hangouts." Nearly two decades after these places had been razed to make way for waterfront redevelopment, they lived on in the collective memory of the gay men who frequented them.[2] Taken together, contemporaneous nightlife columns, crime exposés of homosexual hangouts, and oral histories corroborate Robert's characterization of the waterfront as a vibrant center of queer nightlife in mid-twentieth-century San Francisco.

For gender- and sexual-transgressive visitors and locals alike, the water-front enabled cross-racial and cross-class encounters in a concentration of establishments geared toward accommodating and entertaining an ongoing parade of sailors, longshoremen, and military personnel in the city.[3] Although the operator and business names sometimes changed, there were at least seven locations on a short stretch of the Embarcadero flanking Market Street where the queer clientele remained: 144 Embarcadero (Chili's, Admiral, and 144 Club), 109 Steuart (Sea Cow and Crossroads), 90 Market (Castaways, Talk of the Town, and Last Resort), 82/88 Embarcadero (Barrel House and Headhunters), 111 Embarcadero (Jack's Waterfront Hangout), 226 Embarcadero (Jack's Waterfront, Edgewater Hotel, and Original Don's), and 1 Market Street (Ensign Café and Broken Drum). In addition, the former Army and Navy YMCA, renamed the Embarcadero YMCA when it began to cater to merchant seamen and naval personnel, anchored the block with the most significant concentration of gay bars.[4] While there were other hubs of queer nightlife in the city, particularly in the Tenderloin and North Beach, the waterfront stood out as the most concentrated, vibrant, and enduring during the 1940s and 1950s.

Why did the "budding" waterfront have "many a gay bar" during this period? Was queer life along the Embarcadero in the 1950s really "even wilder" than the city's gay bars in the swinging 1970s? If so, how could that be? As scholars have shown recently, Cold War anxieties fueled a state-sponsored ideology of normative sex and gender relations that privileged heterosexual marriage and parenthood to the detriment of overt expressions of same-sex desire and gender variance.[5] During the 1950s, the most blatant forms of sexual paranoia emanated from what Margot Canady called the "straight state," with the bureaucratization of homosexuality as immoral, pathological, and anti-American.[6] The key to understanding why the Embarcadero became so closely linked to same-sex desire and queer life requires more than locating the formation of social identities and sexual communities in particular places. It calls for a closer examination of how queer places developed and transformed during a period of heightened policing of sex and gender norms. The following pages reconstruct when and where same-sex social and sexual encounters proliferated on the Embarcadero waterfront, by drawing on oral histories with gay men, nightlife guides that intimated changing clientele, and accounts of anti-homosexual crackdowns by federal, state, and local officials published in press and government reports. Paradoxically, the national security pressures that propelled anti-communist raids also created the conditions for the concentration of queer life in this area.

This chapter traces how the San Francisco waterfront became a "budding" area for men who organized their lives around social and sexual relations with other men during the 1940s and 1950s. I argue that the emergence and persistence of what were later recognized as gay bars occurred not despite but because of the actions of the state to identify and contain the threat of suspected subversives during the Lavender Scare. In the late 1940s, left-leaning maritime unions in San Francisco, which had become more racially integrated and queer during the war, became the primary objective of a new national security program designed to remove homosexuals and other suspected subversives from Pacific ports. In San Francisco in the early 1950s, the expulsion of homosexuals from the maritime labor force, as well as away from port facilities operated by the military, flooded seamen's hotels, sailor bars, and maritime hiring halls on the Embarcadero with an unknown, though significant and recognizable, number of gay men. As the screenings against alleged subversives unfolded in nearby docks, warehouses, and hiring halls, the queering of many seamen and longshoremen hangouts gained momentum. By the mid-1950s, the seamen's haunt most associated with left-leaning maritime labor unions no longer catered to sailing crews and work gangs. Instead, they became pickup bars in a gay cruising strip in what was once the heart of the city's sailortown quarter. While there were a few attempts to round up homosexuals on the waterfront in the mid-1950s, by the decade's end, the area was primarily treated as a vice containment zone as police prioritized eliminating queer nightlife from other parts of the city.

SAN FRANCISCO'S MARITIME QUARTER

In geographer David Hilling's analysis of the demise of sailortowns around the world with the advent of containerized shipping, he described San Francisco's maritime quarter as "the Embarcadero and the grid of streets that developed north of Market Street, with Pacific Street and the adjacent streets providing the core area."[7] One hundred years of real estate speculation, land reclamation, and harbor improvements shaped the contours of the commercial and administrative hub of the city's port operations. The city's maritime commercial and labor interests reclaimed land from a shallow cove to create a five-block, semicircular area that fanned out from a new intersection at Market and the Embarcadero. In the late nineteenth century, state harbor commissioners oversaw the construction of an integrated system of piers, wharves, and warehouses that fixed the shoreline and underpinned blocks of new land reserved for sailortown land uses. As a result, the Embarcadero became the new "city front," with seamen's hotels, bars, and hiring halls clustered near the foot of Market Street. Wholesaling activity developed in the nearby Commission District to accommodate produce and other goods entering the city by boat.

Located at Market Street and the Embarcadero, the San Francisco Ferry Building anchored the maritime district as the principal gateway to the city and the administrative hub for managing harbor traffic. The ferry terminal served as the primary portal to the city for commuters and visitors before two new bridges linked the peninsular city to the wider region in the late 1930s. On the ground floor, legions of daily commuters, tourists, and business travelers passed back and forth between the boat slips and streetcar lines that radiated out from the foot of Market Street to the rest of the city. At the height of ferry service in the 1930s, the San Francisco Ferry Building was second only to London's Charing Cross train station in commuter traffic, with 170 ferries arriving daily, carrying 150 million passengers annually.[8] On the upper floors, business leaders, state officials, tourism promoters, harbor pilots, and trade organizations coordinated the port operations and maritime activities that flowed through and along the roughly seven-mile-long integrated complex of piers, railroad tracks, and warehouses at the water's edge. In one suite of offices, state harbor commissioners managed the publicly owned port facilities, including leases on wharves, finger piers, and seawall lots reserved for warehouses and railyards served by the Beltline Railroad and its many spurs extending inland. The Chamber of Commerce maintained a private, oak-paneled reception room in another suite for visiting business leaders and dignitaries. In adjoining exhibition spaces, a 450-foot-long map illustrating the state's distribution of economic activity, while next door, the California Bureau of Mines extensive collection of mineral specimens afforded visitors an overview of California's commercial and natural resources.[9]

Within a short walk from the Ferry Building, federal officials, shipping companies, and wholesalers oversaw different aspects of maritime commerce. At the US Customs House, federal agents inspected cargoes moving through the port, collected import duties and taxes, and policed smuggling and revenue fraud under the supervision of the port director. At the Maritime Exchange, shipping firms coordinated industry initiatives to expand trade routes, improve port operations, and reduce labor costs. In ornate office towers lining lower Market Street, major shipping and railroad companies, including the Southern Pacific, Santa Fe Railway, Matson Navigation, Dollar Steamship Line, and Alaska Commercial, orchestrated the movement of goods through sea lanes and overland routes that converged in San Francisco and other Pacific ports. A mix of warehouses, small-scale manufacturers, and import-export firms occupied most of the central blocks of the maritime quarter. Produce wholesaling activity dominated five blocks of lower Washington Street. The western margin of the produce market, near the central business district, had a mix of food importers, printing firms, and modest office buildings filled with design firms.

The northern portion of the maritime quarter and the adjacent Chinatown and North Beach neighborhoods were full of social spaces where San Franciscans and the transient maritime workforce congregated and mingled. Lower Pacific and Jackson Streets, known as the Barbary Coast, were the heart of the city's oldest nighttime entertainment district and filled with the most permissive bars, nightclubs, and restaurants for much of the nineteenth and twentieth centuries. Public morals campaigners and temperance activists dismantled a containment system of city-sanctioned prostitution in the late 1910s and effectively dispersed the sex industry from this area to the Tenderloin.[10] During Prohibition, cafés, restaurants, and hotel dining rooms became speakeasies, nightclubs, and members-only drinking clubs.[11] By the late 1930s, the area was renamed the "International Settlement" as an unofficial, organized attempt by local merchants to capitalize on the Golden Gate International Exposition, a World's Fair to celebrate the city's two newly built bridges.

The Embarcadero, opposite the Ferry Building, was lined with low-rent hotels, coffee shops, taverns, lunchrooms, barbershops, cigar stands, and liquor stores catering to a mix of daily commuters, long-distance travelers, merchant marines, dockworkers, and enlisted men passing through and along this threshold to the city. The three-block stretch of the Embarcadero south of Market Street known as "The Front" was San Francisco's principal "sailortown." It contained a familiar mix of businesses, accommodations, and organizations common in other ports.[12] The Army and Navy YMCA, surplus stores, and uniform shops accommodated and outfitted naval personnel on shore leave. Bars, coffee shops, lunchrooms, cigar stores, and newsstands catered to men working on and off of the piers and wharves along the waterfront.

Permanent and transient housing for sailors was a vital component of the mix of land uses on The Front. While port workers lived throughout the city, deckhands, marine cooks, and engine room "firemen" preferred to stay near the waterfront while "hanging out" in their "home" port between stints at sea.[13] Cabin stewards on passenger liners, radiomen, and officers opted for a higher class of residential hotel in the Tenderloin or the slopes of Nob Hill. Historian Clayton Howard has shown that residential hotels, particularly those associated with the city's seafaring labor force, would be tagged as an obstacle to postwar economic development. Unlike the suburban home, single-room-occupancy lodging for unmarried transients was neither "family-friendly" nor did it provide the right kind of privacy to facilitate heteronormative social reproduction.[14] As city officials tried to stem the tide of suburban out-migration by middle-class white families, residential hotel districts and the dense circuit of bars embedded with them became primary targets of urban redevelopment.

More than places for food and lodging, the bars, hotels, and restaurants along The Front also functioned as formal and informal sites of labor organizing in the maritime trades.[15] In the 1930s, nearly 5,400 longshoremen loaded and unloaded cargo daily on the city's waterfront.[16] Many of these men found work in a "shape up" hiring system controlled by shipping firms. During the Waterfront Strike of 1934, longshoremen on the Embarcadero spearheaded an end to this casual labor system, in which crowds of laborers gathered on the piers in Pacific ports in search of work assignments from shipping agents.[17] After shutting down all shipping activity up and down the West Coast, San Francisco labor leaders secured the right of longshoremen in Pacific ports to negotiate long-term labor contracts with shippers and manage their own system for rotating job assignments among a regularized roster of work gangs.[18] The turning point in the strike came when police rushed an estimated six thousand strikers gathered in front of the International Longshoremen's Association's hall on Steuart Street next to the Audiffred Building and killed two men on "Bloody Thursday."[19] The ILA's waterfront hiring hall was active through the early 1950s, although it never completely ended casual labor practices on the waterfront. In 1937, roughly one in five longshoremen signed up weekly for a slot on a job board and waited for a work assignment that paid a fraction of the union wage. While these men waited for work, they stayed in nearby residential hotels and lodging houses and frequented waterfront bars and lunch counters, looking for employment.

After the 1934 strike, union organizing intensified and spread to other specialized maritime tradesmen in the bars, taverns, restaurants, and hiring halls on the Embarcadero. Marine cooks and stewards, engine room workers, deck crews, radio operators, and other maritime laborers organized their own maritime trade associations, secured legal collective bargaining rights for the members, forged alliances with other trade unions, gained leverage in negotiating labor contracts with shipping companies, and established their

FIGURE 1.1 From its hiring hall near the foot of Market Street, the Marine Cooks and Stewards Union dispatched crews to the waterfront to honor labor contracts it negotiated with shipping firms. Before the Lavender and Red Scares, this racially integrated union, which included a significant number of "queens," had a remarkable degree of agency in improving working conditions for its members by remaining organized and united. (AAD-5676, San Francisco History Center, San Francisco Public Library.)

own hiring halls. Workers who catered to the needs of other crewmembers and passengers at sea made the most significant advance, in setting up a more equitable hiring system.

In particular, the Marine Cooks and Stewards Union (MCSU) "transformed an all-white, all-male racist union into one that was mostly men of color that included great numbers of visible queens."[20] The head of the MCSU estimated that "queens" accounted for roughly one-third of the membership, or five thousand men, in 1936.[21] The MCSU's hiring hall near the foot of Market Street became its social, organizational, and administrative headquarters for contracting out its racially diverse, sexual- and gender-transgressive members to ships along the Embarcadero (see figure 1.1). Although MCSU members worked aboard all kinds of Pacific-sailing vessels, the union dispatched the largest number to passenger liners, on which they comprised the largest segment of the crew. While at sea, these men would work under their ship's chief steward as waiters, cooks, pastry chefs, bakers, messmen, pantrymen, butchers, porters, cabin attendants, bellhops, janitors, hairdressers, laundrymen, and bartenders.[22]

The overrepresentation of queens in the MCSU, including many queens of color, reflected prevalent gender and racial hierarchies within the maritime labor force. As Allan Bérubé has shown, passenger liners feminized certain kinds of labor when they staffed their vessels, opening an employment niche for queens to work at sea. "Hotel-like" service work in the steward's department was considered ideal for gay men, given prohibitions against hiring women as crewmembers.[23] The Alexander Line hired only African American men—many of whom were gay—as cooks, waiters, and cabin stewards detailed to tend to the personal needs of passengers and crew. The Matson Company, which operated a fleet of luxury liners, staffed the passenger decks with white gay men. On the same ships, Matson relegated men of color, which always included a contingent of gay men, to the hidden service corridors below deck. Within this gendered and racialized labor hierarchy, white men catered to passengers, African Americans prepared food, Chinese crew laundered, and Filipinos cleaned. In some ship dining rooms, 60 to 70 percent of the staff were easily recognizable as gay men, who self-identified as "queens"—some with feminized nicknames such as Mother Shannon, Grace Line Gertie, Miss Effie, and African Queen.[24]

THE EMBARCADERO AT WAR

At the start of World War II, the War Department designated San Francisco as the primary West Coast headquarters for moving troops and matériel into the Pacific theater, which led to sustained changes on the waterfront.[25] For the duration of the war, military officials took operational control over most of the piers and bulkhead buildings in San Francisco, as well as shipping facilities around the Bay and along the seacoast of Northern California. Fifty major steamship lines operated out of the San Francisco piers before the war. As part of the war effort, these companies converted most of their vessels to army cargo ships and troop carriers. Over the course of the forty-five-month-long war, this fleet transported over 1.6 million soldiers and more than 23.5 million tons of cargo through San Francisco Bay.[26] Nearly all of the soldiers and more than a third of the cargo moved through port facilities located in San Francisco itself.

Across the country, port cities near military installations experienced a boom in businesses catering to servicemen and -women stationed nearby, preparing for deployment, or enjoying shore leave. An influx of military personnel in Chicago, New York, Philadelphia, Washington, DC, Miami, and New Orleans, as well as the Pacific port cities of Seattle, San Francisco, Los Angeles, and San Diego, soon overfilled hotels, lodging houses, and hostels and fueled the expansion of nighttime entertainment districts. On a typical weekend in San Diego, forty to fifty thousand sailors flowed into the city on shore leave.[27] A similar number of soldiers and sailors headed to the downtown "Loop" in Chicago, looking for a good time.[28] In San Francisco, the Tenderloin and North Beach experienced an unprecedented wartime revival of dining, dancing, drinking, and prostitution.[29] The waterfront teemed with activity as merchant mariners and military personnel flowed through and along the Embarcadero.

In many large and medium-size cities, queer servicemen passing through or on leave could reliably find bars and public places to meet one another. In veteran John Nichols's essay about gay life during World War II, he described the kinds of places where these men met, and gave notable examples in cities across the country. His typology included men's bars in finer downtown hotels that required strict discretion among patrons; servicemen's hostels with lax surveillance of shower rooms; gay house parties hosted by men with lots of friends; public parks that provided anonymity for meeting strangers; and straight-owned bars often involved in funneling money to crime syndicates or law enforcement.[30] "Out-of-Bounds" warnings from military brass served as an unintended guide for gay servicemen looking for a night on the town.[31] With a destination in mind, nearby locker clubs helped them evade military police by providing a place to change out of and store their uniforms.

Throughout San Francisco, hotel bars, United Service Organizations (USO) canteens, cocktail bars, beer halls, movie theaters, bus stations, pinball arcades, pool halls, locker rooms, bathhouses, and public parks all served as places for men to seek out sex with other men.[32] While the Tenderloin had more places for the gay crowds, the most well-known nightspot, the Black Cat, was in North Beach. The waterfront, however, stood apart as the city's most reliable overt cruising ground. The wartime mobilization amplified the distinctive homosocial culture forged earlier by working-class men in the maritime trades by turning the hotels, bars, and restaurants along The Front into a queer outpost of the city's nightlife offerings. The mix of hotels, hostels, and rooming houses had long provided temporary and permanent lodging to seamen and dockworkers who wanted to be close to the finger piers, waterfront bars, and union hiring halls where they might secure their next position. Many lodging places had ground-floor bars where men socialized, exchanged job leads, and arranged their personal affairs. Other bars like the Mohawk and Denny's Barrel House were more directly connected to union organizing. Servicemen, merchant marines, longshoremen, and civilians crossed paths during the war and socialized in these waterfront seamen's haunts. A significant but indeterminable fraction of these men cruised for sex on the street, in bars and clubs, or in hotels and hostels.

The Embarcadero YMCA and the Ensign Café anchored a particularly active two-block strip along The Front where men sought sexual encounters with other men during the war.[33] The Embarcadero YMCA was the most permissive in the country, with an active shower room twenty-four hours a day.[34] For example, soon after Paul Wonner enlisted in the Army in 1941, the former art student often headed to the Embarcadero YMCA, where it was "easy to find sailors to play with." The slender eighteen-year-old recalled being particularly lucky with "big and protective" sailors who had difficulty with—or preferred not to have—sex with women.[35] Nearby, the Ensign Café was the only bar where men had sex on the premises. John Nichols recounted how the internal configuration of the Ensign enabled sexual encounters in the basement underneath a seemingly deserted first-floor tavern. He explained, "Although the bar was laden with beer bottles, few customers seemed to be standing around drinking. A trip to the basement john revealed why."[36] What struck him was not the bar itself but how men in the know could use such a public space to seek out sexual encounters with other men without attracting the attention of unsuspecting patrons or law enforcement.

During the war, the San Francisco waterfront became more integrated by race and sexuality relative to other port cities due to a tight labor market and nondiscrimination policies in left-leaning maritime labor organizations that diversified their membership rolls. These changes applied above all to the country's two most left-leaning unions, the International Longshore and Warehouse Union (ILWU) and the Marine Cooks and Stewards Union (MCSU). Both were headquartered in San Francisco, had roots in the 1934 Waterfront Strike, and included a sizeable number of Communist Party members.[37] In a show of national unity and an ideological stance against fascism, the ILWU followed a no-strike pledge, grew its ranks, and adopted a maximal production approach to help win the war.[38] In San Francisco, under the leadership of Harry Bridges, this approach called for the rejection of racial discrimination within the ranks of the local ILWU. In the last year of the war, the ILWU's San Francisco waterfront local number 10 added six thousand men, half of whom were African Americans previously employed in the shipyards.[39] By the war's end, nearly 22 percent of unionized longshoremen working on the San Francisco waterfront were Black, which reflected not simply the high demand for dockworkers but anti-racist hiring policies. In contrast, the ILWU's Portland local maintained race-based hiring policies and had no registered Black members at the war's end.[40] The intense demand for dockworkers also opened up opportunities for gay men to work as longshoremen on the waterfront as well.[41]

The already racially integrated MCSU followed a similar pattern in the growth and diversification of its membership. The MCSU had nineteen thousand members at the war's end. Anecdotally, more than one-half were African American.[42] It also likely had a higher proportion of gay men, including men of color, within its ranks. Men dishonorably discharged from the Navy for homosexual misconduct found a spot in the merchant marines as culinary workers.[43] Its long-standing stance against "queen-baiting" made it an attractive opportunity for wartime employment for men barred from serving in the military.[44] Although it is impossible to know precisely how many gay men joined the MCSU during the war, historical evidence suggests that it was likely in the thousands, given the growth of its membership rolls. Most of these men would have considered San Francisco their home port and secured work assignments from the MSCU hiring hall on the Embarcadero.

THE EMBARCADERO BRANCH OF THE YMCA

Throughout the 1940s and 1950s, the Embarcadero YMCA was the social and sexual hub for queer life on the waterfront (see figure 1.2). By the late 1940s, as nationwide crackdowns on homosexuality intensified, YMCA officials began to express concern about the declining moral conditions on the waterfront. As a result, the YMCA Advisory Council called for recreational programs to occupy the more than a hundred thousand "young, merchant seamen" staying in the city when "the ships are not sailing and there is no income."[45] They hinted at deteriorating social conditions among idle merchant marines, which they blamed on the corrupting influence of sailor bars in the area. They hoped to "make the YMCA the focal point along the Embarcadero instead of the bars with a slate of new programs."[46] Ironically, the men who stayed at the YMCA contributed to the queer nightlife scene on the sidewalks and in the bars along the Embarcadero.

After the war, the Embarcadero YMCA became a particularly active zone of sexual solicitation for a changing mix of men arriving at, living in, and passing through the city.[47] Although troop deployments tapered off in the mid-1940s, a steady stream of men, including merchant marines, active military personnel, returning veterans, and new migrants, easily found sexual partners at the YMCA. First-person recollections of the waterfront reveal that the Embarcadero YMCA was a de facto, unregulated gay bathhouse throughout the 1950s.

Early in 1949, Tom Redmon, his partner Gary, and their friend Jimmy moved to San Francisco from New York City and spent their first nights at the Embarcadero YMCA.[48] They arrived penniless after a cross-country Greyhound bus trip and spent the twelve dollars they got from selling two pints of blood to rent dormitory beds in the YMCA before feasting at a nearby cafeteria. Redmon and his partner were an interracial couple who spent the next three years in the city. Redmon's first impression of San Francisco was that "the YMCA was a bath house. You'd check in there and go to the third floor and you had it all day . . . The Golden Gate Y was good, but the Embarcadero Y . . . just like the Sloane Houses in New York . . . was a noted whore house, male whore house."[49] Not actually a brothel, the Embarcadero YMCA was well known for its lax policing of sexual solicitations among men.

Redmon and his partner were not the only ones enticed by the sexual permissiveness found in the Embarcadero YMCA. Its internal configuration allowed a parade of men to try their luck seeking same-sex connections. Gerald Fabian, for example, had begun visiting bathhouses in San Francisco as a teenager in the early 1940s. After the war, he returned to partake in the expanded terrain of gay cruising in the city and found the Embarcadero "so open . . . so easy" for seeking sexual pleasure. Rather than try his luck at other cruising spots on the waterfront, he "headed straight for the YMCA and spent the night because it was so good."[50] The YMCA's internal arrangement provided a mixture of public and private spaces that facilitated a fluid economy of sexual encounters with minimal risk of exposure. Men would catch the attention of potential partners in the public showers, in the hallways, and "in the john" before leading them back to their private rooms. In other instances, the configuration of the rooms themselves aroused homoerotic spectatorship. Some men left their doors open to catch the eye of a passerby, while others cruised the hallways seeking open invitations to cross into private spaces.

In the early 1950s, the Embarcadero YMCA functioned as a queer hostel for men visiting the city to explore the growing circuits of sexual tourism.

Chicago-based writer, academic, and aspiring tattoo artist Sam Steward spent the summers of 1953 and 1954 in San Francisco cruising for sex on the waterfront. On his first visit, he kept a detailed journal of sixty-three sexual encounters during the forty-two days he stayed in a "front cubicle on the 4th floor" of the Embarcadero YMCA.[51] Although many of his "releases" took place in the private rooms of other men lodging there, he also cruised for sex in his black leather jacket in the many nightlife spots in the city. Among the places he found success, he listed "Chili's, [a] queer low-level joint on the Embarcadero"; "356 Taylor, [a] club full of queens," and "Keeno's, a fantastic queer joint" in the Tenderloin; the Black Cat and the Paper Doll in North Beach; and the "doorways filled with toughs, available for $$" along Market Street.[52] When Steward returned in 1954, he discovered that the management at the YMCA had begun discouraging sexual activity among its guests. Steward wrote in his journal that there was a new "furtiveness everywhere" and that "everyone walked with eyes almost painfully (certainly maidenly) downcast," because the management now enforced a strict "Christian atmosphere."[53] The management's new policies excluded outside guests on the upper residential floors, imposed a curfew that limited after-hours interactions among guests, and prohibited loitering.[54]

The crackdown orchestrated by the YMCA's moral crusaders was short-lived, however. Howard Buckley, who had worked as a mail carrier at the Navy Pacific Fleet headquarters in Pearl Harbor in the early 1950s, stayed briefly at the Embarcadero YMCA in the summer of 1955 during a stop-over for his final six months of service in Southern California.[55] While in the shower, he was sexually aroused at the sight of a man who entered after him. The man, an Air Force captain, signaled his receptiveness, and the two spent the night together in the officer's room, just down the hall from Buckley's.[56]

The YMCA was not only popular with traveling servicemen and out-of-town visitors. Local men headed to the waterfront to find masculine working-class sexual partners. For instance, during the 1950s, Paul Goercke frequented the YMCA as one of his Friday night destinations. While a music student at Berkeley, Goercke explored queer life on the waterfront, hoping to meet men transiting or visiting the city.[57] As he recalled years later, he usually started the evening dining at Gordon's before moving on to either Jack's Baths or the Embarcadero YMCA, which he described as "the maddest place you ever saw."[58] He mentioned that administrators of the YMCA posted warning signs throughout the building about room occupancy limits,

FIGURE 1.2 The Embarcadero YMCA, seen here in 1958, catered to merchant marines and military personnel by providing temporary accommodations, exercise facilities, and meeting rooms in a handsome building that stood out along a strip of seamen's hotels and bars on the waterfront. (AAE-1051, San Francisco History Center, San Francisco Public Library.)

to prevent sexual activity among visitors. The night managers, however, largely ignored them. Similarly, Robert Dinsmore remembered wandering over to the YMCA or the restrooms at the Southern Pacific headquarters on his lunch hour for anonymous sex. After the Navy dishonorably discharged him in 1955, he settled in San Francisco and took a job in a downtown department store selling men's shirts. Around that time, he often headed to the YMCA for the "wild sex . . . going on in every bathroom in the place."[59]

While queens in the maritime trades and sexual solicitation at the YMCA provide two explanations for why the waterfront was so closely associated with queer life during the 1940s and 1950s, they alone are insufficient for understanding why the Embarcadero became a queer nightlife strip lined with gay bars—as Robert claimed and other sources corroborate—during this period. From where did a critical mass of queer patrons who turned sailor hangouts into gay bars come? The answer lies with changes in the maritime labor force, fueled by national security concerns, that radically changed the composition of who hung out in the mix of seamen's hotels, bars, restaurants, and nightclubs along the Embarcadero by the mid-1950s.

THE LAVENDER SCARE AND THE SAN FRANCISCO WATERFRONT

During the first years of the Lavender Scare, the San Francisco waterfront was ground zero in the efforts of the straight state to identify and neutralize the alleged homosexual threat to national security at the onset of the Cold War.[60] According to the *New York Times*, the port of San Francisco was the first and only shipping center where three military branches purged suspected subversives from the waterfront.[61] The only similar program was in Boston, where the anti-communist National Maritime Union scrutinized the security credentials of its members in an internal purge in 1950.[62] On the West Coast, the purge effectively destroyed the Marine Cooks and Stewards Union (MCSU), which right-wing critics characterized as "a third red, a third black, and a third queer."[63] In truth, some members were all three. By the mid-1950s, after several rounds of port screenings, many of these men were replaced by a predominantly white, heterosexual, and stridently anti-communist cohort of marine cooks and stewards, who built their own hiring hall in a different part of the city and took over dispatching crews to the waterfront.

Domestic Cold War politics profoundly impacted San Francisco as ideological and moral purges in the name of national security reshaped the city's maritime labor force. In the late 1940s and early 1950s, the United States emerged as the ideological and military opponent of the Soviet Union and China in a global contest over the political and economic foundations of a new era of internationalism. Domestically, a new politics of suspicion targeted suspected enemy agents of foreign adversaries working subversively to overthrow the political and economic order of the United States. Partisan ideologues in government amassed political capital by exercising state power to remove communists, alleged communists, resident aliens, and left-wing trade unionists from occupations associated directly with national defense and border security. Moreover, anti-homosexual purges in the armed forces, the State Department, the Pentagon, and the White House became the cornerstone of a campaign to allegedly prevent foreign influence, under the threat of blackmail against government officials in national security positions.

While scholars have uncovered the impact of the Red and Lavender Scares on gay men and lesbians in the military and the federal government, they have paid less attention to the consequences of anti-homosexual campaigns in the maritime labor force or on the places displaced workers ended up.[64] In the late 1940s and early 1950s, a coordinated, federally orchestrated screening program targeted the Port of San Francisco and other Western ports, expelling thousands of suspected homosexuals from the civilian maritime labor force and the armed services. As a result, a disproportionate number of gay men ejected from the maritime trades and military remained or took up residence in San Francisco, a relatively "wide open" port city with a strong tradition of socially progressive labor organizing.

In the late 1940s and early 1950s, the Chinese Revolution and the specter of the further advance of Communism on the Korean peninsula heightened national security concerns in the United States over the vulnerability of Pacific ports. In contrast to their eastern counterparts, West Coast maritime trade unions were more sympathetic to, if not ideologically aligned with, the goals of the revolution. San Francisco, in particular, was seen as the greatest national security concern because of its strong tradition of maritime union organizing and successes in formalizing labor contracts with shipping firms. Specifically, the ILWU had one of the highest proportions of registered members of the Communist Party, consisting of eight hundred men on its roster of thirty thousand longshoremen and warehouse workers.[65] During the mid-1930s, the longshoremen in San Francisco successfully rallied to change unfair hiring practices by shutting down the shipping industry up and down the Pacific Coast. The ILWU ended its wartime no-strike pledge in 1947 and again negotiated labor contracts with the shipping companies.[66] Opposition within the ILWU to US intervention on the side of Chinese nationalists fueled concerns about the safety and security of Pacific ports.[67] In addition, the racially integrated, queen-friendly, left-leaning MCSU posed a triple threat to port security, given the narrowing racial, sexual, and ideological constructs of loyalty to the nation.

In the summer of 1950, the San Francisco waterfront became ground zero in the overlapping state efforts to expel suspected subversives, including people of color and homosexuals, from the West Coast maritime labor unions. In June, President Truman's commerce and labor secretaries convened a meeting of maritime union leaders and leading ship owners to secure their cooperation in barring merchant mariners associated with the Communist Party from port facilities.[68] The commerce and labor secretaries got the cooperation of all but the MCSU and the ILWU, the two powerful left-wing maritime unions with deep organizational roots in San Francisco. In retaliation, federal officials developed and implemented a new port-security program to screen suspected subversives off the San Francisco waterfront.[69]

On the afternoon of July 31, 1950, at pier 37, Coast Guard officers with "official information from Washington" compared the crew manifest of the cargo ship *Anchor Hitch* against a list of "poor security risks." The officers took papers from the thirty-six crewmembers and "whisked [them] by courier to a locked cabin" where they "checked [them] against a typewritten list of names." According to a contemporary press account, the typewritten list came "presumably from the FBI." Soon after the Coast Guard started the first security checks of seamen's papers against a secret list of suspected subversives, the Army and Navy set up concurrent screening programs at all San Francisco Military Port facilities.[70] Port officials throughout the city disseminated application cards to local union halls. Members voluntarily brought the completed cards to the Ferry Building, where Coast Guard officials affixed a photograph and fingerprint of the applicant before sending the card to military screeners at Fort Mason. Based on which cards came back with a stamped approval for "emergency" service, the Coast Guard decided which dockworkers would or would not have access to port facilities and which merchant marines could work aboard commercial sailing vessels.[71] By September, Coast Guard officials had processed 6,600 applications for security credentials required to work on the waterfront. In October, Truman expanded the program by authorizing Coast Guard officials to screen all vessels, harbors, ports, and waterfront facilities for subversive activity.[72] He directed port directors across the country to issue port-security cards to all maritime laborers with satisfactory "character and habits of life." Because the screening list remained secret and authorities did not provide specific accusations when denying individuals port-security cards, verifying whom the program targeted and on what basis with much precision is impossible.[73] According to Bérubé, screeners removed nearly all left-wing stewards from West Coast ships over the next several months. Three out of four were African American. In one instance, three out of five white stewards known to be gay were barred from boarding a Matson liner when they all reported for duty.[74]

The MCSU raised the strongest objections to the port screening program.[75] This multiracial, queer, left-wing union quickly understood the program's threat to its members. In addition to ending individual careers, it could be divisive within the ranks. Two days after the pilot program in San Francisco, sixty-five MCSU members aboard the steamer *Alaska* refused to sail out of Seattle without assurance that a "third party" would not review their sea papers. After a twenty-four-hour standoff, the shipping company fired and replaced them with a new crew willing to submit their papers to scrutiny.[76] The following week, nine MCSU crewmembers aboard the passenger liner *President Cleveland* refused to sign off on documents required of vessels prior to setting sail. The men were part of the steward's department, which constituted nearly two-thirds of the entire crew.[77]

Truman's port screening program destroyed the careers of a disproportionate number of African Americans and gay men, many of whom were members of the MCSU or the ILWU. In June 1950, just as Truman's port screening program began, the Navy maintained a list of eight thousand suspected homosexuals, while the Army had a list of five thousand.[78] In May 1953, the Coast Guard declared the screening virtually complete, having reviewed the security credentials of 354,000 seamen and 270,000 dockworkers. As a result, port officials expelled over 1,800 seafaring personnel and more than 900 longshoremen from the maritime labor force.[79] African Americans comprised an estimated 60 to 70 percent of the MCSU and ILWU members who were denied port-security clearances.[80] Half of the MCSU members flagged as national security threats and barred from future employment were union delegates elected to represent the interests of crewmembers during sea voyages.[81] It is impossible to know precisely how many of these workers were barred from the maritime labor force based on their sexuality. Nevertheless, many maritime workers likely were ferreted out by officials cross-checking port-security cards against the lists of suspected homosexuals maintained by the Army and Navy.

Soon after President Eisenhower took office, he ordered his own port screening program. In the spring of 1953, he called for rescreening all government employees and civilian contractors working on ships, in harbors, at ports, and in waterfront facilities, using an updated list of suspected subversives. He expanded the list to exclude all personnel with "any criminal, infamous, dishonest, immoral, or notoriously disgraceful conduct, habitual drug use of intoxicants to excess, drug addiction, sexual perversion, or financial irresponsibility," as well as those with a history of "treatment for serious mental or neurological disorder without satisfactory cure."[82] By the end of 1955, screeners denied security clearances to nearly 1,850 of 427,182 civilian sailors and 1,935 out of 397,206 dockworkers.[83] It is impossible to know what percentage of the roughly four thousand men excluded from the civilian maritime labor force during the first half of the 1950s were gay. Over the same period, the Navy dishonorably discharged 5,656 enlisted personnel on charges of homosexuality.[84]

While the port screening program denied suspected homosexuals security clearances to work in the maritime trades, a major reorganization of labor unions, fueled by anti-communist, anti-Black, and antigay members, ejected suspected subversives from hiring halls. In 1953, an organizational battle broke out between left- and right-wing groups over who would control the hiring halls for cooks and stewards and represent their interests in contract negotiations with shipping firms. Fractured by anti-communist, anti-Black, and antigay elements within its ranks and in rival unions, the MCSU membership split into three factions. While one breakaway group of white members aligned with a right-wing union of white sailors, a second multiracial group affiliated with the left-wing ILWU.[85] The third group consisted of most of the Black stewards and a few allies left behind. Gay stewards split across the different factions. In 1954, the right-wing faction won the organizational battle to represent cooks and stewards in negotiating contracts, by demonstrating that it had attracted the largest number of members.[86] The reorganization of the union had the same effect as the port screenings. It excluded a significant number of men who were Black, leftist, queer, or some combination of the three from employment on the San Francisco waterfront.

Maritime bars in the Embarcadero also helped drive the formation of racially mixed, queer drinking publics. Two news items—one published before the screenings and purge began and the other after—show how waterfront hangouts were sites of struggles for inclusion for Black stewards in the MCSU. One place where a racially mixed, queer crowd hung out on Embarcadero was the bar associated with the Admiral Hotel. Located two doors down from the YMCA, this seamen's hotel had a tavern on the first floor with a backroom known as the Sailor Boy. In his unofficial guide to slumming, *San Francisco Chronicle* columnist Herb Caen frequently made coded references to the city's nightlife scene, laced with innuendo and double entendre. For example, in June 1947, he drew attention to "Two of the Embarcadero's more colorful hangouts—the Ensign Café, at Market[,] and the Admiral, opposite Howard, where you'll rarely see an Ensign and never see an Admiral."[87] Caen's short mention of the Ensign and the Admiral implied that the two bars had become popular among African American queens. By claiming you would rarely see a real sailor or officer at the two places, he telegraphed that the Black cooks and stewards who became a majority in the MSCU in the last days of the war had turned the Admiral into a hangout for queerly classed, "colorful" seamen.

Five years later, as race-baiting began to create factions within the MCSU, the Admiral was the site of a backlash against the racial and queer integration of the maritime labor force. In 1952, the manager of the Admiral tavern refused to serve lunch to two Black men in the independent MCSU—one an elected union official. In defending her racist decision, the manager stated: "I have been serving Negroes, like anybody else, but lately several have come in and acted abusive and drunk and then I just don't pay 'em any mind." The two men, who were already facing employment discrimination at the hands of government screeners and rival unions, filed a $10,000 suit for "grievous humiliation and embarrassment."[88] With the port screenings and MCSU purge in full swing, Black stewards were no longer welcome at the Admiral tavern. The racist denial of service at the lunch counter and the subsequent civil rights suit reflected similar fights for racial justice in the South. In this instance, however, it was not about integrating white spaces. Instead, it stemmed from the efforts of a faction of white stewards, aided by rival unions and federal agencies, to wrestle work opportunities away from the multiracial, queer-friendly, and left-leaning union members that controlled the MCSU hiring hall.

THE QUEERING OF WATERFRONT HANGOUTS

One significant consequence of the more intensive port screenings and union purges in San Francisco was that displaced maritime workers—disproportionately queer and people of color—fueled the expansion of a homoerotic, nighttime marketplace of cruising, sex, and slumming on the waterfront.[89] As one anthropologist noted in the 1960s, many of the men expelled from work in the port and aboard civilian ships congregated in "home territory bars" of sailors and longshoremen that served as informal hiring halls and organizational hubs.[90] In particular, the seamen's bars just off the lobbies of or adjacent to residential hotels along the Embarcadero developed into hangouts for a significant, albeit unknown, number of queer men drummed out of the maritime workforce and Navy. These places had a steady stream of both queer men who formerly worked at sea or on the waterfront and trade queens who were sexually attracted to these idled maritime laborers.

Oral histories, when cross-referenced with other sources, provide a glimpse of the expansion of the racially mixed queer hangouts that drove the pleasure economy of the bars, hotels, and other haunts previously embedded exclusively in the city's maritime economy. In 1951, Larry Howell, a twenty-six-year-old self-described "sissy," arrived in San Francisco with some friends for what he thought would be a two-week visit from Los Angeles.[91] He had met Tommy and Frankie, a gay couple from Brooklyn, in the hotel where he was living in Southern California. Tommy was a "middle-aged gruff seaman who shipped out on freighters overseas" with steel-gray hair, and Frankie was a "real cute Italian boy" in his twenties. After Tommy returned from a trip to Hong Kong, he had trouble getting another work assignment and decided to seek work aboard a ship leaving from San Francisco. Tommy's difficulty finding work and his decision to head north were likely direct consequences of the federal policies and labor practices that pushed suspected homosexuals out of the merchant marines. Howell accompanied Tommy to several rough trade bars along The Front—including "a sleazy place called the Ensign Club," Madam Chili's, Lennie's, and the Sea Cow Café—where out-of-work merchant marines were open to casual sex with other men in exchange for food, money, or a place to stay.[92]

Eugene Carles, a native San Franciscan and former Navy sailor who identified as a trade queen, sought out sex with masculine, straight-seeming sailors on the waterfront in the 1950s. He recalled:

> The Embarcadero . . . was still all shipping . . . in those days . . . The produce market and everything was down there with lots of industry you know. I used to get a lot of people when I was . . . half gassed [and] wandering around looking for a piece or something . . . People getting off the midnight shift from some of those printing companies down there . . . Off Market on and off the waterfront, sailors down on the waterfront. Box cars. Any port in the storm.[93]

For self-identified trade queens like Carles, the possibility of sexual connections with masculine-presenting seamen and laborers was part of the allure of the waterfront before the area was redeveloped.

One of Carles's favorite sailor bars was Chili's, on the first floor of the four-story Marin Hotel (see figure 1.3).[94] Chili's was a "drinking man's bar" next door to the YMCA, "where the seamen and the people who worked on the Embarcadero went before it was a gay bar . . . [located in] . . . that row of flophouses and things where the seamen used to stay."[95] Both the YMCA and the Marin Hotel spanned the full depth of the rectangular waterfront block, with the main entrance on the Embarcadero and back entrances on Steuart Street. It was a "raunchy place," and Chili, who ran the place, was "a weird looking thing" who wore lots of makeup and was always "on heroin or something."[96] Gerald Fabian, another regular patron, recalled that Chili "looked like a drag queen" and had been a madam during World War II. One of her "girls" ran a place in the Tenderloin called the Sundown Club on Mason Street, where both gay and straight sailors and marines could procure sex.[97] Glen Price, who also frequented the establishment, could not help but notice Chili's racial ambiguity and extravagant clothing: "I never did know what nationality she was. I think she was a mixture of everything under the sun because her hair was as kinky as a Negro's hair and it stuck out like this. And she had sequins, all that stuff, on her outfits . . . I'd say well what are you today, Chili? And she'd say, I'm a butterfly queen, she'd say, flicking about."[98] He also added about the patrons and atmosphere, "It was just a mishmash of everything and, of course, lots of merchant seamen came there."[99]

Chili's was not what would now be called a gay bar but a seamen's hangout that facilitated all kinds of commercial transactions, including sexual exchanges, for sailors in town between stints at sea. Price was such a reliable fixture at Chili's that he became a money handler for the hustlers who operated out of the bar. Price recalled dealing with four or five "characters," most of them Black men, who engaged in sexual commerce and petty crimes on the waterfront. Periodically during the night, they would stop by Chili's for a beer and put money in his pocket for safekeeping. He never asked where they got their money. He suggestively revealed, however, that in terms of sexual preference, "they went for everything."[100] Sometimes even, they "rolled people or robbed them of something."[101] At the end of the evening, they would return and collect their evening haul. Eventually, Chili introduced Price to Charles Hofftonson, a chief steward for American President Lines. Not long after, Price stopped going to Chili's to pursue what turned into a thirty-year-long relationship with Hofftonson.

Seamen's hangouts like Chili's were more than leisure places of drinking or making social, and sometimes sexual, connections. They performed a crucial role in the city's "underground" labor market and economy. Queer sailors like Tommy, the "gruff seaman" who befriended Howell, went to

FIGURE 1.3 In the 1940s and 1950s, "Chili" ran a small bar in the Marin Hotel at 144–146 Embarcadero (seen here in 1970), where she catered to a racially mixed crowd of sailors and dockworkers. She had a reputation for facilitating sexual encounters among men in the maritime trades and "trade queens" who cruised the waterfront. (TOR-0100, San Francisco History Center, San Francisco Public Library.)

Chili's to seek out news about possible job prospects, compare experiences at sea, and inquire about the hiring conditions.[102] Hangouts also served as informal banks for some gay seamen and patrons. For example, Bob Ross described how the owner of the 57 Powell Club in the Tenderloin kept accounts for gay men in the maritime trades.[103] Ross described this relationship of mutual trust:

> It was a gay bar and all these people were queens but if they get off the ship and they have like $9,000 in paid out cash, or $10,000 . . . they'd go to Maurice's. They'd give him the money and they would drink it down or borrow from [it] . . . When they ran out of money, most of them went back to work . . . He never screwed them over, so he had quite a business going for many, many years.[104]

In effect, these men entrusted Maurice to safeguard a large portion of their earnings while they waited for another job at sea. Ross explained, "The Merchant Marines was big business in this town. And all these queens who worked for the Marine Cooks and Stewards, the Masters Mates and Pilots, everything else, used to hang out at Maurice's 57 Powell . . . Most of them lived in those hotels between, you know, stints on ships."[105]

Seamen's hangouts like Maurice's 57 Club and Chili's developed out of a particular sexual division of labor when queens had a sizeable share of work as stewards on ships sailing out of San Francisco. These informal social hubs were a product of San Francisco's maritime economy. During the late 1940s and early 1950s, as port screenings and union purges excluded more and more queer men from the maritime labor force, many gay men denied port-security cards or purged from union rolls spent more time in "home territory bars" like Maurice's and Chili's looking for work. By the late 1950s, the labor system that produced these bars unraveled as employment prospects in maritime trades dimmed. As a result, a number of former seamen's hangouts, particularly on the waterfront, took on the character of gay bars with a consumer rather than an occupational logic.

Perhaps the most significant waterfront hangout in the history of maritime union organizing on the West Coast, and another important queer spot, was the Sea Cow Café (see figure 1.4). Formerly known as the Mohawk Café, the Sea Cow Café had been the strike headquarters of the International Longshoremen's Association (ILA), led by Harry Bridges, during the waterfront strike of 1934. The strike led to the creation of a union-controlled hiring hall system throughout the maritime trades.[106] In the ground-floor commercial space below the union offices, the Mohawk served as one of the ILA's strike kitchens, feeding dockworkers during a work stoppage that escalated on Bloody Thursday with the killing of two men—a marine cook and a longshoreman—by the police on the sidewalk next door.[107] The dead men lay in repose on the second floor. Dockworkers paid their last respects over the weekend before escorting the bodies down Steuart Street for a funeral procession down Market Street. In a subsequent general strike, nearly ten thousand laborers joined the twenty-five thousand maritime workers striking for the right to operate their own hiring halls.[108] By 1937, the Mohawk Café had become Jack and John's Lunchroom, run by Jack and John Balovich. The same sidewalk became the scene of a standoff between rival factions of the ILWU, as longshoremen decided between affiliating with the AFL or CIO. In 1954, the Balovichs lunchroom became the Sea Cow Café around the time the ILWU initiated plans to abandon the central waterfront location and build a new headquarters at the western end of the Embarcadero near Fisherman's Wharf.

By the mid-1950s, the Sea Cow was less a union-affiliated home bar for longshoremen than a hangout for gay merchant marines and men attracted to them. The Mattachine Society, a homophile organization founded in Los Angeles in 1950, compiled a directory of thirty-five gay hangouts in West Coast ports to distribute to participants at its 1954 convention in San Francisco.[109] The closely guarded convention guide was dominated by San Francisco attractions, including three bathhouses, three restaurants, and various bars, nightclubs, and cocktail lounges.[110] Indicative of the changing sexual economy of the waterfront, the guide characterized the Sea Cow as an excellent place for gay men visiting the city to find "Beer, Wine, and Seamen."[111]

Another working-class bar on the Embarcadero that gained a queer clientele in the 1950s was Jack's Waterfront Hangout. It was the preferred cruising spot for trade queens, like San Jose native Richard McClure, interested in hypermasculine men. McClure recalled:

It was a rough trade hangout. And trade queens exclusively went there. This is where the leather scene was born. In that environment. Dock workers, truck drivers, dock hands and all that stuff. Merchant seamen. Black gang guys they were called . . . meaning they worked . . . around the engines and . . . get black [from] engine oil [that] can make you pretty dark [in] the black part of the ship . . . down in the hold.[112]

The mix of regulars he recalled matched the kinds of land uses in the area. Jack's was located on the Embarcadero adjacent to the wholesale produce market, where agricultural goods came into the city by truck and were off-loaded by longshoremen and warehousemen. Not far from Jack's was the headquarters of the Marine Firemen's Union, which represented "black gang guys," or groups of laborers often covered in oil and soot from working in the engine room aboard ships. As McClure's characterization reflects, waterfront hangouts were differentiated by occupation, underscoring their importance as critical sites of trade union organizing. The men who frequented Jack's were considered "rough trade" because they were more masculine than the queens who hung out at The Admiral, Maurice's, and Chili's. The waterfront workers who hung out at Jack's were unbothered by, or perhaps drawn to, the trade queens like McClure. Out of these social and sexual interactions, Jack's likely was where "the leather scene was born."[113]

In another sign that waterfront hangouts were becoming queerer in the mid-1950s, Army veteran Leonard "Lennie" Mollet took over the former Silver Dollar tavern at 36 Embarcadero and briefly operated the 36 Club in late 1954.[114] A plumber from Massachusetts, Mollet settled in San Francisco in 1950 after finishing his military career in the Pacific. Only days after he posted a public notice that he had acquired a liquor license for the 36 Club, Army-Navy officials labeled the place a "hangout for homosexuals" and added it to its out-of-bounds list.[115] Nevertheless, Lennie's 36 Club briefly drew working-class men to the waterfront tavern for several months before city officials purchased and razed the modest two-story for a parking lot.[116] Mollet's short-lived 36 Club marked the start of his nearly forty-year career as "the longest [operating] gay bar owner in town."[117]

FROM SEAMEN AND SERVICEMEN TO CLERICAL WORKERS AND BUSINESSMEN

In the mid-1950s, the queer cruising strip frequented by merchant marines, dockworkers, and naval personnel near the foot of Market Street developed into a circuit of gay bars popular with downtown office workers. Arch Wilson, an Army stenographer during World War II, came to San Francisco initially in 1953 and took a short-term clerical job before moving to the city permanently in 1955.[118] Through his new job at the headquarters of the Southern Pacific Railroad, he quickly met other gay men. As Wilson recounted years later: "I was meeting people from Southern Pacific where

FIGURE 1.4 The Sea Cow Café (flanked by 7-Up signs in 1957) was located on the first floor of a longshoremen's hall that had been at the center of maritime union organizing on the West Coast from the 1930s to the early 1950s. From the mid-1950s to the mid-1960s, the Sea Cow, later known as Crossroads, was a popular queer hangout among homophile leaders and trade queens. (AAK-1663, San Francisco History Center, San Francisco Public Library.)

there were lots of queens . . . There were lots of people who had fled the merchant marine working for Southern Pacific. Not to mention former service people like me, lots of gays in San Francisco . . . lots in Southern Pacific."[119] Jim Kepner also recalled working on freight accounts in the basement. Not only did he remember working alongside two long-haired men who were "obviously lovers," but he developed a crush on a "willowy redhead" in the Statistical Department.[120] A perceptive female friend and coworker picked up on Kepner's awkwardness and helped him to engage other gay coworkers and find gay bars in the area. The incident underscored the queerness of the Southern Pacific as a workplace where gay men built social networks with other gay men relatively openly and with the help of colleagues.

The Southern Pacific Building was a prominent, block-long, ten-story edifice on the south side of Market Street, only a half-block from the Embarcadero (see figure 1.5). During the 1950s, a prominent neon sign crowned the building's central tower. At night, the oversized "SP" letters on the forty-by-seventy-foot sign cast a red-and-blue glow over the foot of Market Street and dominated the lower Market cityscape from 1954 to 1962.[121] Playing on the initials emblazoned on the sign, gay men nicknamed the building the "Swish Palace" for the large contingent of gay men employed in clerical positions. Jim Duggins, a Navy journalist stationed in the Pacific during the Korean War, learned about the Swish Palace when he first visited the city in 1954.[122] Four years later, he moved to San Francisco. He recalled that Southern Pacific "still had hired only male secretaries. And they had a big, big ["SP"] sign on top of the building . . . that everyone claims as 'Swish Palace' because the place was full of male secretaries, maybe a thousand of them. And at 4:30 when they got off, people claim that they flew out of those windows (laughter). 'Cause there were, you know, suddenly 500 or more male secretaries let out on Market Street, and suddenly you got a gay village on the street."[123]

By the mid-1960s, many of the former seamen's hangouts near the waterfront that developed into a circuit of gay bars were gone—razed to make way for the Golden Gateway urban renewal project. Legions of gay clerical workers, however, continued to grow as the city's economy—and employment base—shifted away from its maritime footings. Several gay men recalled how large numbers of gay clerical workers continued to dominate pockets of the downtown business district. Jim Kirkman, who had arrived in the city in 1965 and worked at Bechtel, attributed Southern Pacific's policy of hiring male secretaries as an attempt to allay the jealousies and suspicions of wives of executives who often traveled with their assistants. He described a similar phenomenon of gay men leaving work en masse from their office jobs in the financial district: "I worked at Bechtel in those days, and there were so many gay [men]. . . at five o'clock when the elevators emptied out, you would've swore you were in a gay bar, so obvious."[124]

Duggins also noted that the YMCA continued into the 1960s to be a popular place for gay cruising during off-work hours, albeit without the older connection to the maritime and military economies. He characterized it as a "health facility" that drew married businessmen seeking sex over their lunch hour or before returning to their wives in the suburbs on Friday afternoon.[125] Gay men who had lovers also frequented the YMCA as an inconspicuous place to seek out sexual encounters as part of the "noontime" and "Friday afternoon" crowd. David Harrell's reminiscences of the YMCA suggest that it continued as a sexual "gateway" to the city for newcomers into the mid-1960s. In early 1965, when he moved to San Francisco, Harrell

FIGURE 1.5 The Southern Pacific Building (upper right with "SP" sign on top) was nick-named the "Swish Palace" for the large number of gay male clerical staff who worked there in the 1950s. These men were part of a new class of workers who transformed seamen's hangouts on the waterfront into gay bars. Like the changing bar crowds, the Embarcadero Freeway (under construction in 1958) reflected the city's declining economic dependence on its port facilities. (AAD-6335, San Francisco History Center, San Francisco Public Library.)

stayed several nights at the Embarcadero Y while looking for more perma-nent housing. He chose the Y because it was convenient to his new job at Standard Oil, where he worked as a typesetter printing statistical reports. Harrell arrived from a small town in Kansas. He had worked at the local newspaper until the local postmaster found magazines with male nudes in his mailbox and told his employer. At the urging of a straight friend from college, he moved to San Francisco to start over after his first job ended in public humiliation. He had been to San Francisco on a short summer vacation but "didn't have any concept of [the city] being a gay center."[126] During his short stay at the YMCA, however, where "all these people [were] patrolling the bathrooms that don't live here," he "suddenly became aware, this is really homo heaven."[127]

"THOSE BUDDING DAYS"

The Embarcadero waterfront near the foot of Market Street became a racially diverse, queer margin of the city during the middle decades of the last century. During the 1930s and 1940s, queens working as marine cooks and stewards organized and secured gains in wages, job security, and political influence within the West Coast hiring hall system. With the decasualization of the predominantly male maritime labor force, queer men congregated in home territory bars where they could learn about employment opportunities, find solidarity with fellow union members, and fulfill their personal needs and desires. During World War II, the influx of troops brought an increasing number of queer servicemen through the city, intensifying the association of the waterfront with queer bars and same-sex cruising. As Cold War tensions mounted in the late 1940s, the San Francisco waterfront was the epicenter of a coordinated effort by the Coast Guard, Army, and Navy to systematically exclude homosexuals from the merchant marines, waterfront work crews, and naval military service. The security screenings of port workers by federal officials and the reorganization of labor unions in the city destroyed the livelihoods of an untold number of suspected homosexuals in the maritime trades. As job prospects dried up with the dissolution or relocation of union hiring halls, former labor hangouts developed into a nightlife circuit where displaced port workers, returning servicemen, and civilians organized their personal and social lives around same-sex desire. Before city officials razed them to make way for the Golden Gateway urban renewal project, these hangouts were important sites for a queer counterpublic to develop among owners, staff, and patrons during the late 1950s and early 1960s.

2

THE BIRTHPLACE OF MODERN SAN FRANCISCO

In the 1950s, Berkeley's Aquatic Park was "a gathering spot" for men from fifty miles around who came for sex in the park's four public restrooms.[1] According to the local police and city officials, the bathroom walls were covered with "lewd writings and drawings, including names, dates, and numerous 'propositions' for immoral acts." These crude sexual invitations surrounded glory holes in the partitions between toilet stalls. Most upsetting to the officer reporting on the potential danger of this behavior was that some restrooms lacked signs indicating whether they were for men or women. City officials struggled to "stamp out" the search for sexual thrills that took place in and around the bathroom. The park's sole maintenance worker could not keep up with cleaning the facilities. Periodic fresh paint became a canvas for new vulgarities. Police patrols were outmanned, unable to deter men from having sex in the restrooms, nearby bushes, and parked cars. Berkeley officials deliberated over how to deal with such a flagrant example of queer sex in public spaces, including a proposal to raze the three worst facilities and refurbish the remaining one next to the park office.[2] Across the Bay from Berkeley, San Francisco leaders wrestled with the same question about how to temper the voyeuristic lure of these facilities and control the growing number of queer hangouts. On waterfronts on opposite sides of the Bay, expressions of same-sex desire among men in public spaces had become a concern that was hard for local authorities to ignore. Could these disorderly places be straightened up with targeted policing, or was demolition the answer?

As efforts to straighten up the restrooms at Berkeley's Aquatic Park suggest, targeted policing and radical modifications to the built environment were two remedies that city officials used to constrain the sexual subcultures that threatened the heteronormative public sphere of the United States in the 1950s.[3] Neither approach was effective in containing San Francisco's growing sexual countercultures, although it was not for lack of trying by local leaders. In the 1950s, state and city officials enacted new liquor licensing guidelines, undercover surveillance, vagrancy laws, and "saturation" policing to close gay bars and "clean up" public cruising areas.[4] Alarmist coverage of the law enforcement struggles to contain the homosexual threat, however, cemented rather than undercut San Francisco's reputation as a "Queer City."[5] The redevelopment agency followed up by razing several residential hotel and rooming house districts, long considered a public nuisance and breeding ground for social ills.[6] Rather than rebuilding San Francisco for heterosexual families, urban redevelopment produced a new urban geography by driving gay bars and queer people away from the margins of downtown and into outlying neighborhoods.[7] Precisely how targeted policing and urban redevelopment worked hand in hand as tools to contain and eliminate queer land uses merits closer attention—particularly in the case of seamen's hangouts that developed into gay bars in San Francisco during the 1950s.

Across the country during the 1950s and 1960s, pro-growth coalitions of local business elites, elected officials, and planning and design professionals marshaled the local redevelopment authority and federal resources to reorganize patterns of urban land uses in the interest of stimulating economic growth in the urban core.[8] Urban scholars have shown how urban redevelopment initiatives physically transformed the San Francisco waterfront during this period.[9] Less understood is how local elites mustered the political will and governing capacity to carry out these transformations.[10] In his discussion of the Golden Gateway project, urban geographer Jasper Rubin highlighted the relative success of local actors in exercising redevelopment authority to reshape waterfront land uses. His focus on the ascendance of urban renewal as a political agenda led him to conclude that the project of "cleansing, washing away the dirty bits of urban society," faced "little criticism" from the wider public.[11] These "dirty bits of urban society," principally the queer nightlife crowds on the waterfront, reveal much about how pro-growth proponents persuaded the public to prioritize waterfront redevelopment over competing projects. Scattered among reams of archived records and personal recollections maintained by government officials as well as gay community historians are clues about how redevelopment proponents at times publicly decried, while also privately encouraged, the transgressive sexual economy at the foot of Market Street in order to rationalize an aggressive program to remake the area into "the birthplace of modern San Francisco."[12]

This chapter reconstructs how law enforcement and pro-growth proponents played overlapping and complementary roles in adding queer drinking establishments to the very top of the city's urban renewal agenda. Alarmed by what they viewed as deteriorating social conditions on the Embarcadero during the 1950s, a new group of civic leaders spearheaded an expansive urban redevelopment project to raze much of the maritime quarter. At key decision points, waterfront hangouts figured prominently in their efforts to expand the project's geographic extent, alter the route of a planned freeway, and secure funds for a waterfront park. While these hangouts occupied a small portion of the urban renewal area, they played a crucial role in deepening the involvement of corporate and banking executives in urban planning priorities and projects.

THE LIMITS OF BAR RAIDS, STREET SWEEPS, AND CLEAN-UP DRIVES

In the late 1940s and early 1950s, San Francisco law enforcement and state liquor agents set their sights on the queer and racially mixed waterfront bars where suspected subversives in the maritime trades congregated. During this period, the term "hangout" first became shorthand to stigmatize these places in the city's labor economy. In 1950, for example, the *San Francisco Chronicle* tagged the Marine Cooks and Stewards Union (MCSU) hiring hall as "a notorious hangout for left-wingers," to describe the targets of the federal port screening program in the city.[13] Soon, local officials tagged bars where queer men in the maritime trades and naval forces congregated as "hangouts for homosexuals."[14] Periodic dragnets, bar raids, and street sweeps became blunt instruments of the straight state to cordon off homosexual cruising strips from port and military officials. In these roundups, law enforcement cited queer individuals with various criminal acts, including cross-dressing, vagrancy, sexual solicitation, and disorderly conduct. If port or military personnel were caught in these activities, they would be screened out of the labor force.

The most problematic meeting place for idle merchant marines was a nightlife operation run by Sol Stoumen on the northern edge of the business district. When Stoumen took over the Black Cat in 1945, the gay clientele who frequented the bar included merchant marines and longshoremen.[15] Gerald Fabian, a patron of the establishment, recalled that the Black Cat attracted "a cross-section of people from North Beach . . . longshoremen and workers and dockworkers and people from the Embarcadero, because it was in that area where those people stayed; they stayed in those hotels around there . . . It was kind of a rough place but it had a kind of working-class feeling about it."[16] In the summer of 1947, local law enforcement raided the Black Cat based on a "claim from a young war widow that she had been raped by four men who met her at the Bohemianesque bar."[17] Then, in the fall, police arrested Stoumen and five others on a mix of assault, vagrancy, and narcotics charges. These two incidents of police action against the Black Cat were local manifestations of a national crackdown on vice and sex crimes that had not yet focused explicitly on targeting homosexuals.[18]

In the late 1940s, gay bar crowds in North Beach and on the waterfront were an open secret that garnered occasional public comment but little cause for concern. In late 1947, *San Francisco Chronicle* columnist Herb Caen called out the queerness of Black Cat patrons, smirking that "many of the 'artists' that hang around the Black Cat . . . have [not] painted anything besides their eyebrows or lips."[19] Five months earlier, Caen had implied that the gay crowds were getting bigger at two sailor bars on the Embarcadero waterfront, the Admiral and the Ensign Café.[20] His brief asides about the change in clientele at these three seamen's hangouts suggest that queer nightlife crowds of merchant marines had begun to turn these drinking establishments into pickup spots where they sought out same-sex social and sexual relationships. The Black Cat would be the first of these sailor bars to be explicitly and categorically recognized as a "gay bar" by patrons and the local press. However, as the next chapter will show, the Ensign Café had a more sexually transgressive, queer social scene than the Black Cat and Stoumen's larger nightclub on the waterfront.

With the backing of politically powerful state liquor interests, Stoumen was unfazed by his 1947 arrest. Not only was he able to keep the Black Cat Café open, he soon expanded his enterprise to cater to the growing number of gay men in the city. By 1949, Stoumen had taken over the nearby Old Grotto restaurant with a back barroom with sawdust floors known as the Red Lizard. According to a nightlife guidebook, after Stoumen arrived, he "encouraged the fruit and the place went to hell."[21] With a singing chef, the restaurant resembled a Prohibition-era "pansy" club. Army psychologist Stuart Loomis remembered the backroom as a "very, very crowded and popular gay bar."[22] Charles Gillman, who came to San Francisco in 1949 as a nineteen-year-old, also found the Red Lizard to be a "pretty wicked" pickup spot, where men performed oral sex under the table "not in the back of the bar, but in the front of the bar."[23] Gilman also learned about other queer nightspots from his fellow file clerks in the offices of American President Lines, which he noted was full of gay men.[24] Stoumen's expansion into the Old Grotto–Red Lizard, on the ground floor of a nearby seamen's hotel, was likely a move to address another recurring charge leveled by the liquor control agents. Rather than offering a full food menu, he merely put out bowls of pretzels.[25] By taking over the restaurant, he had access to a kitchen only steps away from the Black Cat. It was a strategy he would repeat in the early 1960s to expand his nightclub operation to lower Market Street.

Sol Stoumen's legal troubles began in 1949 when the Lavender Scare sparked gay-baiting in West Coast labor unions. The factionalism within the racially mixed, queer maritime culinary trades that ultimately destroyed the MCSU also sparked a labor dispute at the Black Cat. That year, his expanding queer nightlife operation—which benefited from a growing number of out-of-work queer seamen on the waterfront—got the brunt of the city's panic response to a so-called homo invasion.[26] Stoumen employed queens as waiters and kitchen staff at the Old Grotto. His critics viewed his hiring practices as a cynical move to turn it into a "beehive of perversion."[27] At the same time, the anti-homosexual screening program that sowed division within the ranks of the Maritime Cooks and Stewards Union also affected the non-maritime bartender and culinary worker's union. The culinary union pressured Stoumen to sign a closed-shop labor agreement that would have given the union more control over dispatching workers to the Old Grotto.[28] Wishing to continue to hire queer waitstaff that "encouraged the fruit," Stoumen refused, even rolling out a carpet for antigay picketers in front of the Black Cat.[29] The local liquor licensing administrator, George Reilly, sided with the protesters and pressured Stoumen to sign the closed-shop agreement. The prolabor Democrat hoped ridding the bohemian bar of homosexuals would help launch his run for mayor. When Stoumen refused, state liquor control authorities, acting on accusations of "idle, lewd, and dissolute conduct" by Black Cat customers, suspended Stoumen's liquor license indefinitely.[30] The state agents denounced the bar as "a hangout for persons of homosexual tendencies."[31]

Over the next two years, Stoumen, with legal representation from American Civil Liberties Union lawyer Morris Lowenthal, successfully beat the charge in a case that went to the State Supreme Court and established the constitutional right of homosexuals to public assembly. Although Stoumen won the case in 1951, he relinquished ownership of the Old Grotto to a new operator, who "eliminated the Red Lizard . . . which was getting sort of a name for itself."[32] Nevertheless, the 1951 court ruling in Stoumen's favor marked the start of a four-year "break with rigorous policing" that enabled "queer conviviality and sexual transgression to consolidate in the city's Tenderloin and North Beach districts."[33] Stoumen's successful defense of his hiring practices and his right to cater to queer patrons demonstrated to city leaders the limits of bar raids as an effective policing tactic to "clean up" the city's homosexual problem.

The period of relative permissiveness that came with the Black Cat legal victory began to break down in 1954 when city officials tried to clamp down on sexual solicitation in parks and other public spaces. As the Coast Guard and Navy screening programs targeting West Coast ports and military facilities intensified, gay men excluded from the merchant marines and armed forces found their way to and settled in San Francisco in significant numbers. As a consequence, public sexual solicitation among men soon became more prevalent and harder to ignore in the city. In June 1954, a sex crimes detail of twenty uniformed officers "swept through known gathering places throughout the city in a roundup aimed at homosexuals."[34] At the time, the thriving gender- and sexual-transgressive scene on the waterfront was well known to authorities, if not the general public. Lieutenant Bearden, head of the sex crimes detail, characterized lower Market Street as a known gathering place "where men dressed as women parade the sidewalks late at night." After police swept through the area, he told the public: "One arrest on lower Market Street involved a man with a prior record who was impersonating a woman and accosting servicemen."[35] The 1954 sweep was one of the last publicized citywide "roundups" of homosexuals loitering in public spaces. The sensationalized coverage drew unwanted attention to cruising areas and reinforced San Francisco's reputation as a queer city. Law enforcement soon changed tactics to keep the issue out of the headlines. They beefed up undercover entrapment of gay bar patrons on solicitation charges, which garnered both individual arrests and evidence needed to revoke liquor licenses.

After the June 1954 street sweep, downtown business interests called for stronger government action to deal with the influx of queer men in the city. For them, the threat was not an issue of national border security or sexual danger on the waterfront but the cause and effect of declining downtown property values. Economic pressures ultimately motivated urban boosters to crack down aggressively on queer waterfront establishments. At an October 1954 conference of business leaders and property owners in the retailing and hotel industries, commercial building owners blamed the proliferation of queer land uses in the mid–Market Street area and the Tenderloin for their difficulties finding and keeping legitimate businesses as tenants.[36] The chair of the Downtown Association's city planning committee set up the meeting to address the problem of "cheap bars, honkytonks, 'fire sales,' and theaters that specialize in lewd motion pictures" in the downtown shopping district. He also cited the encroachment of "phony sales, auction sales, and penny arcades where the sale of hot dogs in open storefronts is combined with shoeshine parlors." Finally, in a veiled reference to an emerging gay cruising ground in the Tenderloin, he railed against the "undesirable" bars where the armed services continually complained of "the presence of panderers and the mulcting of servicemen." One of these "undesirables" they could have unknowingly been referring to was Otto Bremerman, a self-proclaimed trade queen who had lots of success soliciting sex from "the sailors or soldiers or marines [who] would stop in the little arcades there on Market Street."[37]

The alarm among San Francisco business leaders and local officials over flagrant sexual solicitation on Market Street near the downtown shopping district signaled a change in anxieties about homosexuals in the city. During WWII and the onset of the Cold War, military and Coast Guard brass viewed gay men first as a public health problem and later as a national security threat.[38] At the conference, government officials, business leaders, and property owners expressed panic that the growing queerness of the city was indicative of a downward slide in land values in the urban core of an expanding metropolitan region.[39] They cast the willingness of some property owners to tolerate "undesirables" as an economic development problem. For these urban boosters, economic recovery was synonymous with stamping out the gender- and sexual-transgressive culture that permeated the once-thriving downtown. For instance, a representative from the district attorney's office argued that the group should work through the property owners to change the nature of their businesses. A Real Estate Board representative pushed back, contending that it was unrealistic to expect property owners to be too selective in accepting tenants. Commercial landlords could not be too picky if they wanted to avoid vacancies and a loss in income. They called for stronger government regulations to clamp down on unlawful business practices and sexual solicitation in the downtown shopping and entertainment districts.

Under pressure from business leaders, elected officials adopted a new regulatory framework for targeting bars, taverns, and nightclubs where "undesirables" congregated.[40] California legislators reorganized and empowered the
state alcohol control authority to become the primary government agency
tasked with containing the influx of homosexuals in California cities. In the
early 1950s, San Francisco assemblyman Casper Weinberger spearheaded
the formation of the Alcoholic Beverage Control (ABC) Board, which had
enhanced powers and stiffer liquor licensing rules.[41] At the start of 1955,
the reformed agency gained the statutory authority to revoke operating
permits from any "resort for illegal possessors or procurers of narcotics,
prostitutes, pimps, panderers, or sexual perverts."[42] The new rules fostered
closer collaboration between local law enforcement and state liquor agents,
incentivized undercover entrapment tactics used by sex crime units to collect
evidence for revocation accusations, and complemented the "saturation"
policing by "S-squads" of targeted problem areas of the city. In its first
two years, the ABC waged an aggressive enforcement campaign to clean
up residential hotel and nightlife districts in cities throughout the state.[43]
In San Francisco, local law enforcement and state liquor agents targeted
three areas: a strip of bars in North Beach, a section of the Tenderloin, and
a concentration of workingmen's hotels in the South of Market area.[44] The
first was on the northern edge of the central business district, with its long
history of nighttime entertainment. The second two targeted enforcement
areas were on the western and southern margins of the downtown shopping
district. This crackdown on "resorts of perverts" effectively put a lid on queer
nightlife in North Beach and the Tenderloin.[45] The ABC focused its energies
on closing down or changing the management of places that had shown
up on the military's off-limits list, including the Beige Room, the Chi Chi
Club, Tommy's Club, Dolan's Supper Club, Silver Rail, the Sundown Club,
the 181 Club, Keno's 47 Club, the 356 Club, Bobby's Three Vets, and the
Silver Dollar.[46] In recognition of his strict liquor code–enforcement crusade,
Weinberger received serious consideration to head the city's redevelopment
agency a couple of years later.[47]

In 1955, the ABC singled out two waterfront bars as "resorts for perverts," Lennie's 36 Club and the Sea Cow. In the summer, San Francisco
police officers raided the Sea Cow in a roundup of homosexuals, which
included the arrest of the multimillionaire John Cabell "Bunny" Breckenridge on vagrancy charges.[48] Breckenridge was an heir to the Comstock
fortune and a well-known swishy eccentric who had recently announced
his intention to undergo "sex-change" surgery in the press. His arrest at the

Sea Cow underscored the degree to which the establishment had become a predominantly gay waterfront "hangout" by the mid-1950s, frequented not just by queer men in the maritime trades but by well-heeled trade queens in the slumming tradition of crossing social, gender, and sexual boundaries.[49] Breckenridge contested the charges by underscoring the absurdity of charging the wealthy queen as a shiftless vagrant. The press coverage reframed the raids as an arbitrary, abusive use of police power to round up sexual- and gender-transgressive bar patrons. The incident signaled the limits of police power to regulate queer nightlife. Because there was nothing illegal about homosexuals patronizing bars, law enforcement would need to gather evidence of disorderly conduct to initiate revocation proceedings against their operators. Local law enforcement and state liquor agents shifted to undercover operations in which officers posed as bar patrons to entrap gay men in the act of soliciting sex on the premises. The policing tactic criminalized homosexuality and generated a record of disorderly conduct needed to shut down "resorts for perverts."

While it is important not to minimize the impact of bar raids, street sweeps, and roundups on the lives and livelihoods of individuals, these policing tactics ultimately had little effect on reversing the proliferation of gay bars in San Francisco, especially on the waterfront. The ABC and local law enforcement did, however, influence the sexual geography within the city by driving queer nightlife crowds away from the Tenderloin and North Beach to the waterfront. Between 1955 and 1959, the waterfront was treated effectively as a containment zone reserved for queer nightlife. After the Sea Cow incident, the ABC did not raid any queer waterfront hangouts on the Embarcadero, nor did law enforcement conduct street sweeps for the rest of the 1950s.[50] Soon after the raid, the Sea Cow changed its name to the Crossroads and continued to attract transgressive crowds over the next eight years. The Crossroads, the 144 Club, and the Ensign Café were joined by two new queer waterfront hangouts in the fall of 1957—Castaways and Jack's Waterfront Hangout. Both opened and operated with the active involvement of local law enforcement and state liquor agents, who collected a regular cut of bar receipts and a share of the stock of liquor. The only casualties during this period were the short-lived Lennie's 36 Club and the Sailor Boy, which were acquired and razed by government officials to make way for highway and parking projects in 1956. The Sailor Boy crowd relocated to the 144 Club, the seamen's hotel bar formerly run by Chili. After Lennie's 36 Club closed, the owner moved his business to a bigger spot farther west along the Embarcadero.

BLIGHT AT THE FOOT OF MARKET STREET

From the 1940s to the mid-1950s, local business leaders and elected officials grappled with how to initiate urban redevelopment in the lower Market Street area. Working under the auspices of the Chamber of Commerce, they looked to Sacramento, rather than Washington, for help with a multipart plan to transform the produce market and central waterfront into an automobile gateway to the central business district. The Chamber touted the passage of the 1945 California Community Redevelopment Law as a boon to efforts to acquire the produce market area for a proposed parking garage and commercial complex.[51] One Chamber working group focused on relocating the produce market, arguing that a purpose-built trucking terminal would improve market conditions and reduce the cost of bringing food to consumers.[52] They tried to convince wholesalers, as a group, to build a more efficient distribution facility elsewhere in the city with subsidies from Sacramento. Another Chamber working group joined forces with state highway engineers to develop plans for a direct freeway connection to downtown with off-ramps feeding into a massive parking terminal slated for the produce market blocks.[53] Yet another group of business leaders eyed the blocks surrounding the parking terminal, for a new Rockefeller Center–style office and showroom complex to promote Pacific Rim commerce.[54] Backers of this new World Trade Center project successfully lobbied for $60 million in state bond financing for the project. However, help from state lawmakers for downtown improvement projects grew more complicated and less likely as urban competition within the state heated up.[55]

From 1954 onward, the influx of merchant marines and naval personnel screened out of the maritime labor force and armed services became the catalyst for targeting nightlife strips as potential candidates for urban redevelopment. The drumbeat for designating these areas as blighted began with salacious crime exposés in the pulp press. Often narrated by police officers, true crime stories purported to provide the public with an insider's account of the degenerate, antisocial conditions in urban vice districts. For example, early in 1954, a national men's pulp magazine published an exposé of the narcotics trade, which characterized the Fillmore District as the city's epicenter of "vice, murder, rape, drug-peddling, lush-working, strip-tease, [and] gaming."[56] This sensationalized account of the transnational flow of drugs into the city identified the bars and clubs of merchant marines who evaded detection by port screeners or labor unions as the primary site of fomenting criminal activity among African Americans and wartime labor migrants to

San Francisco. Within the area of approximately one hundred city blocks, the author singled out the "strand" of Sutter Street between Fillmore and Webster as an "assembly point for merchant seamen . . . where they meet their own kind in bars and clubs [that serve as] unofficial hiring halls." He tagged this strip and these men as the principal vector for trafficking narcotics into the city. "In this district," he wrote, "there is a vicious clique of fringe seamen who use their union ratings chiefly to provide them[selves] with access to Pacific ports and an unscreened return to their home base." "This enables them to load up on narcotics and smuggle them into The Fillmore for distribution to wholesale and retail dealers at great profit to the smugglers." The author portrayed the "thousands of workers [who] came to the city from the Old South" as victims of drug peddlers who exploited the laborers' "inclination to find new thrills with their scratch [wages]."[57]

While the article underscored the goals of the port screening program and labor purge that destroyed the Marine Cooks and Stewards Union, it shifted attention from the docks, wharves, and union halls to target the home territories of merchant seamen while they were ashore. The Fillmore had a segregated wartime housing district for recent African American migrants to the city. It was tagged as the city's first slum clearance project under the state redevelopment legislation in 1947.[58] The article called out the "area to shun" by the street boundaries—which coincided with blighted blocks the city targeted for redevelopment. This crime exposé served, in effect, as urban renewal propaganda that characterized the specific spatial, racial, and gendered boundaries of a problem area deemed too far gone for rehabilitation. It also captured a new antipathy of law enforcement and city officials toward the floating population of racially diverse, queer, and left-leaning maritime laborers spending more time in San Francisco in the wake of the successful port screening program and labor union purges.

As government officials and real estate investors got more involved in expanding urban redevelopment plans, the same destructive discourse of blight stigmatized other parts of San Francisco to launch an even more ambitious program. City officials soon turned to another "area to shun," the city's queerest concentration of seamen's hangouts and residential hotels at the foot of Market Street. This pro-growth coalition helped to popularize the notion that the concentration of queer people negatively impacted property values and posed an existential risk to the neighborhood. In the spring of 1954, the Chamber of Commerce and its allies waged a sustained drive to sideline several flagging rebuilding projects to make the maritime quarter the city's top urban renewal priority. The drive began with a visionary sketch of what the area could become and ended with the legal designation of twenty-eight blocks of warehouses, hotels, offices, and small factories as blighted and subject to condemnation hearings. To make a case for replacing the historic core of maritime San Francisco with a landscaped, freeway-connected complex of office and residential towers, they stigmatized the existing mix of land uses in the area. They treated gathering places of merchant marines not merely as disorderly, undesirable businesses to be policed but as a menacing queer land use that anchored larger "problem areas" and threatened urban development. In short, the narrative of blight turned the increased queerness of the waterfront into the root of the problem. City leaders agreed and set aside several already approved redevelopment projects to make razing and rebuilding the Embarcadero waterfront its new top urban renewal priority.

Pro-business newspapers like the *San Francisco News* soon began aggressively marketing urban renewal proposals in the area. In the early spring of 1954, Arthur Caylor, a columnist for the newspaper, outlined a new approach and vision for rebuilding the entire maritime quarter in the lower Market Street area.[59] Inspired by Boston's plans to replace the West End neighborhood with residential towers in a park-like setting and by Pittsburgh's Golden Triangle development, Caylor advocated for a similar project on the Embarcadero using state tideland oil revenues. He was inspired by the cooperation of local business leaders in Pittsburgh and Pennsylvania state officials. He proposed a similar partnership to transform the derelict waterfront into an expansive, heritage-themed, state-funded park with a freeway interchange and an expansion of the central business district.[60] In San Francisco, Caylor pushed for eliminating warehouses, wharves, and rail facilities using public monies, to create a favorable setting for private investors to construct modern office buildings.

Although Caylor miscalculated the support from Sacramento, he accurately predicted the basic design elements of what would become San Francisco's Golden Gateway urban renewal project.[61] Caylor's vision for remaking the waterfront anticipated the construction of the Embarcadero Freeway and the redevelopment of much of the adjacent maritime quarter during the 1960s and early 1970s.[62] In 1954, however, when Caylor proposed the project, he stressed how the whole area could be reborn as a postmaritime, automobile-oriented extension of the central business district. He wrote:

Suppose the whole string of now useless wharves were made usable for other purposes. Suppose the Embarcadero were freed of the state's

Belt Line Railroad on the north side of Market Street and paved to make a wide esplanade with the freeway as a second deck. Suppose the ramshackle buildings along the west side of the Embarcadero were replaced by handsome modern structures extending up into the present commission district.[63]

He hoped the right mix of park and freeway expenditures from state park commissioners and highway engineers would stimulate private investment to rebuild the adjacent blocks of maritime-oriented land uses. Where the foundations of the city's maritime economy were growing more outmoded and queer, urban redevelopment now promised to turn the area into a symbol of an aesthetically pleasing, business-friendly, and forward-looking city.

Over the summer of 1954, the *San Francisco News* kept up a steady drumbeat of calls to redevelop the waterfront, focusing particular attention on visual blight, neglect, and dilapidation in the blocks across from the Ferry Building.[64] The paper, often aligned with the Chamber of Commerce's interests, soon began to refer to Caylor's proposal as his "dream" for the waterfront. The paper's editors portrayed the Ferry Building as a "crumbling ruin" and tagged the area around it as "an eyesore in our very front yard."[65] In the summer of 1954, the *News* published a pair of photographs taken from the Ferry Building looking toward the buildings lining the Embarcadero on either side of Market Street.[66] The caption anticipated that what had once been the "city's front" would again become the "center of downtown" and become the "birthplace of modern San Francisco." Both the text and photos framed the lower Market Street area as the prime target for redevelopment, given its dilapidated appearance and history of neglect. According to the paper, this "edge of San Francisco its citizens forgot" had become "the drab harborfront nobody cares about," filled with "clutter and decay." Discourses of blight would come to typify representations of the area over the next several years. In particular, redevelopment proponents reinforced the notion that nobody cared about this marginal, neglected area. While they worked out an area-wide renewal plan to raze and rebuild not only the central waterfront but also the adjacent produce market, they stigmatized the area to discourage piecemeal, private investment in the environs of the Ferry Building.

Port officials piled on by highlighting the declining conditions in seamen's hangouts in lower Market Street and intimating the growing queerness in the area. In August 1954, San Francisco Port Director and Brigadier General Robert H. Wylie characterized the hotels, bars, and cafés in the lower Market

Street area as outmoded and useless, reflecting the waterfront's deteriorating economic conditions, as he told the *San Francisco News* reporter:

> The decline of property values in this waterfront section and along lower Market [Street] is a tragedy in the city's life . . . What San Franciscans today don't realize is that this area once served a useful purpose. It had restaurants, respectable saloons, and many sailor hotels to suit an era when seamen drew meager wages and lived floating and rootless lives. That need has past [*sic*]. This derelict San Francisco waterfront is not representative of the seamen's life of today. It serves no purpose in today's scheme of waterfront needs. The seaman of today is with his family out in the Richmond or Sunset District, when he is ashore. Or he is taking his girl out to one of the better restaurants or hotels in the city. Or he is swapping talk in his handsome union headquarters. Neither sailors nor longshoremen need the run-down district that is the edge of San Francisco across from its piers and wharfs.[67]

Wylie spoke of a newfound suburban respectability among modern seamen who lived in outlying areas. They had attained middle-class respectability by cultivating stable heterosexual relationships and commuting to downtown union headquarters like other professional men. Most importantly, they steered clear of the old maritime quarter on the waterfront. The "handsome union headquarters" he referred to was the new Sailors' Union of the Pacific (SUP) Hall, several blocks away from the lower Market Street area. The SUP had successfully reorganized West Coast maritime unions by breaking up the Marine Cooks and Stewards Union (MCSU). As head of the port, Wylie had overseen military transportation from West Coast ports during World War II and the onset of armed conflict on the Korean peninsula.[68] In that capacity, he had also overseen the screening of homosexuals out of the merchant marines and off the waterfront, actions that had destroyed the racially and queerly mixed MCSU years earlier and driven queer, out-of-work maritime laborers to settle in the city.

Wylie's characterization of the Embarcadero waterfront as blighted coincided with efforts by the Chamber of Commerce and city planners to establish the legal and planning rationale for designating much of the historical core of the maritime quarter as the top urban renewal priority. As city planners finalized a proposal to declare both the produce market and Embarcadero waterfront blighted, federal, state, and local health inspectors scoured the nearby area for code violations. They found "dirty water running in gutters where open boxes of fruit were displayed, animals lying on fresh produce, and garbage littering the streets."[69] The public health director called for cooperation from police, fire, and building inspectors to strictly enforce all city codes. Out of the targeted enforcement campaign, public health officials condemned and razed the first building in the area. They labeled the forty-room Colchester Hotel a "public nuisance" and ordered the evacuation and demolition of the entire block, citing the dilapidated state of the structures and the mix of incompatible uses.[70] The waterfront seamen's rooming house, which had a tavern on the first floor, abutted a potato warehouse. It would be the first of fifteen lodging houses and residential hotels for single seamen, comprising nearly 1,400 dwelling units, demolished in the area over the next ten years.[71] Caylor weighed in that it was a "shame to waste [lower Market land] on potatoes" when it could be transformed into "something that would safeguard San Francisco against the dangers of decentralization."[72]

As the public reports of the blighted waterfront appeared in the *San Francisco News*, the Chamber of Commerce struggled behind closed doors to map out a redevelopment initiative to dramatically scale up several flagging postwar improvement projects in the lower Market Street area. A Chamber committee had been trying to convince produce merchants to move out of their downtown wholesaling district, an eight-block section of Washington Street just off the Embarcadero.[73] Another committee had sights on the underlying land to build a major office and convention center complex to promote Pacific commerce and shipping industries.[74] The World Trade Center project was stymied by intrastate urban rivalries and the reticence of the produce merchants to move.[75] After the WTC group shifted their proposed project to the foot of Market Street, their initiative stalled due to freeway design conflicts, more intrastate rivalries, and a lack of interest from potential tenants.[76] The port screenings and union purges sparked several violent labor conflicts on the waterfront that likely undermined the WTC project.[77]

In the fall of 1954, the Planning Department, with oversight from the Chamber, drafted a proposal to declare the produce market blighted. The proposal looked remarkably like an expanded version of Caylor's vision for redeveloping the entire lower Market Street area.[78] Planning Director Paul Opperman called for declaring not only the eight blocks of produce warehouses as blighted, but a much larger twenty-eight-block area that included "hotels, union halls, chandlers, import-export firms, a few garages, bars and cafes, and some parking lots."[79] He reasoned that the expansive blight declaration would incorporate all of lower Market Street, complement the planned Embarcadero Freeway and its ramps, and ensure that redevelopment projects within the area would not be "submerged in the surrounding conditions of blight."[80] The stated pretexts for declaring these blocks blighted included congested streets, high commercial vacancies, defective design, aging structures, obsolescence, and small lot sizes. Left unsaid: many waterfront bars, clubs, and hotels within the proposed boundaries were not vacant but had experienced a growth in "undesirable" queer patronage at the time.

Based on Opperman's recommendation and with the support of the Chamber of Commerce, city officials declared the entire twenty-eight-block area blighted in February 1955 under the California Community Redevelopment Law (see figure 0.3).[81] Clearly, the redevelopment area boundaries were drawn not to coincide with the extent of the produce market but to incorporate the increasingly queer land uses on its margins. All or a portion of eleven surrounding blocks—none of which had produce dealers—were included "to allow the freedom in developing a change of character of this general area."[82] The westernmost parcel within the project area boundary was the "Montgomery Block," a nineteenth-century commercial building that had become an artist colony filled with residential studios. Residents of the "Monkey Block" anchored the bohemian and queer public culture that developed in North Beach after the repeal of Prohibition.[83] The western portion of the redevelopment area also included the former Red Lizard bar—located next door to the Montgomery Block and across the street from the Black Cat. In the southern portion of the redevelopment area, the four waterfront blocks facing the Ferry Building were composed primarily of hotels, coffee shops, and taverns, as well as the Embarcadero YMCA, maritime union halls, barbershops, cigar stores, and laundries that catered to servicemen, merchant marines, and dockworkers. At the time, many of these establishments had become well-known queer nightspots for drinking and cruising.

Blight declarations incentivized state neglect and disinvestment. Improvements by property owners could reverse the blight designation, which provided the legal basis for condemnation proceedings. If owners rehabilitated buildings, secured good tenants, or embarked on small-scale redevelopment, they could undermine state-led, area-wide redevelopment projects by questioning the blight label or making land assembly too expensive. Planning officials in San Francisco recognized this paradox. For example, the Redevelopment Agency declared a tract of temporary wartime housing blighted, with hopes of convincing the produce merchants to build a new food-wholesaling facility there. When federal housing officials evicted the remaining tenants and made plans to raze the buildings, the planning director convinced them to delay demolition, insisting that "unoccupied ramshackle housing units [are] evidence of blight."[84] In another instance, the department rejected strict code enforcement of health, building, and traffic ordinances in the produce market, because it would encourage owners to improve their property and undermine the legal basis for acquiring and razing the structures by eminent domain.[85]

This paradox of blight and neglect helps explain how queer waterfront hangouts were occasionally publicly reviled as evidence of urban decline while, at the same time, they thrived and expanded in numbers during the 1950s and early 1960s. In 1954, both strict code enforcement crackdowns on produce merchants and drives on deviates in the area coincided with the search by city leaders for an actionable plan to replace the maritime-oriented land uses with an expanded downtown. However, it would take five more years before the Redevelopment Agency started purchasing property in the produce market area and Embarcadero waterfront. In the interval between the blight declaration and land assembly efforts, city officials mostly took a hands-off approach to law and code enforcement while working to redevelop the area. As the next chapter shows, state liquor agents and local law enforcement used their policing powers to exploit queer nightlife crowds at the Ensign Café, Castaways, and Jack's Waterfront Hangout, stopping by regularly to take a cut of the bar's receipts and an occasional bottle of liquor. Soon after financing and legal authority for a comprehensive waterfront redevelopment scheme was in place, eminent domain proceedings rather than code enforcement actions swept queer hangouts off the Embarcadero.

THE REDEVELOPMENT BOOSTER CLUB AND FREEWAY PARK

On the heels of the blight declaration, a new group of corporate executives and bank officers took an interest in the Chamber of Commerce–backed vision for transforming the maritime quarter into an expanded central business district. This group, which urban planner Chester Hartman nicknamed the "Redevelopment Booster Club," got increasingly involved in marshaling political support for an aggressive, federally backed urban renewal program on the waterfront. They reshuffled the city's urban redevelopment priorities, underwrote new urban design studies and project proposals, lobbied local and state officials for funds, and rallied the public to embrace the basic elements of Caylor's vision for a modern automobile gateway into downtown San Francisco.[86] This pro-growth coalition advocated for freeways, a regional mass transit system, and urban redevelopment projects that would turn San Francisco into the administrative and financial center of the Bay Area metropolitan region. Members of the booster club included corporate executives and bankers who headed the Bay Area Council (BAC), the Blyth-Zellerbach Committee, and "their brethren" in the Chamber of Commerce.[87] They sidelined rival local business leaders like hotelier Benjamin Swig, real estate developer Louis Lurie, and directors of the Downtown Association, all of whom prioritized redevelopment initiatives in the South of Market area to expand the downtown shopping and hotel district over Caylor's dream for the waterfront.

Between 1955 and 1960, San Francisco's redevelopment club coalesced around a campaign to secure funds to transform the low-rise blocks of sailortown land uses at the foot of Market Street into a waterfront park. The park was a critical component of Caylor's dream of stimulating private investment on the waterfront with a state-funded freeway and maritime heritage park. This coalition of businesses and bankers made six attempts to secure public funds to raze and rebuild the strip of waterfront hangouts across from the Ferry Building. They made three attempts to convince state park commissioners and highway engineers to pay for the park. When those efforts failed, they went to San Francisco voters twice with a bond-financing resolution. After those spirited campaigns came up short, pro-growth urban boosters leaned on the Board of Supervisors to set aside money from the general fund. They pitched each of these attempts to raze the waterfront blocks as a different park design proposal that would mitigate the visual blight of the Embarcadero Freeway. Although each proposal promised potential aesthetic improvements to the Ferry Building area, the imperative for creating a waterfront park was the queer cruising and nightlife strip along the Front. As state officials and voters stymied their proposals to repurpose the area around the freeway at the expense of these emergent queer land uses, this pro-growth coalition underwrote, vetted, and championed the Golden Gateway urban renewal project as San Francisco's best hope for reversing declining downtown property values. As the city's in-kind contribution to the cost of redevelopment, the waterfront park would be key to unlocking federal urban renewal funds for the Golden Gateway. Once boosters secured the funds to build it, the planned park ushered in a series of sweeping, large-scale urban rebuilding projects that started with lower

Market Street but grew over the next several decades to include stalled urban renewal projects in other parts of the city.

Before this booster club coalesced in the mid-1950s, local business leaders, elected officials, and state highway engineers had already ironed out the routing and design details of a planned Embarcadero Freeway crossing in front of the Ferry Building. The waterfront freeway was a small but essential component of a proposed urban freeway system that included a downtown loop for distributing incoming traffic to a series of parking terminals on the margins of the central business and shopping district.[88] The Embarcadero segment of the planned loop included a set of ramps that would replace the produce market and stimulate the revitalization of surrounding blocks. The BAC, an organization of corporate executives formed during World War II to advance regional planning and industrial development initiatives, championed the project as a critical new link between the Bay Bridge and downtown.[89] It would be critical to the BAC's effort to transform San Francisco from a major Pacific port into the financial and administrative center of the expanding metropolitan region. In the early 1950s, state highway engineers presented preliminary plans for the overall design and routing of the proposed freeway at a public hearing before the Board of Supervisors, planning officials, and business leaders.[90] The concept included a double-deck structure along the Embarcadero from Howard to Broadway with four lanes of one-way traffic on each level. The narrow footprint of the stacked structure would "prevent interference with port activities."[91] The Chamber of Commerce urged the State Highway Commission to approve the design concept and prepare final engineering drawings for the project.[92] With little public discussion and no press coverage, the San Francisco Board of Supervisors unanimously approved an agreement with state highway officials to construct the Embarcadero Freeway as a straight, double-decked structure along the waterfront connecting the Bay Bridge to Broadway.[93] Soon afterward, the State Highway Commission formally approved the new freeway segment and scheduled the start of land acquisitions and construction for 1954.[94] The 1.3-mile segment would "promote distribution of traffic to and from the financial district and the waterfront industrial areas."[95] The lead highway engineer hailed the project as "an outstanding milestone" and "the first freeway outlet offered to centers of employment, largely concentrated north of Market Street."[96]

With both the freeway plans and the blight resolution for the adjacent blocks in place, elected officials and business leaders turned to the next element of Caylor's vision for redeveloping lower Market Street: a state-funded historical park that would stimulate private investment in the area. Marshaling the resources for the park would prove to be much more challenging, partly because of a series of rival design proposals for the foot of Market Street championed by city officials and business leaders behind the WTC project. In March 1955, the Board of Supervisors predicted that the Embarcadero Freeway could have "an undetermined effect on the general economy of [the] entire downtown area."[97] They warned that the freeway would be a source of blight rather than a boon to property values. With suitable landscaping, however, they asserted the freeway could be "an opportunity of beautifying this area and affording a much-needed recreation project for the benefit of many thousands of our citizens." In August 1955, the mayor appointed a "Citizens Committee for a Ferry Building Park" to oversee the preparation and presentation of a park design proposal to state park officials.[98] Led by Crocker First National Bank President Jerd Sullivan, the eight-member committee included the heads of the Redevelopment Agency, the City Planning Department, the Downtown Association, the Chamber of Commerce, and the State Board of Harbor Commissioners.[99] The Committee employed consulting architects and landscape designers to prepare and publish a park design proposal, which its leaders presented to the California State Park Commission in October 1955.[100]

The Committee could not agree on where to situate the park to mitigate the impact of the freeway and enhance the façade of the Ferry Building. Proponents of the flagging World Trade Center project had big plans to replace the Ferry Building with an office tower and commercial exhibition complex. They backed plans for a straight, double-deck freeway directly in front of the Ferry Building that would harmonize with their ambitious plans for the area. The WTC architect called for replacing the waterfront blocks at the foot of Market Street with a twelve-acre plaza and park that would minimize the visual impact of the roadway. During the process of developing the Ferry Building Park proposal, a new group of business leaders—headed by Committee chair Jerd Sullivan and allied with the BAC—rejected the WTC plans and offered an alternate proposal for how to configure the freeway and the park. Architect Vernon DeMars and landscape architect Theodore Osmundson recommended a modification to the right-of-way of the freeway, ostensibly to create an "appropriate setting" for the Ferry Building.[101] Instead of building a straight-line freeway along the Embarcadero, DeMars and Osmundson called for curving the roadbed away from the waterfront to open up space for the park between the freeway and Ferry Building (figure 2.1). The lack of agreement between the two factions doomed the

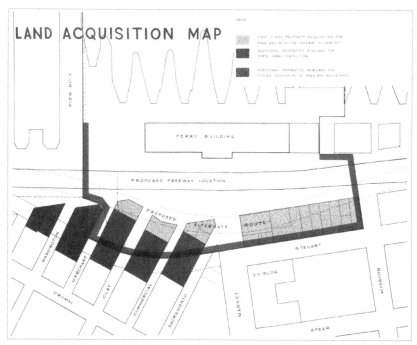

Figure 2.1 In 1955, a citizen's committee of business leaders proposed curving the right-of-way of the Embarcadero Freeway to secure state highway resources to raze the expanding queer nightlife circuit at the foot of Market Street. One of the two queer hangouts in the alternative route was acquired and demolished by highway officials even though the curved path was not adopted. (Ferry Building State Park, proposal, 1955, San Francisco History Center, San Francisco Public Library.)

1955 Ferry Building State Park proposal and undermined the prospects for a state-funded park. The California State Park Commission opted to fund a rival proposal for a maritime museum at San Francisco's Aquatic Park. Located two miles west of downtown near Fisherman's Wharf, the winning project proposal had a unified group of backers, carefully considered plans, and mooring facilities for historic ships.[102]

Both the publicly and privately circulating rationales for the 1955 park proposal reveal much about the preoccupations of its proponents over what they saw as deteriorating conditions at the foot of Market Street. In its published proposal, the Ferry Park Committee took direct aim at the waterfront with a two-page photo montage of the Embarcadero frontage under the heading "blight and decay degraded the area."[103] The image captured both "Lennie's 36 Club" and the Ensign Café, two hangouts

BLIGHT AND DECAY HAVE DEGRADED THE AREA

Figures 2.2A & 2.2B In an unsuccessful attempt to secure funds to raze the entire block, proponents of a Ferry Building–themed state park denounced "blight and decay" in a stretch of the Embarcadero (beginning at Mission Street) that had a growing queer nightlife scene in the mid-1950s. (Ferry Building State Park, proposal, 1955, San Francisco History Center, San Francisco Public Library.)

that anchored the Embarcadero queer nightlife circuit (figure 2.2). On the previous page, a full-page photo of a small group of men loitering under a neon sign for the Ensign's second-floor cocktail lounge provided a pedestrian's-eye view of the waterfront cruising strip (figure 2.3). With no written description of the scene or reference to the nature of the bars, the illustrations implied that the high concentration of bars, nightclubs, and idle men alone was evidence of "blight." The two bars featured in the 1955 Ferry Park proposal were known queer hangouts when the Committee argued for state highway funds to raze them. In the spring of 1953, state liquor agents made an unsuccessful attempt to shut down an unauthorized basement bar and an upstairs after-hours club linked to the Ensign Café at 1 Market Street.[104] The second hangout, Lennie's 36 Club, opened in the fall of 1954.[105] The Armed Forces Disciplinary Control Board soon

Figure 2.3 Proponents of a proposal to raze a large swath of the Embarcadero prominently featured the Broken Drum, a new queer hangout, in an unsuccessful attempt to gain support from state park and highway officials. (Ferry Building State Park, proposal, 1955, San Francisco History Center, San Francisco Public Library.)

added this new homosexual gathering place to its list of bars "off-limits" to military personnel.[106]

While the Ferry Park Committee was developing its proposal for state park funds, a well-timed, lurid exposé directly implicated gender- and sexual-transgressive nightlife as the source of deteriorating conditions at the foot of Market Street. *Men*, a national monthly pulp magazine that promoted heteronormative virility, prominently featured the lower Market Street area in a 1955 crime-fighting exposé about San Francisco. "Don't Call Us 'Queer City'" provides a vivid example of how city officials responded to a noticeable uptick in sexual solicitation among men on the Front. Although Lt. Eldon Bearden denied that San Francisco had become more "queer," the story suggested otherwise. He drew attention to the growing queer nightlife circuit at the foot of Market Street and, in doing so, introduced a new trope of sexual predation to justify waterfront redevelopment:

> Homosexuals had flocked into the City from all parts of the United States. They were everywhere . . . On lower Market Street, near the waterfront's Embarcadero, the "queen" homos were bustling with activity. A "queen" wears female garb to trap a soldier or sailor who has imbibed too much. Striking up a friendly conversation with a serviceman, it isn't long until the two are in a cheep [sic] hotel room. The "woman" then gives a song and dance about "her" physical condition, which is slightly askew at the moment. Usually the serviceman awakens, the next morning, with a buzzing head and his money gone.[107]

In this salacious portrait, Bearden asserted that the waterfront was bustling with homosexual and gender-transgressive criminals preying on putatively heterosexual servicemen. Unable to fathom that soldiers and sailors themselves might be willing participants, he portrayed the waterfront as a danger zone where "'queen' homos" tricked heterosexual men, unaware of their dangerous surroundings and the deceit of gender transgressors. Bearden's characterization of lower Market Street as a zone of unchecked moral perversity and emasculating sexual peril complemented similar discourses of visual blight, functional obsolescence, and sanitary danger that had already primed the area to be the city's new top urban renewal priority.

Betraying the preoccupation of the Ferry Park Committee with redeveloping the growing queer nightlife circuit on the Embarcadero, DeMars and Osmundson were explicit about the rationale for the curved freeway plan in a letter to Mayor-Elect George Christopher about the 1955 park proposal. To persuade the mayor, they used coded anxieties about queer hangouts:

> A decision in favor of a curved freeway will initiate clearing of blighted blocks adjacent to and in the redevelopment area, years ahead of any action that will ensue in the wake of a decision to accept the straight freeway alignment. This is for the simple reason that the curved freeway *requires* clearance and acquisition of blighted blocks (at state expense) while the straight freeway plan can proceed without any clearance of blighted properties. The straight freeway creates no compulsion or pressure to start the clearance of blighted properties, in the immediate vicinity of the Ferry Building.[108]

In effect, DeMars and Osmundson recommended reconfiguring the freeway right-of-way to expedite the acquisition and clearance of the queer hangouts along the Embarcadero. It was not the visual impact of the freeway that concerned them the most but an imperative to raze the blocks of waterfront bars, nightclubs, and seamen's hotels frequented by queens and "homos."

Although the Committee could not win approval for the curved freeway, they convinced state highway officials to acquire and raze two queer hangouts along the Front. State officials evicted Leonard Mollet from the 36 Club in October 1955 and turned the building into a parking lot.[109] They also took possession of and razed the Admiral Hotel—home to the Sailor Boy tavern popular with marine cooks and stewards. That waterfront parcel was slated for a short bend in the freeway where it turned from Howard Street onto the Embarcadero. Lennie's 36 Club and the Sailor Boy were the first of several queer waterfront hangouts demolished to make way for the Golden Gateway urban renewal project. Other queer establishments, like the Ensign Café, which would be one of the last parcels vacated and razed, had a more complicated role in waterfront redevelopment.

Despite the setback in 1955, proponents for area-wide redevelopment soon gained a strong supporter in City Hall. In his first year in office, Mayor George Christopher championed the BAC's efforts to transform San Francisco into the financial and administrative hub of the metropolitan region, as well as the Chamber of Commerce's vision of making the produce market an automobile gateway to the central business district.[110] In 1956, however, there were multiple obstacles to making these interrelated plans a reality. After several conferences failed to convince the produce merchants that they would be fairly compensated for their property, the mayor ordered a series of intensive crackdowns on health and safety code violations to try to break the impasse.[111] First, a breakaway group of merchants dug in deeper and threatened to leave the city if forced to relocate involuntarily. Then, owners of condemned properties around the produce market—including hotel operators—tried to remove the blight designation for landholdings.[112] At the same time, the San Francisco Redevelopment Agency, packed with his predecessor's appointees, favored a smaller, piecemeal approach to waterfront redevelopment with assistance from Sacramento rather than Washington.[113] Finally, a scandal over corrupt real estate practices in the city's first urban renewal project area further dimmed the prospects of federal urban renewal assistance on the waterfront.[114] Christopher's political ally and chief administrative officer appointee resigned over the scandal. The prospects for urban redevelopment in lower Market Street were dim even as local business leaders viewed such a forceful tool to eliminate queer land uses as a growing imperative to reverse the downward slide in downtown property values.

During the second half of the 1950s, downtown business interests meeting behind closed doors took charge of much of the planning and design work necessary for securing federal urban renewal assistance to redevelop the produce market and Embarcadero waterfront. Undeterred by the failure of the 1955 Ferry Park proposal, they repeatedly failed to attract public support for a waterfront park. They saw the project as the key to unlocking federal dollars and private investment to raze and rebuild the area. The Chamber's Redevelopment Coordinating Committee hammered out the legal, technical, administrative, and financial details of how to initiate urban renewal on the waterfront.[115] This redevelopment booster club grew larger in August 1956 when paper manufacturer J. D. Zellerbach and investment banker Charles R. Blyth formed the Blyth-Zellerbach Committee (BZC).[116] They shared the same compulsion of the Citizens Committee for a Ferry Park to expedite waterfront redevelopment by starting with the foot of Market Street. The BZC spearheaded a second attempt to reconfigure the Embarcadero Freeway plans to secure highway funds to raze the queer hangouts across from the Ferry Building.[117] They tried to convince state highway engineers to submerge the roadbed beneath an expansive plaza that would eliminate the same blocks targeted in the 1955 park proposal. Their strategy was not to draw attention to the existing queerness of the area or raise the alarm about urban decline. Instead, they made a positive case for the project with design sketches of the proposed plaza and predictions of the new investments it would bring to the surrounding area, including the produce market area. Moreover, they came out in support of pursuing federal urban renewal assistance to rebuild the entire twenty-eight-block blighted area (Area E), rather than just the produce market. The BZC, however, came up short. State highway engineers rejected the 1956 tunnel-plaza proposal as too costly. The mayor quashed the proposal, adding that it would slow progress on freeway construction.

The redevelopment booster club, with the BZC leaders serving as its most prominent public spokespersons, waded deeper into the initiative to rebuild the waterfront, with a third attempt to secure state park funds to rebuild the foot of Market Street. With a "gift" of survey and planning funds from the BZC, the Planning Department hired architect Mario Ciampi and the architectural firm Skidmore, Owning, and Merrill to collaborate on a design proposal for a Ferry Building park and a general redevelopment plan

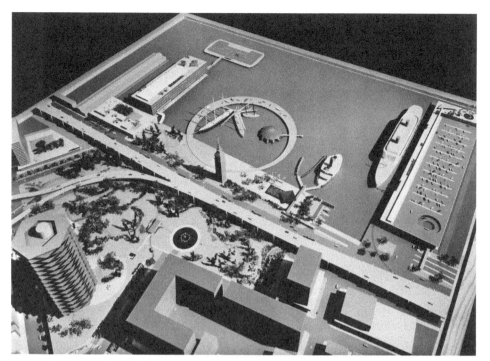

Figure 2.4 Undeterred by failed attempts to raze and rebuild the Front, corporate and banking executives commissioned an expansive area-wide redevelopment in 1957. Architect Mario Ciampi and landscape architect Lawrence Halprin envisioned a sweeping public plaza at the foot of Market Street that would attract private investors interested in redeveloping the prized commercial parcel in the area. (San Francisco Ferry Park, Mario J. Ciampi Records, College of Environmental Design Archives, University of California, Berkeley.)

for lower Market Street.[118] When the BZC presented Ciampi's 1957 scale model for harmonizing the park, freeway, and urban renewal plan, the State Park Commission panned his vision for a Ferry Building State Park (figure 2.4).[119] His ambitious scheme called for leveling not only the waterfront blocks across from the Ferry Building but also most of the terminal itself, to create an expansive plaza right up to the water's edge.

After three failed attempts to secure state park funds to raze the blighted waterfront blocks, the redevelopment booster club turned to San Francisco voters. In 1958, the mayor and the Ferry Park backers tried to rally support for a bond measure to cover the cost of purchasing and razing the two low-rise waterfront blocks at the foot of Market Street. Although the vote was ostensibly about funds for the park plan, it soon became a referendum on downtown redevelopment. J. D. Zellerbach's brother, Harold, headed the mayor's "Citizens Committee for Ferry Park Bonds" to promote the passage of Proposition C.[120] The kickoff event was a noontime rally at the proposed site of the park, with speeches from the mayor and leaders of the Committee. For the event, the Committee constructed a temporary facsimile of the park "including park benches, landscaping, bandstand, public address system, [and] a fountain."[121] Nightclub performers and an orchestra provided respectable entertainment to an estimated crowd of five to ten thousand.[122] As before, the redevelopment boosters promoted a positive vision for the future of the area rather than focusing on present conditions or indicators of blight. Addressing the crowd, Mayor Christopher stressed how voters could launch the city's redevelopment plan for the entire Lower Market–Embarcadero district by endorsing the park funds. The rally kicked off a two-week-long campaign of canvassing for votes using a mobile three-dimensional diorama of the proposed park mounted on a flatbed truck that toured every neighborhood and district in the city. The committee also sought endorsements from thirty civic and neighborhood clubs, distributed a hundred thousand printed brochures, and sent thirty press releases to local papers. The *Call Bulletin* recommended a "Yes" vote because the bonds would "enhance surrounding property values."[123] Despite the effort, with 155,495 votes for and 94,801 against, the measure failed to reach the two-thirds majority for passage.

Undeterred, the redevelopment boosters returned to the voters a second time for funds for the park in 1959. The new bond drive committee included representatives from the Bay Area Council, the Chamber of Commerce, the Downtown Association, and the Blyth-Zellerbach Committee. This time around, however, they made minor adjustments to their pitch by pandering to maritime laborers and explicitly linking the planned park with their ambitious urban renewal plans for lower Market Street. Conscious of the overwhelming representation of downtown interests on the bond drive committee, Mayor Christopher added an officer from the local chapter of the AFL-CIO Marine Cook's Union as cochairman.[124] The committee also retained local architect and city park planner Ernest Born to draw up plans for the park.[125] He presented sketches of a new revenue-enhancing park that would replace "three blocks of rundown, decaying, tax-eating structures."[126] In a press release in support of the bond measure, the mayor stressed the relationship between the park and the Golden Gateway—the proposed urban renewal plan for Area E under review in Washington at the time.[127] The bonds, he argued, would be matched with a federal grant and loan totaling $5.5 million that would transform "two of the most important

Figure 2.5 Federal urban renewal officials required San Francisco to finance a new park at the foot of Market Street before releasing funds to redevelop the rest of the Golden Gateway—the common name for urban renewal project E-1. (*In the Golden Gateway: The Time Is Now!*, San Francisco Redevelopment Agency brochure, 1960, San Francisco Public Library.)

[blocks] in the entire Golden Gateway Project" into "the most imposing skyscraper office buildings" in the city. Perhaps reflecting voter skepticism about urban renewal in general and growing rejection of freeway-oriented development in particular, the Ferry Park bond measure failed for the second time to gain the needed two-thirds majority.[128]

Project boosters finally secured funds for the park in 1960. As a prerequisite for initiating land acquisitions for the Golden Gateway, the Board of Supervisors set aside $653,000 from the general fund as the first of three annual installments to pay for the waterfront park (figure 2.5).[129] By 1962, when all of the funds were available, the Golden Gateway urban renewal project was well underway, with most of the blocks cleared, new buildings taking shape, and plans for an additional set of freeway ramps into the heart of the area moving forward.

THE DRAB HARBORFRONT NOBODY CARES ABOUT

In July 1954, the *San Francisco News* characterized the Embarcadero water-front as the "drab harborfront nobody cares about," a mischaracterization that overlooked the layered history registered in the photographs and obscured the vested interests of an array of existing users and redevelopment proponents (see figure 2.6).[130] The panoramic photograph of the foot of Market Street did not depict neglect but a scene where the future of the city was unfolding with a great deal of interest from multiple current and potential users. In the foreground, suburban commuters, more of whom were arriving at the Ferry Building's regional bus terminal than its ferry slips, dodged car traffic to reach streetcars queued up in a rail loop, ready to head back down Market Street. A different set of tracks for the beltline railway passed under the streetcar loop on their way to piers all along the waterfront. Some of the railcars these tracks carried delivered fruits and vegetables to a freight terminal in the nearby wholesale produce market. Almost visible on the right side of the page is the hiring hall where the Marine Cooks and Stewards Union had, for years, dispatched crews to ships along the waterfront—as had other maritime unions in the area. Men working as marine cooks and stewards had recently split into three factions, each preparing for an upcoming election to determine which faction would control the hiring hall. On the left side of the page, several seamen's hang-outs along the Embarcadero anchored a growing queer nighttime cruising circuit. In addition, government officials and business leaders were actively trying to transform the "drab harborfront" into something else. Architects for the World Trade Center project were hard at work drafting plans for an office and exhibition hall for the area. State highway officials, working with Chamber of Commerce input, were drafting engineering drawings for a waterfront freeway that would, as the caption promised, fill the fore-ground of the photograph. Finally, a new redevelopment booster club was beginning to work out how to turn the area into the "birthplace of modern San Francisco," modeled on Pittsburgh's Golden Triangle development.[131]

During the 1950s, queer land uses on the waterfront reordered planning

Figures 2.6A & 2.6B As redevelopment boosters devised plans to transform the maritime quarter into an extension of the central business district, their allies at the *San Francisco News* characterized the waterfront as a marginal zone that "nobody cares about" in a panoramic view of the foot of Market Street taken from the Ferry Building. (AAB-3549 [*top*] and AAB-3548 [*bottom*], San Francisco History Center, San Francisco Public Library.)

priorities and projects in the lower Market Street area by convincing corporate and civic leaders to embark on a robust urban redevelopment agenda beginning with the Front. Just after the *News* ran its opening salvo against "the drab harborfront," the Blyth-Zellerbach Committee emerged as the principal underwriter and advocate for an expansive proposal to transform lower Market Street into an automobile gateway into downtown San Francisco. Federal urban renewal assistance for the project was contingent on securing state or local matching funds to turn a strip of bars, seamen's hotels, barbershops, liquor stores, and union halls into a waterfront park. Razing the blighted blocks was imperative to make the area more attractive to private investors. Beginning in 1955, the BZC made five failed attempts to secure funds for a Ferry Park, each time with a new design proposal for how to repurpose the queer cruising strip at the foot of Market Street. On the sixth attempt, in 1960, they finally secured funds for a modest city park, unlocking federal funds for area-wide waterfront urban renewal. Over this period, the BZC emerged as the leading proponent of the Golden Gateway, the centerpiece of its ambitious urban renewal agenda to secure San Francisco's primacy as the financial and administrative hub of a growing metropolitan region. After the BZC steered the city through the legal, administrative, design, and financing obstacles to urban renewal on the waterfront, they set up a new urban research and lobbying group that became the city's official citizens' participation organization for urban redevelopment. Representing corporate and real estate interests, the San Francisco Planning and Urban Renewal Association (SPUR) succeeded the Chamber of Commerce and the San Francisco Planning and Housing Association to become the primary advisory group for urban planning issues.[132]

As the BZC deepened its involvement in advancing the Ferry Park project, an interesting shift occurred in the policing of queer waterfront hangouts. When business leaders, elected officials, and city planners initially set their sights on redeveloping the central waterfront along with the produce market, the Sea Cow, Lennie's 36 Club, and the Ensign Café figured prominently in coverage of citywide roundups of homosexuals and depictions of urban blight. Public crackdowns on these queer nightlife spots helped make the case that the waterfront was blighted under the state's urban redevelopment statute. The perception of blight—and official declaration of its areal extent as a legal and administrative matter—kicked off a long process of marshaling the resources and authority to acquire and raze much of lower Market Street. As redevelopment proponents made repeated efforts to sort through precisely how to rebuild the area, it was expedient to perpetuate blight conditions on the waterfront and in the produce market. The five-year-long process of securing the resources and authority to raze and rebuild the waterfront opened up a space for queer nightlife to flourish along the Embarcadero. While the BZC struggled to marshal the resources for a waterfront park to replace the queer cruising strip, the Ensign Café, the 144 Club, the Crossroads, Castaways, and Jack's Waterfront Hangout mostly escaped the spotlight and grew in popularity. During this transitional period between the first design concepts for the area and the first land acquisitions, local law enforcement and state liquor agents treated the central waterfront as a managed vice district to isolate and control queer drinking publics.

By the early 1960s, these waterfront hangouts slated for redevelopment took on a new significance. Once the redevelopment officials began acquiring buildings for the park and the associated Golden Gateway project, the short period of relative permissiveness abruptly ended. State liquor agents and local law enforcement unleashed a raft of license revocation actions against gay bar operators while pressuring commercial landlords to evict gay bar tenants before selling their landholdings to the city. The queer drinking publics in these bars responded by forming what one well-known gay bar host called "some kind of union," an organization that challenged multiple forms of repression by the straight state.[133] The following three chapters reconstruct the distinctive origins, remarkable persistence, and ultimate demise of the three most prominent queer nightlife operations on the waterfront: The Ensign Café, 90 Market, and Jack's Waterfront. These were the most significant queer waterfront hangouts that developed in the wake of the exclusion of homosexuals from the maritime trades and naval forces at the port of San Francisco. While the former remained firmly embedded in the city's system of managed vice controlled by local law enforcement, the latter two developed into nationally significant sites of group identity formation, where queer drinking publics forged new forms of collective organizing for sexual-minority rights.

3

HANGING OUT AT THE ENSIGN CAFÉ

In a 1964 essay, Guy Strait, then publisher of the city's first gay newspaper, the *LCE News*, made a clear distinction between "the ordinary homosexual hangout" and "gay bars." In "What Is a Gay Bar?" he described homosexual hangouts as transactional, alcohol-fueled pickup spots where patrons lacked a social connection to the city's gay community. In contrast, he claimed that gay bars were legitimate commercial enterprises with responsible managers, a "self-respecting" clientele, community purpose, and a "rather decorous" atmosphere. Strait estimated that, of the twenty-five to thirty gay bars in the city at the time, three-quarters had started as homosexual hangouts. Many of these homosexual hangouts began as straight bars that started to struggle financially when the wartime mobilization ended. Facing mounting debts and falling revenues, their owners hired gay staff to draw in a new crowd and revitalize the business. Jack's Waterfront Hangout, he wrote, "was such a little dump on the Embarcadero that it could not possibly exist. No self-respecting homosexual would go down on the waterfront but this place starved as a straight joint and made a killing as a gay bar." In addition to these social and operational differences, Strait emphasized that the unequal treatment each type of establishment received from local and state authorities was infuriating.[1] The Ensign Café, he asserted, was "the leading homosexual pickup spot in the city . . . for a number of years" and enjoyed "one of the highest walk-in businesses of all bars in the city," but local law enforcement and state liquor agents largely left it alone. In contrast, he lamented, a gay bar just around the corner with "no higher percentage of homosexuals" was "under constant fire from the Department of Alcoholic Beverage Control," even though its managers kept "a watchful eye for possible violation of the law."[2]

The permissive approach authorities took toward the Ensign Café had everything to do with local efforts to manage the growing queer nightlife crowds on the waterfront during and after World War II. With the tacit support of law enforcement, the Ensign was the most notorious and longest-lasting hangout for sexual- and gender-transgressive patrons in San Francisco from the 1940s to the mid-1960s.[3] With many of the physical and operational aspects of a Prohibition-era speakeasy, the Ensign was the product of an underground transactional economy of containment and control in which overt sexual activity was tolerated on the premises by the management and law enforcement. Michelangelo "Mike" Caldaralla, who oversaw the bar-nightclub-liquor-store complex, repeatedly avoided serious trouble with law enforcement over his thirty-year career in the illicit liquor trade. In the few instances authorities cracked down on the Ensign, Caldaralla quickly reestablished himself and reopened the bar with an even more permissive iteration of his nightlife operation. Throughout the 1940s and 1950s, under Caldaralla's management, working-class patrons of the Ensign Café expected a night of overt sexual solicitation—and even sexual encounters. In the early 1960s, the upstairs cocktail lounge became popular with butch lesbians and transgender people, because it was one of a few venues where local police rarely bothered them.

The Ensign Café was never a part of the city's network of gay bar operators that came together to fight against corrupt policing practices and a raft of liquor revocations.[4] Caldaralla never advertised in gay newspapers or bar guides, nor did he host any fundraisers for the gay community. In fact, despite its popularity, the Ensign never appeared in Strait's gossip column of queer nightlife—unlike the Black Cat, Jack's Waterfront Hangout, and a handful of other gay bars on the Embarcadero. In a rare reference to the Ensign, Bill Plath, a prominent gay bar owner and community leader, disassociated his business from Caldaralla's nightlife operation. In an oral history, he specified that the Ensign "was never part of the gay bar scene. That was a sex operation . . . [run by a] straight owner that paid no attention to what was going on, and he knew damn well what was going on with the Ensign. But you could never classify it as a gay bar. I never think of it as a gay bar. Sex bar, oh yes."[5] Plath had personal and economic reasons to disassociate gay establishments from the Ensign. In the early 1960s, Plath cofounded the Tavern Guild, a local association of gay bar owners, managers, and bartenders that sponsored fundraisers for social causes and legal aid, cooperated with police to keep patrons in order, and endorsed candidates for political office. He viewed the Ensign—which never got involved with the Tavern Guild or its initiatives—as purely catering to the sexual urges of its queer patrons rather than serving as a place for gay socializing and community mobilization. While Plath's disdain for the Ensign reflected his racial, gendered, and socioeconomic biases as a white, gay businessman, it also revealed the pragmatic concern of gay bar operators to restrict sexual solicitation, not to mention sex acts, on the premises to avoid the liquor license revocation proceedings.

As a holdover from an exploitative system of queer nightlife that implicated local law enforcement, state liquor agents, and alcoholic beverage distributors, the Ensign Café operated under a different set of rules than the gay bars that formed the Tavern Guild. In the first half of the twentieth century, San Francisco's "open town" policing practices reserved a stretch of Pacific Street and the Tenderloin for gambling, narcotics, and prostitution. In this older system with roots in the Prohibition era, bar managers and local authorities turned a blind eye to reviled forms of sexual expression and gender transgression in exchange for a share of the profits from the illicit, lucrative bar trade. As maritime activity, troop movements, and ferry service all waned after World War II, these same policing practices became an instrument for containing and exploiting queer land uses near the foot of Market Street.[6] This system kept Caldaralla in business for decades under a logic of spatial control that isolated queer nightlife from the general population, confined sexual and gender transgressions to particular locations, and concealed the involvement of state and private actors from public exposure.

Outside San Francisco, illicit cooperation between law enforcement and liquor interests in other cities also enabled gay bars to operate in the shadows during the 1950s and 1960s.[7] In New York City, for example, several organized crime syndicates ran gay bars in and around Greenwich Village with the tacit support of state and local authorities. In the most famous instance, the Genovese crime family transformed the Stonewall Inn into a queer hangout in 1966 and ran it for several years until patrons and bystanders rioted against harassment by the police and exploitation by the operators.[8] As a predecessor of the Stonewall Inn, the Ensign Café had similar social and operational characteristics. However, it did not become part of a milieu for organizing a new sexual identity or mobilizing for gay rights.[9] The story of the longevity and final days of the Ensign Café provides clues about how state actors and liquor interests successfully kept a lid on and profited from queer nightlife crowds before gay bars emerged as a relatively common, legally sanctioned, and consumption-oriented urban land use.[10]

This chapter charts the shifting tactics of state actors during the Lavender Scare in dealing with the influx of queer nightlife crowds on the San Francisco waterfront, by reconstructing the trajectory of Caldaralla's illicit business practices and his role in making the queer waterfront. Under his management, the Ensign Café developed into a so-called homosexual hangout through an ongoing, largely cooperative relationship with law enforcement officials, who adopted an unspoken policy of steering queer nightlife to the foot of Market Street. During the late 1940s and 1950s, the relatively permissive treatment of the Ensign's nightlife crowds helped keep a lid on an uptick in sexual solicitations among men in the city while also serving as a continuing reminder of the imperative to redevelop the waterfront. Understanding how this Prohibition-era holdover survived to be one of the very last businesses shuttered in the Golden Gateway showcases how law enforcement treated lower Market Street as a managed vice district reserved for queer nightlife, while the city's pro-growth coalition drew up plans to raze and rebuild the area.

CALDARALLA'S EARLY CAREER AS A SPEAKEASY OPERATOR

Between the mid-1910s and the mid-1930s, beer and liquor merchant Mike Caldaralla perfected a set of business practices that later helped him run the Ensign Café as a queer nightlife venue with relative impunity. He developed a remarkable ability to skirt legal trouble while running an extensive, profitable, and illicit alcoholic beverage distribution operation under the thinnest veil of secrecy. In 1915, Caldaralla started out serving "near-beer . . . containing more alcohol than is lawful" at a saloon on Pacific Street.[11] By the early 1920s, he was producing, storing, and distributing liquor out of a basement distillery and warehouse beneath the International Hotel disguised as a furniture dealership. The false storefront and signage removed suspicion about the contents of the crates of merchandise his drivers loaded onto delivery trucks in front of the building. After a 1921 fire in his basement distillery, Caldaralla expanded his warehouse into larger quarters near Broadway and Front Street.[12] Under the guise of automobile repair and "express" delivery service, he grew his operation distributing wine and spirits to the area's bars, saloons, and dance halls.[13] He later incorporated his business enterprise as the "Golden Gate Grape & Juice Co" in order to obscure the nature of the business and shield himself from charges of unlawfully producing and selling alcoholic beverages. For decades, Caldaralla would continue to use similar concealment tactics and legal strategies to insulate himself from liability for operating the Ensign Café as a hangout for homosexuals and an after-hours club. Several decades later, he deployed the same measures when he used deceptive signage, sham façades, and hidden interior spaces to transform the Ensign Café into a homosexual hangout with separate bar, restaurant, and nightclub spaces.

Caldaralla's interactions with law enforcement during Prohibition followed a pattern of public exposure of criminal activity followed by exoneration from wrongdoing. On at least three occasions, he was cleared of involvement in the illicit liquor trade despite solid evidence of his role in running a criminal enterprise. In 1926, a second fire in the basement of the International Hotel exposed his underground distillery and warehouse. Federal agents decried the flagrant operation of "an illicit liquor establishment in the basement of a building . . . within a few rods of the Hall of Justice and two blocks from Prohibition headquarters." Caldaralla successfully avoided prosecution by claiming he had "sublet a part of the basement to an unknown lessee." It was a remarkable evasion given that "Caldarall's [sic] name was on boxes and signs found in the place."[14] Subleasing bar spaces and club rooms to third parties became another hallmark of Caldaralla's business practices that enabled him to actively manage waterfront liquor distribution networks and retail outlets with impunity.

Two years later, he again avoided criminal prosecution for participating in the illicit liquor trade. In December 1928, Caldaralla was implicated in the murder of his business partner at the Broken Drum, a basement speakeasy in the Bay Hotel near the foot of Market Street.[15] After interrogating Caldaralla about the incident, the police cleared him of any wrongdoing.[16] Six months later, the police charged someone else with the homicide and dismissed the incident as a lethal struggle to control the rum trade.[17] Although the shooting exposed Caldaralla's association with the illegal liquor trade, he walked away unscathed. Nearly thirty years later, he received similar leniency after police charged him with discharging a firearm and critically wounding a former employee in a dispute over unpaid wages at the Ensign Café.[18]

The biggest threat to Caldaralla's operation came not from local law enforcement but from federal agents. In 1931, Prohibition agents began cracking down on Caldaralla's illicit liquor distribution network and retail outlets. In September, they padlocked the Studio Club at Caldaralla's

Hotel Claudia as part of a campaign against apartment houses and hotels operating "small resorts alleged to be speakeasies."[19] Six months later, a major raid of Caldaralla's trucking and distillery operation exposed him as a major liquor producer and distributor in the city. Timed to coincide with National Prohibition Director Amos W. W. Woodcock's visit to the city, Prohibition agents raided Caldaralla's headquarters at 941 Front. They also seized two five-hundred-gallon liquor stills, three trucks, and an automobile registered to Caldaralla at his auto repair shop at 83 Broadway. At the shop, the agents arrested fourteen men loading trucks from a storehouse filled with 2,500 cases of fine liquor, including champagne, imported ryes, bourbons, and gins, worth $75,000 wholesale. As on previous occasions, law enforcement cleared Caldaralla of any wrongdoing.[20] Officials dropped the charges for "lack of evidence." Despite his close connection and periodic public association with the beer, wine, and liquor trade, Caldaralla avoided criminal prosecution for producing, storing, and distributing alcohol during Prohibition. He became a seasoned beer and liquor distributor—who had operated with impunity despite several incidents that exposed the illegal nature of his nightlife enterprise.[21] Soon after the repeal of the Eighteenth Amendment, Caldaralla employed the same operational and business practices when he opened a new beer and liquor retailing enterprise at the foot of Market Street, to skirt new liquor sales tax rules and regulations prohibiting after-hours sales.

CALDARALLA SETS UP OPERATIONS AT THE ENSIGN CAFÉ

In 1934, Mike Caldaralla began a thirty-year career as manager of the Ensign tavern in the Merrimac Building, located across from the Ferry Building at the intersection of Market Street and the Embarcadero.[22] His tenure in the building began when he used the refrigerated basement storerooms to distribute Los Angeles–brewed Eastside Beer during the 1934 Waterfront Strike.[23] It did not end until 1965, just before the block was razed to make way for a waterfront park as part of the Golden Gateway urban renewal project. Caldaralla initially catered to the steady stream of merchant seamen, dockworkers, and ferry commuters in the area. During the 1939–1940 Golden Gate Exposition, the Merrimac Building was well situated to attract fairgoers returning to the city by ferry from the fairgrounds on Treasure Island. Eager to capitalize on the new crowds, Caldaralla grew his nightlife operation in the building to include liquor, food, and dancing.[24] He incorporated "Ensign Café, Inc.," a new alcoholic beverage distribution enterprise registered to the first-floor corner storefront at 1 Market Street. The inclusion of "café" in the new name satisfied liquor licensing rules requiring bar operators to sell food along with alcoholic beverages. He began marketing the Ensign with a small classified ad announcing "Turkey Sandwiches as Our Specialty."[25] The real draw, however, was a large dance hall and cocktail lounge on the second floor, accessible via a separate, clearly marked entrance around the corner from his first-floor tavern and liquor store.

Working at times with family members, Caldaralla directly or indirectly controlled multiple liquor licenses registered to "Ensign Café, Inc" and linked to a changing, interconnected suite of commercial spaces in the building.[26] The transferability of these licenses to different people and leasable subareas allowed him to supply beer and liquor to a shifting configuration of commercial spaces in the building. As in the past, Caldaralla used this corporate structure to shield himself and investors from criminal charges when liquor control agents and law enforcement launched raids and crackdowns.[27] While Caldaralla tended the main bar, he subleased the other spaces in the Merrimac Building to different tenants and supplied them with beer and liquor on a percentage basis. Through this arrangement, he reaped profits from alcohol sales while avoiding liability for operating a disorderly house, serving minors, or staying open after hours. In the few instances that local law enforcement and state liquor agents raided one of the subleased spaces, authorities charged the tenant, not Caldaralla, with violating rules governing the sale of alcohol to patrons. Besides legal protection, this spatial configuration and corporate structure allowed Caldaralla to conceal illicit activities on the premises from the casual visitor and offered a degree of privacy to sexual- and gender-transgressive patrons. For queer patrons, the relative permissiveness of Caldaralla's nightlife complex came at the cost of overpriced drinks in exchange for a head start—or heads up—in the event of a police raid.

While Caldaralla operated a small bar and liquor store at the corner in the Merrimac Building, he subdivided most of his commercial space into three interconnected, leasable subareas, including a basement bar, a first-floor restaurant, and a large second-floor nightclub (figure 3.1).[28] Each subarea had a primary street entrance allowing Caldaralla and his tenants to manage the nightlife crowds by controlling access to different parts of the building. An

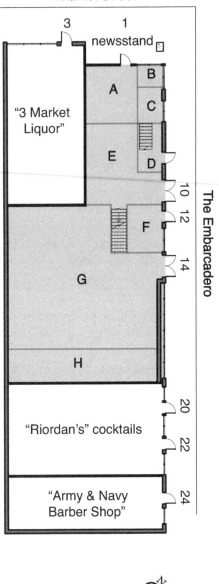

Market Street

3   1

newsstand

"3 Market Liquor"

A

B

C

E

D

The Embarcadero

10 12 14

F

G

H

"Riordan's" cocktails

20 22

"Army & Navy Barber Shop"

24

FIGURE 3.1 In the mid-1950s, Mike Caldaralla reconfigured access to his nightlife enterprise at 1 Market to manage multiple subareas across three floors. In 1960, these subareas included: A) "Ensign Café" bar; B) "CJ Cigars" and newsstand; C) "Ensign Liquor" package sales, with walk-up window; D) unmarked basement bar; E) "Broken Drum" cocktail lounge, on second floor; F) barber shop; and G) "Ensign Club" bar and restaurant, which along with a backroom (H) was concealed behind a false façade. (Map by the author in collaboration with Ursula Roma and Alex Cox.)

25 feet

unmarked building entrance at 8 Embarcadero opened into a small room with stairs to the basement. The basement was a large, unfinished storage area with low ceilings, two bathrooms, and multiple refrigeration rooms.[29] Sidewalk chutes connected the basement to street grade for deliveries of beer, alcohol, and other wares. The basement was an essential part of Caldaralla's operation, because it enabled him to easily supply beer and liquor to his tenants on the upper floors. During World War II, it also served as a space for queer nightlife crowds to gather undetected by the general public. The second entrance along the Embarcadero, at number 10, opened into a small lobby with a staircase to a second-floor cocktail lounge with a stage and dance floor. At different times, this large space served as the Ensign Café, the Treasure Island Club, the Broken Drum, and the Ensign Club Room in its last incarnation. Lastly, a third entrance at 14 Embarcadero provided direct access to a first-floor bar and restaurant space known at different times as the Ensign Café and the Market Street Café. After a major reconfiguration and enlargement of the first-floor commercial spaces in 1950, this storefront gained a false façade that concealed the revelry inside and enabled Caldaralla to create an adjoining backroom completely undetectable from the street. This space may have facilitated overt sexual activity on the premises by affording participants additional time to quickly compose themselves, flee the scene, or remain unseen in the event of a police raid.[30] Throughout all the commercial spaces controlled by Caldaralla, patrons and staff could move internally from one area to another, making it easier for him to control the nightlife crowds and for those crowds to avoid public exposure.

During World War II, Caldaralla again expanded and reconfigured his beer and liquor distribution and nightclub business in the Merrimac Building. Within weeks of the attack on Pearl Harbor, he and his associates prepared for an influx of soldiers and sailors bound for the Pacific. He first relocated the second-floor Treasure Island Club to new quarters in a nightlife strip that had sprung up next to an armed forces hospitality center near Union Square. He then expanded the Ensign Café by applying for a new permit to sell beer, wine, and distilled spirits for the recently vacated "dining and dancing" space upstairs.[31] After a 1942 raid against establishments that facilitated the spread of venereal disease forced the closure of the Treasure Island Club, Caldaralla focused his energies on running the Ensign Café.[32] Located at a prime spot on the busy waterfront, he installed a blue-and-white "Ensign Café" neon sign with the silhouette of a saluting uniformed sailor framed by stylized waves and a chain and anchor to appeal more directly to naval personnel. The new sign projected diagonally over the sidewalk at the corner, making it visible to car and foot traffic along both Market Street and the Embarcadero. For the duration of the war, Caldaralla continued catering to a steady stream of patrons looking for a good time at his multi-story nighttime entertainment complex.

The internal configuration of the Ensign Café—and its popularity with sailors—made it an active sexual cruising spot for men, in and out of uniform, seeking sex with other men during the war years.[33] In particular, the basement was a warren of "rooms downstairs where the guys could carry on."[34] Veteran John Nichols briefly described how the Ensign facilitated sexual solicitation among men on the premises: "The Ensign on the Embarcadero was unique in that although the bar was laden with beer bottles, few customers seemed to be standing around drinking. A trip to the basement john revealed why." He prefaced his description of homosexual sex at the Ensign by explaining that, back then, gay life was "totally unorganized," "not emancipated," and "frequently conducted under cover of secrecy." Nichols claimed that "there was a touch more mystery to cruising because labels were not as prominently worn by either the place of business or its customers. 'Is he?' or 'Isn't he?' was a more tantalizing question." To find places like the Ensign, Nichols and other men compiled a personal city-by-city guidebook based on "volumes of correspondence circulating among friends with look-up recommendations of people and bars."[35]

The basement bathroom at the Ensign Café was just one popular spot in a constellation of places where men sought out sex with other men in cities across the country. During the 1940s, men seeking sex with other men could reliably succeed at fashionable hotel bars, bathhouses, movie theaters, city parks, YMCAs, private parties, and public restrooms in major hubs of wartime mobilization and military deployment.[36] Some participated actively in a nascent gay world by organizing their social lives around places where expressions of same-sex desire and intimate relationships were more acceptable.[37] The Ensign most resembled one of what Nichols identifies as the "cheap taverns, inexpensive transit hotels and penny arcades" located near the bus stations and transit terminals that became popular cruising areas in most cities during the war.[38] In these areas "jammed with servicemen," civilians could quickly gauge the sexual interests of military personnel passing through the city by buying them a drink, offering them a ride, and inviting them home for the night. Due to their larger numbers and low pay, soldiers were the easiest to pick up with an offer for a place to stay, while Navy men and Marines were the most prized for their relative rarity, "body-hugging uniforms," and manliness.[39] As a principal port of embarkation for the Pacific fleet and a major naval supply depot, San Francisco had an exceptionally large stream of military personnel and merchant marines passing through during World War II and the onset of the Korean War. A fraction of these men ensured that the Ensign Café basement was a particularly active, homoerotically charged pickup spot during the 1940s and 1950s.

FROM CRUISING SPOT TO HOMOSEXUAL
HANGOUT

A series of changes at the Ensign Café in the late 1940s suggest that Calda-ralla sought to capitalize on the popularity of gay cruising in the basement by turning the first-floor commercial space into a so-called homosexual hangout. To draw in queer nightlife crowds without facing repercussions from the police, he needed the cooperation of local officials. Several ads in the *Police and Peace Officers' Journal* suggest that he started making protection payoffs to local law enforcement. In February 1946, Caldaralla ran a small classified advertisement in the journal for "Ensign Café, Inc. 1 Market, cor. Embarcadero," which signaled that he was operating with the good graces of local authorities.[40] In October and the following April, Caldaralla purchased two additional advertisements in the law enforcement journal.[41] These payments came soon after Caldaralla was arrested and charged with staying open after hours and selling alcohol to minors.[42] Around that time, he also stepped down as titular head of the Ensign Café corporation and put his nephew in his place. After the advertising in the police journal and his performative shuffle in ownership, he was back in business. From then on, local law enforcement mostly allowed Caldaralla to operate without fear of police harassment or legal retaliation. Just as they had contained illicit nighttime entertainment during Prohibition, they treated the Ensign as a managed vice operation, entrusting Caldaralla to help them control, and profit from, queer nightlife crowds as the waterfront became an increasingly marginal section for the city. As the recollection of an operator of a nearby lesbian bar made clear, the Ensign stayed in business for so long because "those guys were paying off, they had to [be]."[43]

While Caldaralla's advertisements attempted to placate law enforcement, a *San Francisco Chronicle* columnist signaled to gay men that the Ensign welcomed their patronage. In June 1947, Herb Caen, who frequently com-mented on the shifting cultural scene in the city, wrote (as previously cited), "Two of the Embarcadero's more colorful hangouts—the Ensign Café, at Market, and the Admiral Restaurant, opposite Howard, [are] where you'll rarely see an Ensign and never see an Admiral." Characterizing both places as "colorful" and not quite what they seemed followed Caen's practice of pro-moting particular nightlife venues with coded language and gossipy asides in his column. He often directed gay readers to different entertainment venues with campy passing mentions of female impersonators, bar raids, and club openings and closings. World War II veteran Stuart Loomis credited Caen with being an essential source of information for the city's growing number of gay readers during the 1940 and 1950s, adding, "Everybody read Herb Caen in the morning to find out what was happening in the gay life."[44]

By the early 1950s, queer nightlife at the Ensign was going strong, as several operational and physical changes in the Merrimac Building illustrate. When suspected homosexuals drummed out of the maritime trades and the armed forces began to show up in large numbers on the San Francisco waterfront, Caldaralla expanded his illicit nightlife operation at the Ensign. He changed the internal configuration, façade, and tenancy relations of the Merrimac Building to create a private-membership club that catered to gay men. The new, larger commercial space on the first floor merged several adjacent storefronts along the Embarcadero. He subleased this space to a newly incorporated business, "Ensign Club, Inc.," established in early 1949.[45] While the older "Ensign Café, Inc." was set up as a corporation to register multiple liquor licenses at 1 Market, the new "Ensign Club, Inc." was a private social organization that could rent out and operate a nightclub at any location. The directors of the Ensign Club—five married men in their late thirties from Oakland—included a pharmacist, several dockworkers, and a partner in a Reno gaming enterprise who became a statewide liquor sales account manager for Seagram distillers. They specified that the purpose of the club was to "cultivate social intercourse among its members and to inculcate the principles of charity, justice, brotherly love and fidelity" by leasing and operating "clubs, club houses, [and] club rooms" and serving "refreshments of all kinds" to members. As a legal and administrative matter, the club's purpose was to enable the directors—who presumably were all straight—to run a so-called homosexual hangout with cooperation from Caldaralla, who acted as their landlord, alcohol supplier, and fixer for troubles with local authorities. For their part, local and state law enforcement officials presumably got a share of the bar tabs and credit for containing queer bar crowds to an increasingly marginal area slated for redevelopment. The new configuration came on the heels of a proposal to raze a large swath of the waterfront, including the Ensign Café, to build a World Trade Center complex to promote Pacific shipping interests.[46]

In setting up his new enterprise at the Ensign, Caldaralla revived the same tactics he used to develop a network of basement distilleries, alcoholic beverage warehouses, delivery trucks, and speakeasies during Prohibition. He masked the sexual economy that underpinned his new business by creating hidden rooms and configuring discreet, controlled access to interior spaces that preserved the anonymity of patrons and impeded police raids. The build-out of the Ensign Club space into the adjacent storefronts, completed around 1951, tripled the area Caldaralla controlled on the first floor of the Merrimac Building.[47] He hid the space behind a new, sleek, modern façade with five large plateglass windows. Rather than bringing light and sight lines into the interior, the windows were backed by a black wall that concealed the interior space from the street and prevented passersby from seeing patrons inside. A large neon sign for the "Ensign Café Grill" hung above the doorway at 14 Embarcadero. Bold cursive letters announced the "Charcoal Broiler" on white Vitrolite panels above the windows. Behind the façade, the Ensign Club developed into a private-membership club known in some circles for late-night, queer revelry and sexual activity on the premises.

After building out the Ensign Club on the first floor, Caldaralla differentiated and renamed the second-floor nightclub the Broken Drum—a nod to the basement speakeasy in the nearby Bay Hotel that he ran in the early 1920s. When it opened in 1951, the Broken Drum offered Italian dinners, dancing, cocktails, and regular performances by the Gene Ortet Orchestra, all with no cover charge.[48] It may initially have been set up as an alternative to the first-floor Ensign Club, offering dinner and dancing to heterosexual nightlife crowds. It soon, however, attracted a mixed clientele of sex- and gender-transgressive patrons. Because the Broken Drum catered much more to the late-night and early-morning partiers than the dinner crowd, it was known locally as a "breakfast club," a place that violated liquor control rules by serving alcoholic beverages after hours. Not unlike "bottle clubs" like New York's Stonewall Inn in the mid-1960s, the staff at the Broken Drum surreptitiously mixed cocktails for patrons from mislabeled bottles of liquor.[49] Because the windowless lounge, stage, and dancefloor were hidden behind a series of smaller rooms facing the Embarcadero, it was an ideal spot for late-night revelers to carry on until all hours of the morning out of sight.

THE QUEER SCENE AT THE ENSIGN CLUB AND BROKEN DRUM IN THE 1950S AND 1960S

After Caldaralla partitioned the Merrimac Building into a multi-floor nighttime entertainment complex in the early 1950s, the first-floor Ensign Club and the basement below thrived as a so-called homosexual hangout, where a racially mixed crowd of working-class men not only socialized but had sex on the premises. The tearoom trade mentioned by Nichols in the downstairs bathroom during the war years had become the basis for a new commercial enterprise, an underground sex club. Gerald Fabian, a gay man who hung out at the Ensign Club in the 1950s, described the basement as a space "down below the street" that was "subject to the tides" and often got so "sloshy" that "you'd have to wear rubber boots." The upstairs, he recalled, had "a long old Victorian bar" that was not off-limits to military personnel and could be packed with as many as three hundred patrons. At the same time, the downstairs "tearoom" would hold "as many as could pack in . . . as many as could roll up their trousers."[50]

Fabian characterized the basement scene at the Ensign Club as diverse crowds of sailors, marines, and tourists engaging in overt spectacles of transgressive interracial group sex. Fabian explained that "men like contrasts in their sex" and "there were all races down there." When LGBT archivist Willie Walker asked Fabian to elaborate on the "pretty spectacular shows" he witnessed, he shared one example:

> There were things that were just incredible . . . I saw this mulatto, very beautiful mulatto, one time take a leather person of his race up the rear . . . It came, kind of like, off of a canvas or something . . . This particular mulatto, he was just delighted in going through all of the gyrations and the facial expressions and everything, but it was all done for the immense crowd . . . We were all standing around whacking off.[51]

White men like Fabian made the Ensign Club a destination for out-of-town visitors by circulating stories of sexual slumming.[52] This voyeuristic and racialized gaze often resonated with gay migrants and tourists coming from elsewhere seeking sexual pleasure. Fabian explained, "It was so popular with people, they would want to see things like that when they came to San Francisco."[53]

Eugene Carles, who also frequented the Ensign Club in the 1950s, recalled details about the upstairs bar's history and appearance while also commenting on the basement sex scene. He described the Ensign as a former longshoremen's bar "where the seamen and the people who worked on the Embarcadero went." As one of many "straight bars . . . for the people that worked . . . in shipping," it had preserved the appearance of a "drinking man's bar [with] nothing gay looking in it or anything else."[54] Carles recalled seeing a long bar on the first floor covered with empty and half-full beer bottles and nobody there. The action, however, was downstairs in the basement, where the bathroom was "mobbed" with men having sex.

While interviewing Carles, gay community historian Jim Duggins shared his own recollection of the first time he went to the Ensign after moving to the city. In 1958, his friend Otto Braverman took him to see the under-ground sex scene in the basement. Like Carles, Duggins was struck by the empty upstairs bar. He asked Otto, "Why did you come here?" Otto replied, "Well, go downstairs. And I'll give you fifteen minutes and if you don't come back, I'll send a posse." He responded knowingly with a simple "Yeah, it was unbelievable" and "hot as hell."[55] In another recollection, Duggins remembered seeing about seventy people participating in an "outrageous" sex scene in a flooded basement. In contrast to the enormous upstairs bar "with a big railroad sort [of] clock on the wall" and only a couple of people, he described the orgy in the basement as having "water so deep that it would probably have gone over shoe tops."[56]

At the height of Eisenhower's port screening program and the purges in maritime labor unions, the Ensign Club became one of the most popular so-called homosexual hangouts on the San Francisco waterfront. When Bob Ross, a prominent gay community leader, first came to the city in 1953, he visited the Ensign Club. He was on his way from San Diego to Hawai'i as part of his naval deployment in the Pacific during the Korean War. Refer-ring to the lower Market Street waterfront, he remembered that the Ensign Club was of the "two or three little bars in the whole area then about that time."[57] That same year, World War II veteran Arch Wilson arrived in the city to work as a stenographer for Southern Pacific headquarters on lower Market Street. As a "young buck out on the town," Wilson would meet gay men at work and in the bars on the nearby waterfront. He remembered, "There were wonderful little gay bars just off Market, way down near the Embarcadero. Wonderful . . . and places on the Embarcadero, all kinds of joints there were great . . . gay joints and great atmosphere . . . in the 50s." He specified that the Ensign and an after-hours place above it, which he referred to as "the Drum," were popular "gay joints" at the time.[58] These recollections of overt sexual solicitation among men at the Ensign Café confirm the vibrancy of queer social life on the San Francisco waterfront in the 1950s. They suggest that so-called homosexual hangouts emerged not despite but because of anti-homosexual purges, bar raids, and street sweeps that limited queer nightlife to particular, marginalized spaces in the city.

Caldaralla's Broken Drum likely started as a bottle club hosted by "B-girls" who flirted and served overpriced drinks to patrons.[59] At least initially, Cal-daralla seemed to assume that straight men would be his primary clientele. Here patrons were expected to bring their own bottle of liquor, which they could purchase from Caldaralla's liquor store on the first floor. After entering the Broken Drum, they handed the bottle to the bartender or waitress, who would serve and charge the patron for watered-down, expensive cocktails made from that patron's personal stash. The system was intended to insulate Caldaralla from charges of selling alcohol after 2:00 a.m., the cut-off time specified by state liquor agents.

At different points over the 1950s and early 1960s, the Broken Drum garnered a reputation as an after-hours dance club, a transgender hangout, and a female impersonator cabaret. Orvis Bryant remembered "The Drum" as a place with bad "gay" entertainment, including drag performer "Blotchy Blotter."[60] Another gay man, Glen Price, remembered going to the Broken Drum with friends to see Ida Brook, a Black singer who performed there regularly.[61] The Broken Drum had a lot of similarities with the Gourmet Breakfast Club, another queer after-hours club, located in the predominantly African American Fillmore district that briefly stayed in business during the 1950s. Larry Howell recalled how "gays just flocked" to the Gourmet Breakfast Club at two in the morning for drinking and dancing. After entering the building and climbing the stairs to the second floor, patrons paid a heavy-set African American man to enter the "great big room." The doorman would have "a wad of ones in his hands so thick, he could hardly hold it because everybody paid a dollar to walk in." Inside, patrons would get a coffee mug with "nothing but bourbon and ginger ale." Howell was drawn to the place because it had "gay dancing." Although it was filled primarily with gay men, "a lot of gay women [were] there too."[62]

Like the Broken Drum, the Gourmet Breakfast Club typified a new cross-racial and sexual geography of illicit nightlife that developed during the war but faced increasing scrutiny and crackdowns with the postwar transition to civilian control of the city. The Gourmet Breakfast Club, located in the three-story Victorian flat on Post Street, had been the Cherryland restaurant and banquet hall run by a Japanese American sukiyaki chef.[63] The relocation and confinement of Japanese Americans to internment camps and the subsequent influx of African American wartime workers into the neighborhood resulted in the transformation of the Cherryland into a Black-owned jazz club that operated after hours under various names.[64] By 1953, the former Panther Room reopened to cater to gay men in and out of uniform under the management of an African American drag queen. Gay newspaper publisher and columnist Bob Ross later recalled: "It wasn't uncommon to go to Ernestine's fabulous Gourmet Supper Club on Post Street and find sailors and marines dancing with each other. Here was a place you could hold your man good and tight because close dancing was about all you could do on that small floor. Ernestine served only one entrée—homemade biscuits and Southern fried chicken."[65] During a three-month-long crackdown on breakfast clubs in 1953, authorities temporarily shut down the Gourmet Breakfast Club and the Broken Drum.[66] The heightened scrutiny reflected mounting concerns among local and state leaders about the impact of growing transgressive nightlife crowds on postwar urban development. Urban renewal proponents at City Hall and in the business community, in particular, were pushing to redevelop parts of the Fillmore district and the lower Market Street area. The raids on breakfast clubs, and other forms of illicit entertainment, helped make the case that these sections of the city were not just a policing problem but a source of blight.

By the early 1960s, the Broken Drum had become an important social space in San Francisco for female impersonators and transgender people. A twenty-year-old self-described "femme boy" from Johnson City, Tennessee, came to San Francisco in 1959 and began performing as a Marilyn Monroe impersonator at Finocchio's in North Beach. Under the supervision of endocrinologist Harry Benjamin, she soon began transitioning to Aleshia Brevard with hormonal treatments. Brevard later recalled that the Broken Drum and another upstairs place on Turk Street were the only places where transgender and gender-variant residents and migrants could socialize. She characterized the Broken Drum as a relatively safe place she and her friends could go "looking for true love." At the time, she identified as "femme" and did not feel like she was a "part of gay society." Along with her friend "Stormy," who often wore an ermine stole thrown over her bare shoulders, Brevard patronized the Broken Drum because "I belonged with the men that were attracted to me because they appeared for all intents and purposes to be straight." Eschewing gay bars, Brevard and her friend opted to remove themselves from "all that" by perching "queenly" at the bar in the Broken Drum. She explained, "We'd sit and preen and wait for somebody to offer to buy us a drink and take us home." In 1962, she moved to Los Angeles, had gender-affirming surgery, and embarked on a film and television career.[67]

The Broken Drum and Ensign Club did not simply tolerate a more gender-transgressive clientele in the early 1960s—the operators, presumably Caldaralla or his tenants, actively courted trans patrons with strategic advertisements on the outside of the building and in print. New signage on the Market Street façade, an arrow-shaped "Televission [*sic*]" sign hanging over the sidewalk, directed visitors around the corner to the double doors at 8 Embarcadero (see figure 3.2).[68] Above the door, a second sign pointed to the entrance below, with the promise of "Television News on the Hour, Every Hour." The prominent advertisement had a double meaning, as the

Figure 3.2 The layers of signage on the façade of the Merrimac Building in 1961 reflected Caldaralla's years of managing and controlling queer nightlife crowds by partitioning, concealing, and subleasing different commercial spaces. (San Francisco Redevelopment Agency Papers, San Francisco History Center, San Francisco Public Library.)

abbreviation for television, "TV," also served as a shortened form of the now outdated term "transvestite." The slang term circulated among people who produced, read, and corresponded through the monthly magazine *Transvestia*, published sporadically "of, by, and for TVs" in the 1950s and 1960s in Los Angeles.[69] In the October 1961 issue, the editor of *Transvestia* identified the Ensign Café as one of nine nightclubs across the country that hosted regular female impersonator shows.[70] The following year, the Ensign Club openly advertised shows by "Internationally Famous Female Impersonator, Mr. Rudi Del Rio" and "Pantomimist, Mr. Bobbi St. Clair" in the nightlife section of the *San Francisco Chronicle*.[71]

Fragmentary sources suggest that the Broken Drum was also a hangout for butch lesbians. Glenna Lopez, a former "hoochi-koochie dancer" at the Broken Drum, had "a record of morals offenses and other charges dating back to 1953." In 1961, her photograph appeared in the *San Francisco Chronicle* alongside her accomplice and roommate, Judith Corron, after they robbed a food market in a small Sacramento Valley town several hours north of the city. While her second accomplice—Nancy Jordan, an unemployed woman from Oakland—waited in the car, Lopez and Corron threatened the store owner with a .22-caliber pistol and made off with $450. All in their early twenties, the three collaborators were arrested in a bar across from the Chico police station after police officers searched their motel room and found the loot. Corron, a secretary, had a record of suspicion of burglary. She and Lopez lived together in a small second-floor flat in Bernal

Heights in San Francisco. The coverage of the armed robbery highlighted the three suspects' masculine dress: "All three women, police said, were wearing Levi's, canvas shoes and cowboy hats." Side-by-side mugshots of Corron and Lopez framed the criminal duo in a butch-femme dichotomy. With a boyish cropped haircut, T-shirt, and men's brow-line eyeglasses, Corron's perceived and rebellious masculinity was a counterpoint to Lopez's femininity with her long hair, V-cut blouse, and thick makeup. Although the story did not explicitly comment on the relationship between Corron and Lopez, the details about their employment, living arrangement, and the butch-femme framing of the mugshots all suggested that the two were a young lesbian couple immersed in the life of sexual thrills and criminal activity associated with the Broken Drum's after-hours scene.[72]

QUEER CONTAINMENT ON THE WATERFRONT

Mike Caldaralla saw the port screening program and the reorganization of maritime unions that drove displaced laborers to San Francisco as a business opportunity. To reverse the loss of beer and liquor sales that came with the end of the wartime mobilization of troops, he reoriented the Ensign Café to cater to the influx of suspected homosexuals forced out of the merchant marines and armed forces. While police and liquor agents cracked down on the Black Cat and several other gay bars in North Beach and the Tenderloin, Caldaralla was able to run the Ensign Club and Broken Drum with the full awareness of local law enforcement, who turned a blind eye to its more sexual- and gender-transgressive crowd. The tacit support of local authorities, rather than Caldaralla's business acumen alone, explains why the Ensign Café stayed in continuous operation during the height of crackdowns on so-called homosexual hangouts. State and local officials saw the value of containing late-night, queer commerce at the foot of Market Street under his management. When the rare police raid did occur, Caldaralla faced few consequences and was always back in business within a few weeks.

A scrape in 1953 illustrates how all this worked. In early 1953, state liquor control agents raided the Broken Drum and the three other clubs in a crackdown on B-girl, after-hours operations. On a Sunday at 3:00 a.m., sixteen state liquor agents operating in teams of four raided the Kubla Khan in North Beach, Coffee Dan's in the Tenderloin, Bop City in the Fillmore, and the Broken Drum on the Embarcadero. They rousted three hundred customers, made twelve arrests, and served six warrants to tavern owners and bartenders for serving alcohol after two o'clock in the morning. At the Broken Drum, agents ejected fifty patrons and arrested a male bartender, two waitresses, and Mike Caldaralla, whom they identified as the manager. Caldaralla and the staff were each fined $500 and released from custody.[73] Following his arrest, Caldaralla briefly lost control of the Ensign Café. A newly appointed board member to the State Equalization Board (SBE) condemned the usual practice of merely suspending permission to sell alcoholic beverages from operators of disorderly houses, because they were easily removed by the paper transfer or sale of licenses to new operators. Liquor reformers led by California State Representative from San Francisco Casper Weinberger pushed for permanently revoking licenses from operators convicted of code violations. They resolved to close the bars and clubs that had been a recurring problem in the city. In April 1953, the SBE revoked Caldaralla's liquor license for his second-floor B-girl operation, hailing their decision as one of the "the first revocations of on-sale general licenses in San Francisco since 1951."[74]

Caldaralla soon recovered by finding a new tenant to take over running— at least on paper—the second-floor commercial space. The SBE's 1953 revocation order applied to a twelve-year-old license to sell distilled spirits at a cocktail lounge doing business as the Ensign Café and registered at 10 Embarcadero.[75] While the SBE revoked this permit, the state agency left in place a second license, for the sale of beer only, at the same location and under the same business name. Caldaralla transferred the beer license to a pair of merchant seamen.[76] The transfer, which also included a legal name change of the second-floor operation from the Ensign Café to the Broken Drum, went through the approval process without incident. Given that local law enforcement and state licensing officials vetted all permit changes, the successful transfer suggests the tacit support of local authorities for the continuing operation of the queer nightlife complex in the Merrimac Building.

Only five months after the closure of the Broken Drum as an after-hours club, Clarke W. Johnson and Elmer Louis Dense reopened the Broken Drum as a large second-floor beer tavern.[77] In his mid-thirties, Dense was a junior engineer in the merchant marines who frequently sailed out of San Francisco and remained at sea for long periods during the 1950s.[78] Dense would have been a member of a "black gang," a kind of laborer common in some waterfront homosexual hangouts in the 1940s and 1950s. Not a racial but an occupational signifier, the term referred to men who would "work around engines and work around oil [on ships, and] become black."[79] With these subtle changes in the operation of the Broken Drum in 1953, Caldaralla's nightlife complex came to more closely resemble the so-called homosexual hangout recollected years later by many gay men who frequented it around that time. Their recollections included the close association with merchant marines, the enormous size of the main barroom, the many half-filled glasses of beer on the bar, and the distinct separation of activities across multiple floors.

In 1954, in another citywide sweep of after-hours clubs, the Broken Drum was one of eight places served with a written warning by San Francisco District Attorney Thomas Lynch. Police Chief Michael Gaffney reported to Lynch that local district captains complained that these clubs were "creating new problems" and that "new requests for permits to open new clubs" were piling up.[80] Lynch's stern warning marked the end, not the beginning, of efforts to close down the Broken Drum and Ensign Club. Over the next five years, local law enforcement and state liquor agents left the queer nightlife scene in the Merrimac Building alone. There was little incentive to shut it down once the block was declared blighted as part of the Golden Gateway urban renewal project area. Instead, they treated the Ensign and nearby strip of queer nightlife spots as spaces to contain the city's gender and sexual transgressive bar crowds.

The most significant legal trouble Caldaralla faced in the 1950s did not stem from catering to this transgressive clientele or violating alcoholic beverage regulations but from a violent altercation with an employee. On a Friday night in late June 1956, Caldaralla shot one of his relief bartenders, John Mahan, five times after a disagreement over back wages. Mahan stumbled to the nearby Harbor Mission Hospital, where the staff removed two bullets and treated his eight entry and exit wounds. Seventy-three-year-old Caldaralla was arrested and charged with assault with a deadly weapon with intent to kill.[81] During his trial, five San Francisco Police Department officials testified as character witnesses on Caldaralla's behalf. Two police sergeants, an inspector, and two patrolmen representing the central, northern, and southern stations testified that Caldaralla ran a "quiet" place, despite also acknowledging his previous conviction for operating an after-hours club. Chief of Police Frank Ahern was frustrated by the depth of support Caldaralla enjoyed from local law enforcement. The previous year, he had been appointed by Mayor Christopher to "close the city down to organized vice" but was unable to prevent the officers from serving as defense witnesses at Caldaralla's trial.[82]

During the trial, Caldaralla claimed that he acted in self-defense when Mahan leaped over the bar and attacked him for refusing to include overtime pay in his final paycheck earlier in the day. In the cross-examination, the prosecuting attorney tried to prejudice the jury against Caldaralla by asking one of the police witnesses about the nature of the crowds at the Ensign. The officer acknowledged that the establishment was popular among the homosexuals who frequented the Embarcadero:

> **PROSECUTOR:** Did you ever familiarize yourself with whether the Ensign Café, No. 1 Market Street, was a hangout for homosexuals?
> **PATROLMAN:** There has been homosexuals in that place, that I believe were homosexuals—I been in there on various times, as I have been into most bars on the Embarcadero.
> **PROSECUTOR:** Knowing that fact, did that in any way affect your judgment as to the reputation of the defendant for peace and quiet?
> **PATROLMAN:** No . . . because the Embarcadero has got a few homosexuals on it.[83]

At the conclusion of the trial, Caldaralla was convicted of assault with a deadly weapon and sentenced to one year in county jail. He lost an appeal and subsequent petition to the California Supreme Court to rehear the case. While Caldaralla served out his sentence, the Ensign Café's Charbroiler Grill got a new façade, and a former middleweight boxing champion, Kenneth Overlin, took over running the Broken Drum as an after-hours nightclub.[84] Even during Caldaralla's brief time in county jail, his bar-nightclub complex in the Merrimac Building stayed up and running. It was a testament to his decades-long relationship with local authorities, which also allowed him to return to business as usual at the Ensign after serving out his sentence.

URBAN BLIGHT AND QUEER LAND USES

After Caldaralla set up the Ensign Club as a homosexual hangout in the late 1940s, he reconfigured the commercial spaces in the building, secured a club operator to run the place, took out a series of advertisements in the police journal, and garnered a mention in the nightlife column of the *San Francisco Chronicle*. His business dealings suggest that he likely enjoyed the good graces of law enforcement because he shared his profits with local police and state liquor agents throughout the 1950s. As a managed vice operation,

Caldaralla's protection payments, in the form of advertisements and likely "gratuities" to patrolmen, created incentives for law enforcement officers to steer queer nightlife to the Ensign Café.[85] Police graft and vice containment, however, do not fully explain why the Ensign Club and Broken Drum stayed in business until 1965. As the most prominent queer establishment in the center of the city's top-priority urban renewal project area, the Ensign Café was the best illustration of the physical decay, functional obsolescence, and social degradation on the waterfront. When urban renewal proponents flagged the strip of seamen's hotels and bars along the Embarcadero for redevelopment in 1954, they actively discouraged any effort to rehabilitate or repurpose the existing buildings. While they marshaled the resources and capacity to raze and rebuild the area, the Ensign Café, as evidence of urban blight, helped them make their case.

In July 1954, city officials and business leaders began to recast the foot of Market Street not as a special police problem area but a source of urban blight.[86] As we saw in the previous chapter, the *San Francisco News* began a campaign to promote urban renewal by depicting the foot of Market Street as cluttered, decaying, neglected, and abandoned (see figure 2.6).[87] While the accompanying article did not specifically mention the influx of homosexuals on the central waterfront, the photo captured the Ensign Café to make a case for razing and replacing the block with a new Ferry Building Plaza. Six months later, the *San Francisco News* followed up with a cropped, bird's-eye photograph of lower Market Street—with the Ensign Café clearly visible at the center of the frame—to promote the first Ferry Building State Park proposal (figure 3.3). With a "dotted line slashing property frontages on Market Street," the photo editor did symbolically what city leaders hoped the bulldozer would soon do—demolish the waterfront hangout. Specifically, the Ensign served as the primary justification for "beautifying the [city's] eastern gateway."[88] In October 1955, a third street-level photo mosaic of Embarcadero storefronts capturing both Lennie's 36 Club and the Ensign Café was the primary illustration of blight conditions on the waterfront in a formal proposal for state park funds to rebuild the area (see figure 2.2).[89] For added emphasis, a close-up view of the entrance to the Ensign's second-floor nightclub provided visual evidence that "blight and decay have degraded the area" (see figure 2.3).[90] These three images served as the principal visual evidence of blight at the foot of Market Street in 1954 and 1955, when the area was first tagged for redevelopment. By featuring the Ensign Café with these images of urban blight, proponents of waterfront redevelopment drew attention to the city's most recognizable so-called homosexual hangout to

Figure 3.3 The Ensign Café (left side) was the only business visible within the footprint of the proposed Ferry Building State Park in a *San Francisco News* illustration published in February 1955. (AAB-6537, San Francisco History Center, San Francisco Public Library.)

advance plans to redevelop the waterfront and the nearby produce market into the Golden Gateway and Embarcadero Freeway.

The blight label, however, ensured that the Front would develop into the most sexually transgressive, least policed nightlife circuit in the city during the late 1950s and early 1960s. During this period, there was little doubt that the Ensign Café would be demolished as part of the overall transformation of the foot of Market Street to make way for the Golden Gateway urban renewal project. There was uncertainty, however, about precisely *how, when,* and *for what* the waterfront blocks would be razed. As the previous chapter showed, redevelopment proponents struggled during the late 1950s to hammer out plans for a waterfront park that would serve as the city's grant-in-kind contribution to qualify for federal urban renewal funds for the Golden Gateway project. In the interval between the formal blight declaration and the start of land acquisitions for the park, local leaders adopted an unspoken policy of queer containment within the area. As a consequence, the Ensign Café and several new gay bars flourished on the waterfront until the San Francisco Redevelopment Agency began purchasing land and razing buildings on the waterfront.

The blight label that offered a degree of protection to the Ensign Club and Broken Drum lost its potency in 1959 and 1960 with the beginning of land acquisition activities for the Golden Gateway urban renewal project. As the San Francisco Redevelopment Agency began negotiations with landowners over the "voluntary" sale of their property, local, state, and federal authorities came down hard on queer and racially marked after-hours clubs in the city. The Ensign Café and the Broken Drum were prime targets. Alcoholic Beverage Control (ABC) agents began working undercover in 1959, collecting evidence that "sexual perverts were permitted to congregate" at the Ensign Café regularly.[91] In early 1960, undercover federal agents gathered proof of the sale of untaxed liquor at the after-hours clubs leading to a raid by US Treasury Department agents on the Broken Drum and the operators of three other late-night bottle clubs in the city.[92] The revenue agents reported buying $2 mixes and $8 pints of liquor. The bartenders and waitresses held on to the pints and used them to mix cocktails for the agents throughout the morning. The agents smuggled out samples during the night to have a chemist analyze their alcohol content. Broken Drum bartender Bryaine "Tommy" Hunt was arrested for destroying evidence after smashing three bottles against the wall to avoid prosecution. He had taken over the lease from Kenneth Overlin in late February, during the period federal agents were surveilling the establishment. Agents also arrested Overlin at home on the night of the raid. In a series of trials in May, Overlin and Hunt were fined $500 and $100, respectively, for selling drinks without a federal liquor tax stamp.[93]

The state and federal actions against the Ensign Café and Broken Drum in 1959 and 1960 marked only a temporary disruption in queer nightlife in the Merrimac Building. In effect, the ABC's threat to revoke the Ensign liquor license led to a minor shake-up—or perhaps a shakedown—by local police and state liquor agents, but not an end to the illicit liquor trade or queer carousing on the premises.[94] Back on the scene after serving his sentence for assaulting an employee with deadly force, Caldaralla unveiled the Ensign Club Room in September 1960 as a "new entertainment spot" with live performances and dancing between shows.[95] The San Francisco Police Department responded by revoking his dance hall permit on the grounds that the Ensign was a "hangout for homosexuals."[96] The San Francisco Board of Permit Appeals concurred. Nevertheless, Caldaralla moved ahead with opening the Ensign Club Room as a dinner club with live entertainment but no dancing between shows. The *San Francisco Chronicle* subsequently began running regular advertisements in the nightlife section announcing the lineup of performers, touting excellent food, and inviting patrons to "come as you are."[97] Not long afterward, Caldaralla made subtle changes to the façade and ran well-placed advertisements to signal that the Ensign had returned to business as usual. Caldaralla's queer nightlife complex remained in continuous operation until 1965, outlasting a circuit of waterfront gay bars that opened nearby. As chapter 5 shows, only when the Redevelopment Agency approached the very end of the process of land acquisitions, commercial evictions, and building demolitions for the Golden Gateway urban renewal project did this last queer waterfront hangout finally close.

AN ORDINARY HOMOSEXUAL HANGOUT

In 1962, Rod Geddes and several friends took a cross-country road trip from Florida to California to tour national parks, see acquaintances, and visit gay bars along the way. Like many other men drummed out of national security positions as suspected homosexuals, Geddes had recently been fired from defense contractor Martin Marietta after he was seen patronizing a local gay bar. He soon expanded his gay social circle at a new, lower-paying clerical job with the local American Automobile Association branch office, where he assembled "TripTik" roadmaps for the auto club's members. For his own cross-country road trip, however, he did not have the same wayfinding assistance in locating gay bars along his route.[98] The first commercial guidebooks for gay travelers—the *Lavender Baedeker* and the *Damron Guide*—would not be in circulation for a couple more years.[99] So Geddes had to be resourceful in figuring out where to go to meet other gay men in the places he visited. After visiting the popular tourist sites in San Francisco, he asked a cab driver, "Would you take me to a homosexual bar?" The driver dropped him off at the Ensign, a place Geddes later characterized as "my first gay bar in San Francisco."[100]

Geddes's arrival and brief experience at the Ensign provides a window onto the changing social character of homosexual hangouts and gay bars on the waterfront in the early 1960s. Geddes would not have ended up at the Ensign if he had run across a copy of Guy Strait's *Citizens' News*. By perusing pages of gay bar advertisements and reading the nightlife gossip column, he would have been able to choose from among the city's twenty-five to thirty gay bars at the time. The Ensign, however, would not have been among his options, because the *News*'s publisher, advertisers, and readership did not consider it a gay bar. According to Strait, the city's nascent gay community did not regard the Ensign as a legitimate "sociable drinking spot for those of *slightly* different sexual orientation."[101] As a managed vice operation run by liquor interests and backed by law enforcement, the Ensign never joined the social and commercial network of gay bar operators, staff, and patrons that challenged corrupt policing practices and liquor license revocation proceedings in the late 1950s and early 1960s. The Ensign was a product of these practices and remained a primary beneficiary, which meant Caldaralla was never in serious danger of losing his license to sell beer and liquor out of the Merrimac Building. Not unlike the taxi driver who dropped Geddes off at the Ensign, local law enforcement and state liquor agents steered sexual- and gender-transgressive bargoers to Caldaralla's queer nightlife complex at the foot of Market Street.

Geddes's fleeting encounter with the Ensign does not align with the mix of provocative depictions of the sexual character of the place in the 1950s. Geddes was underwhelmed by the Ensign. Not knowing about the downstairs, he stayed in the mostly empty bar upstairs. Had he arrived after 9:30 p.m. in late March, he might have found the space packed for a performance by female impersonator Mr. Rudi Del Rio or pantomimist Mr. Bobbi St. Clair in the first floor "Ensign Club Room."[102] If he had stayed past 2:00 a.m., he might have migrated with the crowd to the second-floor Broken Drum breakfast club and drunk liquor out of a coffee mug. If he had visited in the summer, he might have learned from a bartender or patrons about the Redevelopment Agency's attempts to evict the operators from the building. He might have also met the future Aleshia Brevard, as she unwound in the Broken Drum after performing for the tourist crowd at Finocchio's in North Beach. If he had ventured downstairs when the place was in full swing, he might have stumbled upon the notorious underground sex club. More likely, he might have discovered that, by the early 1960s, the wild orgies in the basement lived on as mythic stories of a homoerotic past rather than as an ongoing source of secretive, sexual pleasure available for the cost of a glass of beer.

Geddes's brief recollection locates queerness at the foot of Market Street when the San Francisco Redevelopment Agency was actively acquiring, managing, and preparing to dispose of properties in the heart of the Golden Gateway urban renewal project area. Although the Agency purchased the Merrimac Building the same year Geddes visited, Caldaralla did not vacate the premises for three more years. Indicative of his continuing support from

local officials, Caldaralla made regular rental payments to his new landlord—
the San Francisco Redevelopment Agency—until just before the wrecking
ball and bulldozers arrived to clear the site. True to his long disassociation
from the gay bar community, he advertised "Good Food, Entertainment,
Floor Show" at the "Ensign Club" in the *San Francisco Chronicle* nightlife
section rather than the *Citizens' News* or the first gay travel guidebooks.[103]
He invited readers to "Come as You Are!" and signed his own name, "Mike
Caldaralla, Manager," signaling to city officials and patrons alike that he
was back in business and in the good graces of law enforcement.

The following chapter shifts focus to a new generation of gay bars in the
lower Market Street area that, unlike the Ensign, resisted the containment
practices that transformed the area into a managed vice district reserved
for queer nightlife crowds. Within and among these self-identified gay
bars, a countercultural drinking public developed when operators, staff,
and patrons challenged the legal and extralegal actions of state actors to
regulate, exploit, and utlimately dismantle the queer world of the waterfront
in the lead-up to area-wide urban renewal. A better understanding of how,
when, and why this counterpublic coalesced provides new insights into
the critical role waterfront urban redevelopment played in gay community
organizing and political mobilizations in San Francisco during the late
1950s and early 1960s.

4

A QUEER HISTORY OF 90 MARKET STREET

On the evening of March 21, 1961, Guy Strait and José Sarria convened a meeting at 90 Market to discuss forming a new gay civil rights organization, the League for Civil Education (LCE).[1] Known as "Elsie" for short, the League would bring together "all persons in the business of supplying food and drink to the Community" to push back against growing incidences of police harassment and revocation proceedings.[2] The goal of the meeting was to demonstrate to law enforcement that gay bar interests and the city's homophile organizations were united in defending gay and lesbian San Franciscans against discrimination. The LCE co-organizers invited representatives from the police department, the state Alcoholic Beverage Control (ABC) Board, the district attorney's office, and the city's two homophile organizations. The police department sent a lieutenant and an inspector to observe the meeting. Several homophile leaders attended as well.[3] The LCE co-organizers held the meeting to legitimize gay bars as a specialized business enterprise and to question the use of state power to target the bars and their patrons with surveillance and criminal prosecution. The mix of attendees signaled the end of the vice containment and control practices dating back to Prohibition. It also marked a new working relationship between homophile groups and bar-based drinking publics in advocating for the legal rights of sexual minorities.[4]

Why did the LCE get started at 90 Market, a gay nightclub complex opposite the Ensign Café at the foot of Market Street? The answer to this question offers a window onto how early-1960s bar-based activism unfolded in the middle of the city's top-priority urban renewal project area. Ninety

Market was a new queer commercial enterprise located in a building slated for redevelopment in the final phase of the Golden Gateway project. Sol Stoumen, the owner of the Black Cat, had recently taken over 90 Market after cooperating in an undercover sting operation that implicated police and liquor agents in extorting payoffs on the premises. After Stoumen assisted with the investigation and trials, he recruited one of his most popular cocktail waiters and drag performers to take over the operation and management of the former Castaways space. Eager to have a more prominent role in the nightlife enterprise, José Sarria oversaw the renovations of 90 Market into the Talk of the Town nightclub and set up his own food concession in the front of the commercial space, where he catered to the daytime lunch crowd. He cofounded the LCE soon afterward to defend his new commercial enterprise from attacks by law enforcement, liquor agents, and area business leaders. In other words, the discrimination he faced as a gay business operator prompted him to rally gay San Franciscans to publicly and collectively demand equal treatment by the state.

From its inception, the League developed what historian Nan Boyd characterized as a novel "political ideology and organizational strategy."[5] The LCE conceived of bargoers as a community of shared interests that, once mobilized, could wield political influence and economic power. Over three years, the group cultivated a spirit of solidarity among gay bar publics by hosting a mix of forums, voter registration drives, fundraising events, and a circuit of themed holiday parties. Supported by advertising revenue, the group's newsletter soon developed into the *LCE News*, a newspaper that became a popular source of local information about legal developments, nightlife happenings, and gossip within the city's queer nightlife circuit.[6] In bars and in print, Guy Strait, José Sarria, and other LCE backers sought to unify drinking publics into a politically engaged, socially minded, rights-seeking, sexual identity–based community. The LCE's efforts to bring bargoers into the public sphere were soon replicated by new homophile organizations that found even greater success and more members by hosting events, publishing newspapers, engaging city officials, and shedding personal anonymity.

In the early 1960s, gay bars in San Francisco underwent an unprecedented transformation to become hubs of group identity formation, political activism, and economic opportunity among a growing population who organized their lives openly around same-sex desire. Crediting the role of early gay travel guides, including one produced by Guy Strait, historian

Martin Meeker pinpointed the "emergence of the contemporary gay bar as a place that had an almost exclusively gay clientele, was owned, managed, and run by homosexuals, and was advertised in gay publications designed to attract gay patrons" in the early 1960s.[7] Although bars with these characteristics were neither new nor unique to the city, they took on a more unambiguous social and sexual identity in San Francisco earlier than a similar shift occurred in other cities. Historian Clayton Howard observed that during the long postwar period in San Francisco, "bars helped bring together an increasingly self-aware queer public."[8] Nan Boyd demonstrated that the formation of this new political consciousness was catalyzed by José Sarria and others who, by mid-century, turned bars in North Beach into a "kind of politicized community center—a site for the development of new political ideas and responsibilities."[9]

This chapter argues that the crucial events that aroused an "articulate, cooperative, and resistant gay and lesbian social movement" in postwar San Francisco were bound up in the establishment of a new queer commercial enterprise at 90 Market.[10] The 1959 mayoral race, the 1960 "gayola" scandal, and Sarria's 1961 run for elective office brought San Francisco's homosexual bar cultures into the public realm ten years before the gay civil rights movement crystallized nationally around the Stonewall Riots.[11] During these formative years, 90 Market played a pivotal role in thrusting gay bars into local electoral politics, challenging corruption in policing queer nightlife crowds, and mobilizing queer drinking publics into a voting bloc. State-sanctioned efforts to steer queer nightlife to lower Market Street in the late 1950s came to an abrupt halt in 1960 when the city started acquiring land for redevelopment. During this brief window of opportunity, several gay entrepreneurs transformed 90 Market into a new commercial complex. When this window slammed shut, they organized to resist efforts to eject them from the waterfront. In retelling this short but pivotal period in San Francisco's queer history, this chapter offers a new vantage point from which to view the origins and methods of queer organizing and political mobilization in the early 1960s. What happens if, instead of focusing on policing practices and legal battles, we focus on the organizational roots of gay bar publics? This shift in focus highlights a vision of queer solidarity and political rights forged by bar owners, drag entrepreneurs, and a diverse clientele faced with dispossession and displacement in the Golden Gateway that, in turn, echoed an older history of maritime trade unionism in the area.[12]

THE POLITICAL SIGNIFICANCE OF "SWISHY" BARS

The 1959 mayoral race in San Francisco was the first of a series of high-profile events that brought to light the political significance of the city's growing gay population.[13] During the 1950s, the city had emerged, along with Los Angeles, as a center of homophile activism during the anti-homosexual purges in West Coast ports. By the decade's end, San Francisco had become the organizational headquarters of two national homophile groups and the center of an emerging gay publishing industry. Leaders of the Mattachine Society coordinated activities among a national network of chapters, produced the group's monthly magazine, and distributed other gay-interest publications through the Pan-Graphic Press and the Dorian Book Service. Meanwhile, periodic bar raids and street sweeps aimed at homosexuals did more to publicize the city's gay population than to check its growth. At least publicly, law enforcement and state liquor agents blamed the city's thriving gay bar scene on legal developments that tied their hands. During Mayor George Christopher's 1959 reelection campaign, his challenger attempted to turn the race into a referendum on the mayor's culpability in the growth of the city's gay population. The tactic backfired. It sparked a public debate about homosexuality and policing practices, which subsequently undercut the power of corrupt officials over queer drinking publics on the Embarcadero.

There was an early warning that the thriving gay bar scene would be a losing campaign issue for any candidate who sought to exploit it for political gain. In the summer of 1958, *San Francisco Chronicle* columnist Herb Caen, a sympathetic ally to gay readers, presented an alternative and more positive image of the changing population: "the Queen City of the Pacific, with more queens arriving every day, drawn, perhaps, by the ceaseless swish of the waves."[14] Early the following year, he cautioned public officials that "queens" would be a factor in the upcoming election: "After a hasty count of the limp-wristers in the swishy bars from North Beach to Thausalito [Sausalito, which was known for its many artists and gay men, spoken with a lisp] . . . , they've got enough votes to recall [Governor] Pat Brown and elect [female impersonator] Walter Hart!"[15] Caen frequently dropped the names of gay bars and nightlife personalities in his column. His campy reference to gay bars as "swishy" played off his earlier comparison of the movement of ocean waves to the sweeping hips of "queens." It also called to mind the nickname for the Southern Pacific Building, the "Swish Palace," based on the large number of gay clerical staff who worked there.[16] With his finger on the pulse of the city's queer scene, Caen's comment was a warning to

---

3 DAYS CELEBRATION — OCT. 3 - 4 - 5
GRAND OPENING
Jack's Waterfront Hangout
Under new ownership of
George Bauman and Mary E. Brown
featuring
Waterfront entertainment after dark
open from 11 A.M. to 2 A.M.
111 Embarcadero . **Showtime 10 P.M., 11:30, 1:00**

Figure 4.1 Gay bartender George Bauman and a friend took over Jack's Waterfront Hangout in October 1957 and revived the failing nightclub with new entertainment. They and their staff brought in a new crowd of gay men that augmented the declining number of seamen, warehouse workers, and truck drivers that hung out there. (Advertisement, *San Francisco Chronicle*, September 28, 1957, 7.)

candidates not to make "swishy" bars or the city's growing homosexual population a campaign issue. He recognized that politicizing gay bars would alienate a growing segment of the electorate, to the detriment of any candidate who called for clamping down further on nightlife crowds.

In the lead-up to the election, the most politically sensitive "swishy" bars were located in the Golden Gateway urban renewal area. After a failed crackdown in 1956 on obstinate merchants resistant to moving out of the produce market, the Christopher administration treated lower Market Street as a marginal area to confine nuisance land uses. In particular, the waterfront blocks across from the Ferry Building became a managed vice district reserved for queer nightlife as plans for the Golden Gateway moved through the approval process and construction began on the Embarcadero Freeway. As the previous chapter showed, law enforcement and liquor agents stood by as Mike Caldaralla turned the Ensign Café into a queer nightlife complex, even after a shooting incident temporarily closed it down. While Caldaralla was away, law enforcement and state liquor agents approved the opening of two new gay bars in the area—Jack's Waterfront Hangout at 111 Embarcadero and Castaways at 90 Market.

Like the Ensign, Jack's Waterfront Hangout had been a straight spot. In September 1957, George Bauman and Mary E. Brown took over the management of Jack's, and turned it into a gay bar (see figure 4.1). In September 1957, they announced a three-night grand opening featuring three

Figure 4.2 Before Castaways opened as a gay nightclub in 1959, the large entertainment complex at 90 Market had been a social club for railway employees, a striptease cabaret, a jazz club (the Downbeat), and an experimental alcohol-free performance venue for teenagers (Dave Glickman's Jazz Showcase, shown here in September 1958). (Assessor's Office Negative Collection, San Francisco History Center, San Francisco Public Library.)

THE
CASTAWAYS
PRESENTS

MAURICE & LA MONT
—
CASS & BEA

RESTAURANT, BUFFET
COCKTAIL LOUNGE

90 Market St.   EX. 7-0694

Figure 4.3 Castaways opened in late summer 1959 with headline performances by female impersonators and pantomime artists Henry Jouron and William Kugler, a nationally touring duo from Florida known theatrically as "Maurice and La Mont[e]." (Advertisement, *San Francisco Chronicle*, August 8, 1959, 8.)

shows of "after dark" entertainment.[17] Bauman, a popular gay bartender from Sausalito, transformed the former hangout for longshoremen, truck drivers, and produce handlers into a popular new place for gay men to congregate. Brown explained that Bauman "brought in his friends, and they brought their friends and so on."[18] In August 1958, local law enforcement took notice of Jack's new clientele. A patrolman on the waterfront beat approached Bauman to discuss the recent "change in atmosphere," making it clear that if he was "going to run a homosexual hangout, he had better see that the police were taken care of."[19] In response, Bauman began making monthly $200 payments to law enforcement to minimize policing of staff and patrons.[20]

In the summer of 1959, Castaways at 90 Market joined Jack's Waterfront Hangout as the second new gay bar to open on the waterfront (figure 4.2).[21] Norman Lee Tullis—the former operator of a gay bar in lower Nob Hill and a gay man in his late twenties—was one of an unknown number of co-owners of the new operation. He brought along one of his gay bartenders, Bryan Lovell Ray, to manage the interconnected restaurant, buffet, and cocktail lounge commercial space at 90 Market.[22] Tullis and Ray transformed the space into what gay newspaper publisher and bar operator Bob Ross later recalled as "a gay bar with a huge, full stage in it, you know, like a regular theater stage in it where [drag queens] used to perform."[23] One of the first nightclub acts at Castaways was Maurice and La Monte, a gay couple who had met in the late 1940s while performing in Florida (figure 4.3).[24] The show was distinct from the drag performances at Finocchio's and the Beige Room, which were glamourous spectacles of female impersonators produced primarily for touristic consumption by the general public. Instead, Maurice and La Monte's "Off the Record" show relied on visual and physical comedy. Dressed in black, they acted out their own ribald pantomimes accompanied by sound recordings of well-known female singers and actresses. Rather than embodying or creating a convincing illusion of their subjects, they evoked different personalities with costume accessories and an array of props and sight gags.

Both local law enforcement and state liquor agents not only were aware of the new gay nightclub at 90 Market, but they had also been actively involved in its opening and continued operation. Before the move to the waterfront, Tullis and Ray ran the Have One in lower Nob Hill as a gay bar, making monthly $20 payments to a beat patrolman. The two men saw the sizeable commercial space at 90 Market as an opportunity to grow their business from a small, crowded bar into a multifunctional performance space. In the spring of 1959, they applied to transfer the Have One's liquor license to 90 Market Street, which required approvals from local police and state liquor agents. With their application pending, a patrolman told Ray that his superiors would reject the license application unless Ray paid him $250 or $300.[25] After he handed over $200 in May, the state liquor control department approved the transfer. The next month, a police sergeant approached Tullis and Ray to demand additional payoffs.[26] Ray relented and started making monthly $150 payments earmarked for a six-way split among patrolmen and district brass. The same month that payments to the police began, a state liquor control supervisor extorted an additional $150 monthly payment to keep investigators away.[27] The payments worked. When the ABC launched an enforcement drive against homosexual bars in May 1959, they limited the scope to four taverns in Nob Hill and the Tenderloin, leaving Castaways and Jack's alone.[28] By combining targeted policing with graft, corrupt local police and state liquor agents effectively drove queer nightlife from the Tenderloin to the waterfront using a mix of rewards and punishments.

Castaways opened as a gay nightclub in a pivotal election year that had significant implications for the Golden Gateway project. The coalition of business leaders pushing the urban renewal plan for lower Market Street strongly backed Christopher's reelection bid. In his first term, they had leaned on him to expedite the completion of the first segment of the Embarcadero Freeway and to advance the Golden Gateway proposal through the application process for $18 million in federal urban renewal funds. Christopher's opponent, San Francisco Assessor Russell Wolden, was skeptical that freeways and urban redevelopment would increase the city's tax revenue, given the loss of "large chunks of taxpaying property."[29] Wolden started his campaign with significant popular support and an opportunity to highlight Christopher's vulnerabilities, including controversial freeway plans and a scandal over slum clearance–related land purchases in the Fillmore.[30] A Wolden victory, however, would jeopardize the final step in securing federal urban renewal assistance. Increasing the election stakes even higher, San Francisco voters would also weigh in on funds for the Ferry Building Park for the second time. After an embarrassing defeat the previous year, a win this time around was crucial to demonstrate public support for the city's application for federal funds for the Golden Gateway.

Rather than take on the pro-growth coalition directly, Wolden framed the race as a referendum on the growth of the city's homosexual population during Christopher's first term.[31] Leading up to the election, a political consultant worked with William Brandhove, a gay man and former marine steward, to compile evidence that Christopher's actions had allowed the city to develop into a national "haven for homosexuals."[32] Specifically, the Wolden campaign developed two lines of attack to portray the mayor as sympathetic to homosexuals. The first charge was that Christopher had allowed San Francisco to become the national headquarters of two homophile organizations, the Mattachine Society and the Daughters of Bilitis.[33] To prove that the mayor was to blame, Brandhove joined the homophile organization and, at the group's 1959 convention in Denver, orchestrated the passage of a resolution praising Christopher's "enlightened administration" and nominated San Francisco as the site of its next meeting.[34] Wolden's second charge, potentially more politically damaging, was that Christopher allowed gay bars to proliferate in the city.[35] To mobilize homophobic sentiment, Brandhove sent postcards to Wolden's supporters with a map of "authenticated homosexual hangouts" that included bars, after-hours spots, steam baths, parks, beaches, public restrooms, and cruising areas throughout the city.

In a fiery radio speech, Wolden called for an investigation of gay bars "principally in the downtown Tenderloin area and in the waterfront district," causing panic among the corrupt cops involved in extorting payments at 90 Market and Jack's Waterfront Hangout.[36] At Castaways, a police sergeant warned bartender Bryan Ray that a Wolden operative was gathering evidence proving Christopher was "involved in a conspiracy to allow gay bars to operate."[37] Ray later testified, "[The sergeant] warned me some fellow is going around taking pictures trying to get evidence that the present regime [Mayor Christopher's administration] was trying to harbor homosexuals. He told me to be on the watch out for anyone who might come in."[38] Ray was so alarmed that he quit and abruptly moved to Phoenix. Norman Tullis took over and continued making the monthly payoffs at Castaways.[39] At Jack's Waterfront, another sergeant told Bauman that in the event of an investigation, he should deny that the bar was a homosexual hangout. The exchange underscored the fear police felt about being caught collecting payoffs. Focusing on the jeopardy to himself and his officers, the sergeant stammered, "It's—we've done our job. We're—we feel we are clean. I'm not worried about anything, because I—I have not done anything wrong." Oblivious to the fact that Bauman was secretly recording the exchange, the sergeant asserted, "If I was doing anything around here, they would come down and set a trap for me."[40] The effort by the two sergeants to enlist the help of the very bar managers they were extorting payoffs from would backfire after the election.

Wolden's smear campaign also alarmed the mayor's supporters in the pro-growth coalition. While Wolden wanted to make the election a referendum on whether the city would be "open" or "closed" to homosexuals, the most consequential outcome would be whether the pro-growth coalition could bring plans to redevelop the waterfront to fruition. An investigation into gay bars on the waterfront would reveal that the ABC and local law enforcement had approved the liquor licenses at both Jack's and 90 Market. It would also reveal that Jack's opened as a gay bar in a building owned by the San Francisco Port Authority. Potentially complicating matters, Christopher's campaign cochair, Cyril Magnin, was president of the state-run agency responsible for harbor operations and facilities.[41] If these details came out during the campaign, they would potentially sink Christopher's bid for reelection and jeopardize the Golden Gateway project. Proponents of waterfront redevelopment had added a second bond measure to the ballot to fund a city park at the foot of Market Street, which federal urban renewal officials would consider part of the local contribution to the Golden Gateway project. A brewing law enforcement scandal involving protection payments from gay bar owners in the top-priority urban renewal area, if exposed during the campaign, would likely have ended Christopher's political career, wrecked plans for the park, and put an opponent of waterfront redevelopment in the mayor's office.

Christopher's backers and local homophile leaders successfully repudiated Wolden's gay-baiting smear campaign.[42] In the city's three major newspapers, Christopher's allies focused on Brandhove's duplicitous interactions with the Mattachine Society. The *San Francisco Examiner*, which had launched the "drive on deviates" on the eve of the previous mayoral race, assailed Wolden's smear tactics, unabashedly claiming that Wolden's charges against the mayor were an attack on the city's reputation. The *San Francisco Chronicle* took a different approach, characterizing the Mattachine Society as a respectable organization maligned by Wolden. In a significant blow to the "conspiracy of silence" around homosexuality, the Mattachine Society publicly demanded that Wolden and radio station WNBC retract defamatory comments about the organization.[43] In stark contrast to the previous decades, during the campaign the sympathetic coverage of homosexuality and sexual minority rights boosted San Francisco's reputation as a relatively tolerant destination for sexual migrants.[44] Mayor Christopher won reelection by a wide margin and used his new electoral mandate to advance an aggressive urban redevelopment program, starting with land acquisitions in the Golden Gateway.[45]

For the gay men who ran 90 Market and Jack's Waterfront, Wolden's call for an investigation into Christopher's handling of gay bars exposed a weakness in the system of graft. Law enforcement and liquor agents were susceptible to criminal charges for extorting bribes from gay bars if the bar operators could marshal sufficient evidence to indict them. If the evidence was incontrovertible and made public, elected officials might side with gay bar operators to burnish their credentials in running a clean town. While the burden of proof was on gay bar operators to expose the payoff system, the risk of punishment would fall on the corrupt officials peddling lax code enforcement. The operators of Castaways and Jack's Waterfront, as well as others who ran gay bars in the Tenderloin, would soon use this to their advantage.

HOW CASTAWAYS BECAME THE TALK OF THE TOWN

After the election, the managers of Castaways at 90 Market and Jack's Waterfront Hangout played a prominent role in challenging the protection payoff system used by police and liquor agents to manage and exploit gay nightlife crowds. During the "gayola" scandal, the gay bar managers and staff turned the table on law enforcement.[46] The operators of the two new gay bars in the Golden Gateway gathered some of the most incriminating physical evidence and delivered the most damaging testimony exposing corruption in the ranks of the police department and state liquor agency. The scandal fueled a shake-up of the police department and a retaliatory crackdown on gay bars and cruising areas in the city.[47] It also had another previously unrecognized outcome. The associated investigation and trials of police wrongdoing created an opportunity for Black Cat owner Sol Stoumen to purchase Castaways—and for his staff to take over running the large gay nightclub-restaurant-bar complex at 90 Market.

In November 1959, a week after the election, Black Cat host and drag performer José Sarria debuted as "Countess Batnick" on the main stage at Castaways nightclub at 90 Market. He guest-starred alongside Maurice and La Monte, who camped it up as Tallulah Bankhead and Bette Davis.[48] Sarria had already cultivated a large following at the Black Cat, where he sang opera parodies on Sundays atop an impromptu stage made of milk crates and café tables.[49] Castaways was a much larger venue, with a permanent stage, a warren of dressing rooms, a large showroom, several bar areas, and kitchen facilities. Sarria and his piano accompanist, James "Hazel" McGinnis, quickly recognized the potential to make more money and be their own boss at Castaways. Sarria and McGinnis quit the Black Cat and brought the gay crowd with them to 90 Market. They hosted twice-weekly performances of the "Castaways Opera Assn." for about a month, until Sol Stoumen persuaded Sarria to return to the Black Cat by offering him a raise (see figure 4.4).[50]

After the 1959 mayoral race, state and local officials launched an all-out war on gay bars in San Francisco. Just after Christopher won reelection, the ABC statewide director announced plans to regulate the hiring practices of bar owners to dissuade them from catering to homosexuals. He asserted, "The bartender is usually the crux of the matter. Certain bartenders approach an owner and offer to bring in the homosexual trade. Then the homosexuals congregate at the bar where the 'queen bee' bartender is at work. When

OPENING FRIDAY NITE, FEB. 26
THE DIPLOMATS
Outstanding pantomine trio direct
from Detroit
6 nights a week - FIRST SHOW 9:30

And... you are invited to an ex-
citing night of show - fun
MARDI GRAS
Tuesday night, March 1
PROPER COSTUMES INVITED, PRIZES

And...THE CASTAWAYS OPERA ASSN.
Presents
JOSE
Each Sun. afternoon with   OPERA
Each Wednesday nite with OPERETTA
JAMES MC GINNIS (HAZEL) CONDUCTOR
Fabulous Sunday Brunch 10 to Four

90 MARKET, SAN FRANCISCO

Figure 4.4 A performance flyer announcing José Sarria's debut, in November 1959, at Castaways signaled the beginning of his involvement with 90 Market. On the back of the flyer, a list of upcoming events (seen here) indicates Sarria planned to move his Sunday afternoon drag operas from the Black Cat Café to the larger venue. (Flyer [back page], folder Performance, 1955–1969, Box 16, José Sarria Papers [1996-01], Courtesy of Gay, Lesbian, Bisexual, Transgender Historical Society.)

we talk to the bar owners, most of them claim they don't know what has been going on."[51] District agents in San Francisco followed up by creating a "confidential listing" of popular bar employees to help law enforcement track nightlife promoters known to "deal in narcotics," traffic in prostitution, or attract homosexual patrons.[52] The policy targeting "queen bee" bartenders was strikingly similar to the systematic screening of maritime workers off the waterfront based on their criminal or sexual history. At the time, ABC officials anticipated a final ruling in a pending case making "any public display which manifests sexual desires, whether they be heterosexual or homosexual in nature" grounds for revoking state liquor licenses.[53] When the ABC won its case in early 1960, the director increased the penalty for running a "disorderly house, based on deviates," from a suspension lasting forty-five days to six months, to a potential permanent revocation for a history of repeated offenses.[54] An ABC administrator for Northern California followed up with a new undercover operation, targeting the twenty-five to thirty "homosexual haunts" in San Francisco, to collect evidence for revocation proceedings. Rather than "raids or rousting," undercover agents would report overt sexual solicitations or conduct on the premises within view or earshot of bar staff.[55]

The scandal intimated by Wolden broke in late February 1960 when internal affairs investigators arrested a police sergeant for extorting protection payments from the owner of the Handlebar.[56] The arrest had a chilling impact at 90 Market. Norman Tullis turned to Sol Stoumen for help.[57] Tullis and Stoumen determined that the best course of action would be to report the payoffs to ABC officials and, like the owner of the Handlebar had done, cooperate in an undercover sting operation to bring extortion charges against the law enforcement and liquor agents.[58] They hoped this shrewd decision would protect Tullis from potential bribery charges and convince the ABC to drop its pending revocation proceedings against the Black Cat.

To safeguard, if not expand, his bar operation, Sol Stoumen approached the upper echelons of the ABC and local law enforcement with an offer to help root out corruption among local officers and agents. Stoumen informed state ABC administrator Sidney Feinberg about the payoffs at a February 19, 1960, meeting in Sacramento.[59] Feinberg arranged for Stoumen to meet with the chief of police, the assistant chief of police, the assistant district attorney, and the ABC chief investigator. At the gathering, Stoumen agreed to "induc[e] 'gay bar' owners to cooperate with the Police Department with exposing, trapping and prosecuting policemen receiving payoffs."[60] An ABC internal affairs investigator supplied Stoumen with "a concealed walkie-talkie transmitter and marked money doused with fluorescent powder."[61] Stoumen waited for local ABC supervising agent Lawrence Cardellini to come to Castaways to pick up the month's payola payment at the beginning of March. After Cardellini did not show and stayed away for two weeks, Stoumen reported the lack of progress back to Feinberg. Feinberg encouraged him to wait until the following month to make another attempt. Stoumen later alleged that Feinberg, as a reward, offered to reduce "the penalty assessed against [Stoumen] in the pending license revocation proceedings."[62]

The scandal that started at the Handlebar in February spread to Castaways in May 1960. ABC district supervisor Lawrence Cardellini was caught accepting marked bills from Norman Tullis in an undercover sting operation.[63] In subsequent questioning, Tullis asserted that public officials extorting money from gay bars was a widespread practice on the waterfront. At a closed-door internal affairs hearing, Tullis testified that Castaways made two separate $150 payoffs each month between June 1959 and February 1960. One went to a police sergeant to avoid harassment of patrons by law enforcement. The other went to Cardellini to avoid inspections and accusations of liquor code violations.[64] Tullis also revealed smaller monthly payments dating back to 1957 at his previous bar in the Tenderloin and another payoff in May 1959 to transfer his liquor license from the old place to 90 Market. The scope of the hearing soon widened to include Jack's Waterfront Hangout. George Bauman testified that he had paid the police $100 a month beginning in January 1959. The amount increased to $200 in May, which he continued to pay until April 1960.[65] Like Stoumen and Tullis, Bauman also cooperated with the internal affairs investigation, secretly gathering recorded audio files of his interactions with police about the unfolding scandal.[66] On the basis of these accusations and the physical evidence collected by Tullis and Bauman, a grand jury charged a district police captain, several sergeants and patrolmen, and a state liquor control supervisor with extorting payments from Castaways and Jack's Waterfront Hangout in May 1960.[67]

Several months later, Castaways and Jack's Waterfront operators and staff served as star witnesses and gave the most damaging testimony against police and liquor agents during two high-profile payola trials.[68] Over four weeks in the late summer of 1960, seven gay bar owners and employees detailed a pattern of police corruption at Castaways and Jack's that implicated the four men on trial and intimated that higher echelons of the force were also involved. Defense lawyers suggested that the bar operators were motivated by either revenge or an effort to keep their liquor licenses. However, they did not deny the payments occurred, characterizing them instead as part of a routine practice of supporting local law enforcement with "gratuities."[69] The jury took only an hour to acquit four police officers for extorting $2,900 from Jack's Waterfront, as well as a sergeant for taking $1,000 from Castaways.[70] In a separate trial in the fall, Norman Tullis and Bryan Ray testified that ABC district supervisor Cardellini extorted roughly $1,350 in monthly payments over nine months.[71] Jurors found the state liquor inspector guilty of a misdemeanor for accepting a single $150 "gratuity" in marked bills from Tullis. The judge ordered Cardellini to pay a $500 fine and reduced a six-month prison sentence to three years of probation.[72]

The gayola scandal had immediate and lasting effects on the city's relationship between law enforcement and gay bars. First, the associated investigation and trials changed how queer nightlife on the waterfront was understood and characterized in the local press, as newspapers adopted less inflammatory language to refer to the places where gay people congregated.[73] Places that had been characterized as "hangouts for homosexuals" or "resorts for perverts" through the 1940s and 1950s became both reputationally and operationally "gay bars" in the 1960s.[74] In addition, the ABC and police force launched an "especially pernicious" undercover entrapment operation designed to intimidate gay-bar patrons and gather evidence for revocation proceedings.[75] As a result, misdemeanor charges against gay men and lesbians from bar sweeps averaged forty to sixty per week, while the number of felony convictions of gay men shot up dramatically. Finally, the city's progrowth coalition, led by the Blyth-Zellerbach Committee, soon spearheaded a government reform initiative to reorganize and professionalize the police force. They succeeded in undercutting entrenched patronage practices with a system of managerial oversight.[76]

Remarkably, the scandal also enabled Sol Stoumen to take over the Castaways complex with the full support of local, state, and federal officials. The morning after the grand jury indicted six police officers, IRS agents began looking into Norman Tullis's tax liability for Castaways.[77] In June, federal authorities seized Tullis's liquor license and bar furnishings to cover $19,773 in unpaid taxes.[78] Soon afterward, Sol Stoumen purchased Castaways for $10,000 and assumed a $39,000 lease liability for the commercial space. The ABC and local law enforcement approved the sale after Stoumen assured them he would run the new nighttime entertainment venue to cater to a "'non-homosexual' clientele."[79] On July 1, 1960, Stoumen started a ten-year lease for 90 Market with building owner Ernest Blumenthal. Under the lease terms, Stoumen agreed to pay $650 per month for the first five years and, subject to renewal, an additional $100 each month for the next five years.[80]

As figure 4.5 indicates, 90 Market was an enormous, multifunctional commercial space consisting primarily of two adjacent storefronts used as a bar and buffet-style restaurant, with a kitchen and two large performance and lounge areas at the back of the building. On the same day Stoumen's lease went into effect, he and two partners formed "Vend-a-Teria, Inc.," a new domestic stock corporation, to operate the restaurant-bar-nightclub complex at 90 Market.[81] The entity enabled the three directors to raise $25,000 by issuing up to 2,500 shares at $10 each, roughly the size of the IRS lien against Castaways. The ABC transferred Ray and Tullis's suspended liquor license to the new business entity. Like the corporation that Caldaralla set up to manage the Ensign Café, Vend-a-Teria, Inc., provided a layer of legal protection for the new iteration of 90 Market.

Soon after Stoumen took over the space and set up the Vend-a-Teria corporation, Sarria started a food concession in the front dining room that operated during the day. Drawing on skills he learned in a restaurant management course at San Francisco State, Sarria set up a lunch buffet

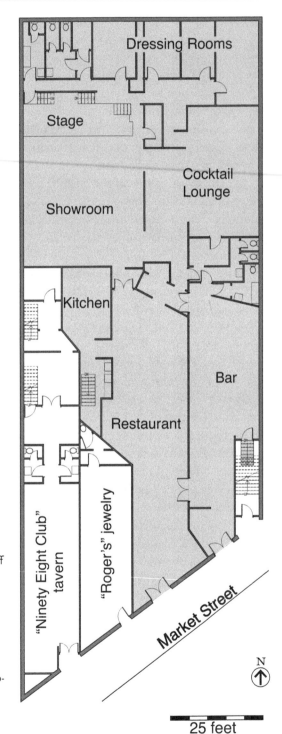

FIGURE 4.5 Stoumen's commercial space at 90 Market included a restaurant in the front, where José Sarria set up a lunch counter, and a showroom in the back, where Sarria and other Black Cat staff staged drag performances. (Layout from 1961 Property Appraisal Report, Acquisition Files, San Francisco Redevelopment Agency Records, Office of Community Investment and Infrastructure. Drafted by the author in collaboration with Ursula Roma and Alex Cox.)

to cater to office workers in the area. Sarria later recalled, "We came up with the idea of selling food by the ounce. Five cents an ounce. And in the middle of the financial district with all the women secretaries, the men secretaries, everybody wanting to eat a fair lunch but not pay a lot."[82] A significant number of his regular customers were clerks from Southern Pacific's "Swish Palace" building across the street and the company's annex office on the second floor of 90 Market. Sarria's lunch counter became an overnight success. He took enormous pride in running it, often sending prepared food to lunch customers at the Black Cat. At times, he fed up to five hundred people.

Over the summer and fall, as the gayola trials captured the headlines, Sarria and the rest of Stoumen's staff at the Black Cat prepared to reopen the former Castaways nightclub at 90 Market. In December 1960, they opened the Talk of the Town nightclub, which consisted of a large showroom called the Stage Room and a separate, more intimate cocktail lounge known as the Living Room (figure 4.6).[83] Contrary to Stoumen's stated intention to refashion the nightclub for "non-homosexuals," the Talk of the Town was set up and managed to accommodate the gay crowds, which had outgrown the Black Cat. Sarria oversaw not just the lunch counter but much of the day-to-day operations of the Talk of the Town.[84] While José Sarria ran the kitchen and hosted drag shows in the showroom, Jim McGinnis accompanied him on the piano and Eddie Paulson managed the bar. By 1961, Sarria was no longer simply an employee of Stoumen or the Black Cat. Instead, Sarria was the vice president and manager of Vend-a-Teria, Inc., while Stoumen served as treasurer.[85] The new arrangement gave Sarria more autonomy. It also insulated Sarria from ABC pressure on Stoumen to fire the most well-known, outspoken "queen bee" who drew gay crowds to his nightlife operation, which briefly stretched from North Beach to the foot of Market Street.

The gayola scandal created significant opportunities and new risks for Stoumen and Sarria's in the early 1960s. On the one hand, they both benefited from Stoumen's cooperation during the undercover investigation and trials. Stoumen expanded the Black Cat operation into the much larger nightclub complex at 90 Market. Sarria opened the Five an Ounce food concession and hosted performances in the much larger venue. The flow of gay men who congregated there during their lunch hour and after work was great for business and symbolized the growing boldness of the city's gay population. On the other hand, the new commercial enterprise also put them in a precarious position. Pending revocation proceedings against the

Figure 4.6 After Sol Stoumen signed the lease for 90 Market, he and José Sarria set up and ran Vend-a-Teria, Inc., out of the bar-restaurant-nightclub space, using several different business names. The first was the "Talk of the Town," depicted here on a flyer with the Ferry Building and Embarcadero Freeway in the background (ca. November 1961). Executives at the Southern Pacific headquarters across the street saw this flyer, or one like it, and warned employees not to patronize the place. Sarria pushed back by cofounding the League for Civil Education on the premises and running for public office. (Flyer, folder Vendateria Papers, 1958–1961, Box 91, José Sarria Papers [1996-01], Courtesy of Gay, Lesbian, Bisexual, Transgender Historical Society.)

Black Cat jeopardized Stoumen and Sarria's investment in the nightclub and restaurant complex. Moreover, state liquor agents and local law enforcement were hostile toward Stoumen for his role in exposing the payola payments at 90 Market. Finally, not all of the neighbors of the new lunch counter were as excited about the steady stream of queer customers walking through the door day and night.

THE ORIGINS OF "SOME KIND OF UNION"

After the gayola scandal, 90 Market became the center of a new, *bar-based* kind of political organizing spearheaded by lunch counter manager and drag entertainer José Sarria. When Stoumen took over 90 Market by purchasing Castaways' liquor license and furnishings and signing a ten-year lease, he was cautiously optimistic that his cooperation with state and local authorities in the payola affair would protect his new nightlife operation. According to Stoumen, in March 1960, ABC administrator Sidney Feinberg agreed to a short-term suspension of revocation proceedings against the Black Cat if Stoumen could produce evidence of payoffs at Castaways. Over the next six weeks, Stoumen later claimed, he "personally prepared the traps which nabbed a number of policemen who had been shaking down bars frequented by homosexuals."[86] As a reward, Stoumen got verbal reassurances from Feinberg that he could "safely" purchase Castaways. In a show of his continuing cooperation, Stoumen convinced Norman Tullis to return to the city from Nevada to testify at the trial against the ABC agent caught collecting "gratuities" at Castaways.[87] Throughout the gayola investigation and trials during the summer and fall of 1960, Feinberg strung Stoumen along, offering assurances of leniency in liquor licensing matters before the ABC in exchange for his cooperation in exposing the payoff system.[88]

Once the trials ended, the ABC reversed course, redoubling its efforts to put Stoumen out of business at both the Black Cat and the Talk of the Town. Feinberg "disavowed and repudiated the settlement arrangement," adding that the agency had gotten all the benefits they wanted from him.[89] When Stoumen protested, Feinberg told him that he should be satisfied with the six-month pause in the revocation proceedings against the Black Cat. Feinberg added that, in the wake of the controversial mayoral race, the Black Cat had become a "symbol" of the gay bar problem and that closing all gay bars in the city "was probably inevitable."[90] Stoumen enlisted the San Francisco district attorney, the assistant district attorney, and Police Chief Thomas Cahill to recommend leniency based on his role in bringing attention to the payoffs and cooperating with the investigation. In a letter to Feinberg, San Francisco District Attorney Thomas Lynch stressed that Stoumen was not implicated in the payola scandal but had worked with special investigators to expose the practice and enforce the law.[91] In January 1961, the ABC director ruled that Stoumen's cooperation had no bearing on the revocation proceedings against the Black Cat. In late March 1961, a Superior Court judge concurred.[92] Over the next several years, Stoumen, with the help of his staff and patrons, waged a legal battle to contest the revocation order. While the appeals process ran its course, Sarria turned to fundraising, social organizing, and political campaigning to keep the Black Cat and his new enterprise at 90 Market going. The latter's fate hinged on the outcome of the proceedings against the former. The stakes were high. If the courts revoked the Black Cat license, Stoumen would also have to forfeit the license for the Talk of the Town.

The commercial success of 90 Market cut against the grain of character- izations of lower Market Street as blighted. It also threatened to complicate efforts to hold down the cost of acquiring land for redevelopment. The language of blight called out physical dilapidation, functional obsolescence, underperforming economic uses, and strains on public expenditures. Cast- aways had been profitable by attracting a new customer base, even with the added expense of protection payments. The revival of 90 Market as the Talk of the Town and a lunch counter demonstrated that the building could still attract investors to revitalize the space and bring in more commercial activity. In particular, Sarria's lunch counter demonstrated that the area's demand for daily food service on the part of gay clerical workers and professionals was growing. Gay community historian Jim Duggins estimated that as many as a thousand male secretaries worked at the Southern Pacific headquarters across from 90 Market. At quitting time, he recalled, a "horde of effeminate men came pouring out of the building," flooding lower Market Street.[93] These men may not have fit the image of a healthy, vibrant city, but the money they pumped into 90 Market could hardly be characterized as blight.

Although Sarria was best known as a host and drag performer at the Black Cat, it was through his association with 90 Market that he came up with the idea for the League for Civil Education (LCE) and his run for office. When Southern Pacific Railway executives threatened to fire any employee caught patronizing Sarria's lunch counter, he snapped back, asserting his right to serve his customers and that of his customers to eat wherever they wanted, free from discrimination by their employer. He later explained:

> The election came about in a funny way. We had taken over 90 Mar-
> ket Street, and I was running a food concession, cooking and serving
> there and delivering food to the Cat. It had regular kitchen facilities,
> very nice, so we cooked there rather than the Black Cat. This was
> about 1960 . . . That's when the Southern Pacific Railway Company

announced on their bulletin boards that anyone coming across to eat in my restaurant would be fired . . . So I went to the manager and said, "You put a notice up denying the right of the people to eat at my restaurant. That's against the law.". . . . So with that as ammunition, I told them that I was going to bring suit against them; defamation of character and this, that, and the other . . . Meanwhile I had come up with the idea that the only way that we could show some strength was to have a voting power, and *some kind of union* [emphasis added].[94]

In other words, it was a threat to his livelihood and that of his lunch counter customers at 90 Market prompted Sarria to mount a political challenge to harassment and discrimination. The defining element of this plan was to demonstrate the electoral strength of the city's gay population by mobilizing gay bar patrons to go to the polls to vote for him in a bid for a seat on the Board of Supervisors. He envisioned the LCE to be a vehicle to unite gay-bar publics that would launch his run for office.

José Sarria, the flamboyant, outspoken son of Colombian and Nicaraguan immigrants, was raised by his mother with the help of the Latino community in San Francisco during the Great Depression. After serving as an officer's aide and cook in the Army during World War II, he returned to the city in 1947 as the port screenings and purges were just beginning. His aspirations of becoming a teacher ended when he was arrested on sexual solicitation charges in the restroom of the posh gentlemen's bar at the St. Francis Hotel in 1952. He then set his sights on being a drag entertainer and bar host. Convinced he could do better than his friend Michelle at an amateur talent night at a nightclub in Oakland, he put together his own act. Michelle, a gay clerical worker recently discharged from the Navy, had come to San Francisco in 1954 during what Sarria characterized as "a big purge of homosexuals from the Atlantic Navy."[95] Sarria won a prize and a two-week engagement to sing "Smoke Gets in Your Eyes." He was able to parlay that into an intermission act at the Beige Room, a female impersonator nightclub in San Francisco's North Beach neighborhood. After the Beige Room closed, he began waiting tables at the Black Cat. In 1957, around the time Jack's opened as a gay bar, Sarria started staging parody operas at the Black Cat to bring in the Sunday brunch crowds. By the late 1950s, he had built up a large following as a bar host. He later described this role by saying, "I became the Black Cat," referring to his ability to draw in patrons.[96] His popularity, and the commercial influence that came with it, was both a remarkable personal accomplishment and an indication of a growing number of San Franciscans who saw themselves reflected in his comedic, affirming vision of gay life in the city.

As postgayola retaliatory bar raids, street sweeps, and liquor license revocation proceedings intensified, Sarria grew more explicitly political in addressing patrons at the Black Cat and 90 Market. He urged the crowds at his performances to work together, stop hiding, and advocate for themselves. Like later leaders in the struggle for sexual and gender equality, Sarria had always been the target of homophobia and transphobia directed at gender-bending, queer, and trans people of color.[97] Behind Sarria's exhortations to his audiences to recognize and exert their political power was his frustration with the complacency and privileges that came with leading a double life—something he never wanted or enjoyed. In essence, he recalled, "I became a bitch, and I started to scream." He focused his energies on organizing the gay bar crowd into a new voting bloc. As he elaborated to one interviewer, "We did not have a say in these laws because we had all these queens coming in here to buy a beer, and then when it was time to vote, they were nowhere around. If they kept sitting on their asses, there wouldn't *be* a place to come and have a beer with their boyfriends."[98] His approach was remarkably similar to—and perhaps consciously modeled on—the labor union membership drives in waterfront hangouts just ten years earlier. The power of labor unions rested in their ability to gain leverage in hiring negotiations by cultivating unity and safeguarding solidarity among a large number of laborers in a particular occupational trade. Sarria adopted the language and strategies of organized labor on the waterfront, drawing queer drinking publics into the political process to demonstrate unity, solidarity, and voting power as a means of gaining equal treatment and civil rights as a legally recognized minority.

In the LCE's first year, Guy Strait and José Sarria visited gay bars to promote the organization and find supporters. In the lead-up to the election, Strait started publishing the *LCE News* as a biweekly newsletter filled with political commentary, legal developments, and nightlife happenings affecting the gay bar scene. The newsletter quickly developed into a newspaper with regular columns and advertisements. As an organ for uniting waterfront bar publics, it served a similar purpose and circulated in the same way as the *MCS Voice*, the marine cook and steward's newspaper that ceased publication in 1953 when the union disbanded. The Black Cat, the Talk of the Town, Jack's Waterfront Hangout, the Headhunters, and the Crossroads became the biggest supporters of the LCE. As we have seen in previous chapters, most of these bars had a relatively recent history of serving as informal social clubs or hiring halls for labor unions. The bars were frequently mentioned in Strait's nightlife gossip column, they paid for advertisements in the *News*, and they cohosted fundraisers and holiday parties that benefited the organization. In contrast, neither the Ensign Café nor the Broken Drum got involved in LCE activities. A holdover of the managed vice system, the Ensign Café run by Mike Caldaralla profited from queer nightlife crowds but never stepped into the limelight as a "gay bar" or openly engaged in political organizing by working with the LCE.

With LCE backing, José Sarria ran for a seat on the San Francisco Board of Supervisors on a platform of "equality before the law." He was inspired to take such bold public action after Southern Pacific executives tried to ruin his lunch counter at 90 Market. For him, this new commercial enterprise reflected his desire to strike out on his own and reap the economic benefits of building such a huge following of gay patrons at the Black Cat. In his declaration for candidacy, he listed his occupation as "Restaurant-Manager" but also insisted he be identified as an "Entertainer-Host" on the ballot.[99] The multiple roles he claimed underscored his real power at the Black Cat and 90 Market—his ability to draw big crowds and drive commercial development.

Sarria's Fall 1961 campaign was a watershed moment in the gay civil rights movement in the United States. In his platform and electioneering, he demonstrated that homosexuality could be the basis for a social and cultural identity that, if mobilized, could wield political influence. In his declaration of candidacy, he quoted an inscription on the front of the new Hall of Justice building to encapsulate his reason for running: "The faithful and impartial enforcement of the laws with equal and exact Justice to all of whatever state or persuasion."[100] He is remembered for rallying gay bar publics to unite around an affirming vision of community.[101] In the lead-up to the election, he rallied his audiences to stand, hold hands, and join in singing "God Save Us Nellie Queens" and proclaimed, "United we stand; divided they'll catch us one by one!"[102] In a 1964 feature story on homosexuality in America, *Life* magazine attributed San Francisco's reputation as "the gay capital" partly to Sarria's rousing performances and run for office.[103]

Sarria's run for office began and ended at 90 Market. As soon as Sarria declared his candidacy, the network of LCE-affiliated bars he and Strait mobilized served as a campaign circuit for him to raise funds, give speeches, and register voters. Sarria delivered campaign posters and calling cards to thirty-five bars in the city.[104] The main donors to his campaign were patrons of the Black Cat, Coffee Don's, Nellie's, and the Crossroads.[105] At the Talk of the Town, he hosted a full lineup of fundraisers, theme parties, sneak previews, and grand openings in October and November. Although he finished in ninth place in the race for five open seats, he drew support from over 5,600 voters.[106] Sarria was an honored guest at the election night party at 90 Market and returned the following week for "An Evening with José" to celebrate his run for elected office.[107] While the campaign headquarters for Sarria was at the Black Cat, 90 Market was where he cofounded the LCE and hosted his most significant events during the 1961 election. Over the next two years, he continued to manage 90 Market while performing regularly at the Black Cat. During this period, lower Market Street was the scene of commercial evictions, liquor license revocations, and violent intimidation, all aimed at dismantling the circuit of gay bars in the area before the bulldozers arrived. Sarria was one of the most prominent members of a network of drag queens that rallied bar crowds to stick together, fight back, and seek out new quarters when the Golden Gateway project claimed the queer world of the waterfront.

When the LCE met for the first time at 90 Market, the city's existing homophile organizations and a nascent gay business association were ill-suited for the kind of bottom-up political mobilization Sarria envisioned. Through the 1950s, the city had only two homophile organizations—the Mattachine Society and the Daughters of Bilitis (DOB). Homophile activists in these relatively small members-only organizations distanced themselves from the bar crowds to project an image of respectability and to avoid exposing particular businesses to public scrutiny.[108] In addition to these homophile organizations, an informal group of gay bar owners, operators, and staff met informally every Thursday to share information about police raids, suspected undercover agents surveilling bars, and patrons passing bad checks.[109] Neither the homophile organizations nor this emerging network of gay bar operators recognized the untapped potential of gay bar *patrons* to wield political power. In a departure from these other groups, Sarria envisioned the primary role of the LCE to be "to reach out to the poor little guy on the street that doesn't have money, that doesn't know the law . . . That's what were are teaching."[110]

The new organizational strategy—mobilizing queer publics into a "community" of shared interests—was transformational in San Francisco. The Mattachine dissolved as a national organization the same month that the LCE formed. The shift was a sign that, in San Francisco, the defense of civil liberties was becoming a more pressing concern than gaining respectability and social acceptance.[111] During the 1960s, sociologist Elizabeth Armstrong found, "defending spaces for sociality became central to gay politics."[112] Many of the new homophile organizations that formed looked more like the LCE than the Mattachine or DOB. Following the LCE, eleven additional groups formed between 1961 and 1968, including the Tavern Guild, the Society for Individual Rights (SIR), and the Council on Religion and the Homosexual. Activists in these groups worked from within and through community-based networks to improve conditions for gay, lesbian, and transgender San Franciscans. They also created dedicated or provisional places where the community shared a sense of ownership and belonging. As a result, many urban land uses—including bars, meeting facilities, dance halls, performance spaces, movie theaters, churches, small businesses, entire commercial corridors, and even whole neighborhoods—became "gay" or "lesbian" in San Francisco during the 1960s.

The most active members of this community—organizers and backers of the LCE's fundraisers, readers of the *LCE News*, and supporters of Sarria's run for supervisor—were the queer waterfront drinking publics that developed in the informal hiring halls and organized-labor social clubs most affected by the Red and Lavender Scares. The fate of these bars was bound up in the story of urban renewal on the waterfront. The city's pro-growth coalition had a vested interest in driving down property values at the foot of Market Street. They accepted queer containment as an effective means of creating and maintaining blight conditions while they ironed out plans to redevelop the area. In the mid-1950s, press accounts of sexual perversity and periodic crackdowns on so-called hangouts for homosexuals shaped public perceptions of declining moral conditions and helped justify the adoption of an expansive urban renewal project area. Once the area was tagged as blighted, local law enforcement and state liquor agents encouraged the concentration and proliferation of queer nightlife crowds in the area. As the next chapter makes clear, these bars closed when the process of assembling land for redevelopment began, with a flurry of commercial evictions, real estate transactions, and liquor license revocations. In this period, the LCE and its members acted collectively to challenge displacement and resist dispersal brought on by urban renewal.

5

THE DEMISE OF THE QUEER
WATERFRONT

In the early 1960s, state actors ended the practice of steering queer night-life to the waterfront and launched a targeted campaign to put the most publicly engaged gay bars in the area out of business. In 1962, a police officer admitted as much to *LCE News* editor Guy Strait, claiming that "there are three centers of resistance: The Black Cat, Jack's Waterfront, and the *LCE News*. When we have taken care of the first two then we can pick you off any time we please. And all the smaller bars will fall into line."[1] The officer's prediction about the closures was prescient. Over the next year, the San Francisco Redevelopment Agency, local law enforcement, and state liquor agents were instrumental in permanently shuttering the circuit of gay bars that stretched from the Embarcadero waterfront to North Beach. Over the previous decade, while business leaders and city officials hammered out area-wide redevelopment plans for lower Market Street, queer containment in the area had helped them make a case for blight and preclude piecemeal, private investment. However, once officials moved forward with assembling and clearing land for the Golden Gateway project, they abruptly ended the practice of treating the Embarcadero waterfront as a nuisance area reserved for queer land uses, with a rapid series of commercial evictions and liquor license revocations.

In cities across the country in the 1950s and 1960s, urban renewal had a disproportionate, devasting impact on communities of color and other marginalized groups. Alarmed by postwar declines in central city land values and tax revenues, local business leaders and city officials made racially biased, heteronormative assumptions about where and how to intervene in the urban land market to reverse the out-migration of white families to the suburbs.[2] At the urging of corporate leaders, bank executives, major property owners, and real estate interests, urban renewal officials in many cities razed African American neighborhoods to build freeways, public housing complexes, market-rate residential developments, university campus extensions, and expanded central business districts.[3] At the same time, they targeted residential hotel districts and nightlife zones as indicators of incipient urban blight and causes of population loss to family-oriented suburban housing tracts.[4] The incorporation of queer land uses in urban renewal project areas was not unique to San Francisco. Urban renewal displaced gay bars and other gathering places in several cities in the 1950s and 1960s.[5] The city's waterfront, however, stands out nationally as a historically significant site of gay community organizing, based on the degree to which bar owners and patrons mobilized and challenged urban renewal–induced displacement in the early 1960s.

Urban historians and legal scholars have highlighted the importance of the Black Cat Café in North Beach in the gay rights movement during the 1950s and early 1960s.[6] The Black Cat was a small bohemian bar in North Beach whose queer nightlife crowds grew during the Lavender Scare. Stoumen welcomed the new business by hiring gay and gender-nonconforming staff and expanding with larger satellite spaces nearby—first at the Pink Rat in the late 1940s and later at 90 Market in the early 1960s. When charged with catering to so-called sexual deviates at the start of the Lavender Scare, Stoumen successfully defended his right to serve gay patrons in a landmark civil rights case decided by the California Supreme Court. By the end of the decade, one of his waiters, José Sarria, emerged as a leading local voice in rallying bar patrons against police harassment and other infringements on civil liberties, by running for public office. Although historians have extensively documented the early successes in challenging state-sanctioned antigay discrimination, the reason the Black Cat continued to be a center of resistance into the early 1960s has been overlooked until now. The Black Cat was in the crosshairs of the San Francisco Redevelopment Agency and state liquor agents because of its close association with 90 Market, a prime piece of real estate in the heart of the Golden Gateway. The closure of the Black Cat in the fall of 1963 is best understood as part of a broader effort to redevelop lower Market Street rather than the culmination of a years-long legal battle over the right to sell alcohol to gay bargoers.

The fate of the Black Cat and 90 Market was intertwined with a network of gay bars along the Embarcadero targeted for closure because they were within or close to the Golden Gateway urban renewal project.[7] On the eastern margin of Area E, Jack's, the Headhunters, the Barrel House, and the Crossroads all faced similar threats of displacement in the early 1960s. During a flurry of undercover sexual solicitation entrapment operations, liquor license revocations, property seizures, and commercial evictions, these waterfront gay bars found common cause with the Black Cat and Sarria. Under the auspices of the League for Civil Education (LCE), they collectively challenged the array of state and nonstate actors aligned against them.[8] Their operators, staff, and patrons had supported Sarria's election campaign, were unbowed by physical intimidation and harassment, collaborated to hold LCE fundraisers, and regularly advertised in the *LCE News*. These "centers of resistance," however, all lost the fight to stay open in 1963. As a result, the once-promising racially mixed and cross-class coalition of bar owners, small entrepreneurs, and drinking publics saw their world demolished. Although the Ensign Club shared the same fate, its owner, Mike Caldaralla, neither participated in LCE's organized opposition to displacement nor attracted the same degree of enmity from local law enforcement. Nevertheless, the Ensign was the last of the postwar queer nightlife venues that flourished along the Embarcadero. Its closure in late 1965 ended the queer world of the waterfront that developed as an unintended consequence of the Lavender Scare.

The San Francisco Redevelopment Agency's archive of real estate appraisals, land acquisition documents, and property management files for Area E provides a window onto how the agency dealt with the mix of queer nightlife establishments within the Golden Gateway project area. During the land assembly phase, urban renewal had the most direct, material effect on the businesses and residents in areas slated for land clearance and rebuilding. Urban scholars, however, have focused on the Golden Gateway's planning and design aspects or urban governance issues rather than the process of acquiring land.[9] This pivotal moment of state intervention in the urban land market generated detailed records of property relations, including land titles, lease agreements, commercial spaces, and business activities. Serving as both an urban planning and queer archive, the administrative records of land assembly in the Golden Gateway reveal how and why gay bars on the San Francisco waterfront became the most consequential sites of gay rights mobilization in the city during the early 1960s. Triangulating SFRA records, oral histories with gay men, and the *LCE News*'s nightlife coverage reveals that state actors discriminated against gay bars when acquiring land for redevelopment in the Golden Gateway, reserving the harshest treatment for places that challenged state power in the courts and at the polls.

This chapter traces the last days of the queer world of the waterfront, when commercial evictions, real estate transactions, and building demolitions destroyed the circuit of bars within and on the margins of the Golden Gateway urban renewal project. For some gay bars, the end came at the hands of SFRA officials who negotiated with property owners over the sale of their landholdings under the threat of eminent domain proceedings. In the process, agency staff devalued property, invalidated leases, ignored subtenants, and seized bar fixtures without compensating their owners. At the same time, in a strip of gay bars just outside Area E's boundaries, liquor license revocations and lease terminations produced the same result. In the process, redevelopment officials, aided by local law enforcement and state liquor agents, punished gay bar publics that challenged the straight state, while rewarding, albeit temporarily, nightlife operators who did not. By the mid-1960s, the queer world that had taken root in the mix of former seamen's hangouts stretching from the waterfront to North Beach was replaced by a modern automobile gateway into an expanded downtown of office towers and residential complexes.

THE GRAND REOPENING AND CLOSING OF JACK'S WATERFRONT

On April 19, 1962, state and local authorities started evicting queer nightlife crowds from lower Market Street, in the process of assembling land for urban renewal. On that date, the San Francisco Redevelopment Agency (SFRA) took possession of the Merrimac Building and ordered the Ensign Club and the Broken Drum to vacate the premises. That same night, the California Division of Highways evicted Jack's Waterfront Hangout from a commercial storefront in the shadow of the Embarcadero Freeway to build an additional set of ramps into the heart of the Golden Gateway.[10] State highway officials had purchased the building three years earlier from the San Francisco Port Authority. That change of ownership had had no effect on the operation of Jack's, as one government agency simply took over as the commercial landlord from another agency.[11] The Merrimac Building stood on land reserved for a new waterfront park, while Jack's was in the right-of-way of a planned set of freeway ramps leading into the heart of the Golden Gateway project area. These evictions initiated the destruction of the queer nightlife circuit that developed in former seamen's hangouts during the 1950s. Over the next two years, gay bar operators on the Embarcadero were embroiled in a losing fight to slow or stop additional evictions. During this brief period, an array of state actors worked not only to eject gay bars from the urban renewal project area but also to undermine their ability to reestablish themselves elsewhere. In this fight, the Jack's crowd and the League for Civil Education stood out as centers of resistance to urban renewal–related evictions on the Embarcadero in the early 1960s.

The crew at Jack's responded to the April 1962 eviction by securing a new place to congregate several blocks east on the Embarcadero. George Bauman and his staff set about reestablishing Jack's at the Seaboard, a seven-story former seamen's hotel with a mix of permanent and transient rooms (see figure 5.1). A troupe of drag performers facilitated the move by hosting a series of private parties, theme nights, and grand reopening events to bring the Jack's regulars back together in the new space. In one of their first events after the eviction, they staged a private fashion show to raise funds for Bauman's new gay hotel and bar enterprise.[12] The unofficial leader of the group was Michelle, who had recently cofounded the LCE along with José Sarria and Guy Strait. Appropriating the legal name of the Golden Gateway—the "Embarcadero–Lower Market Urban Renewal Project Area, E-1"—Strait nicknamed the group the "Hairburners' Association of Lower Embarcadero." Michelle

Figure 5.1 After taking over operation of the Edgewater Hotel and reopening his bar on the first floor, George Bauman promoted his new enterprise to out-of-town visitors—particularly gay men who recognized "Jack's" from reading the *LCE News*. On a matchbook cover, one of the selling points was that the Edgewater was convenient to the "Golden Gate Project [*sic*]." (From the personal collection of the author.)

and other group members were hairdressers who had performed regularly at the former Jack's.[13] The *LCE News* followed their efforts to create a new home for the Jack's crowd with regular advertisements, frequent mentions in its nightlife column, and occasional feature stories. After reopening the upper floors as the Edgewater Hotel, they redecorated the lobby bar with fishing nets salvaged from the former location on the closing night. They continued fixing up the space by painting the walls pink, adding "metallic artificial leaves," and incorporating a "Jack's Wild" playing card motif.

The way the Jack's crowd stuck together with the help of the LCE to secure new quarters was typical of how other gay bar crowds along the Embarcadero responded to eviction. When the SFRA took possession of the Merrimac Building, drag performer Candy Lee ran the Ensign Club on the first floor.[14] As the bar host at the Ensign Club, Lee booked female impersonators to perform and welcomed transgender patrons with a mention in *Transvestia*, a correspondence magazine written "OF, *BY*, and FOR TVs."[15] After the SFRA posted warning signs for unauthorized tenants to vacate the building, Lee suspended the shows and stopped serving alcohol.[16] When the SFRA escalated its efforts to vacate the building, the *News* alerted readers that Candy "is going to move 'right soon.' It seems that the steel ball is going to claim the place he is now in. If those walls could talk what tales they could tell."[17] Soon afterward, Candy Lee led the Ensign Club crowd to the Headhunters, a small bar and showroom down the block run by another LCE supporter and *News* advertiser, Charles "Carlos" Lara. The relocation of the Ensign Club underscored the important role the network of gay bar hosts played when land acquisitions and commercial evictions began in the Golden Gateway. When urban redevelopment claimed the physical spaces and disrupted the commercial relations of queer waterfront hangouts, this network sprang into action, reinforcing the social solidarity of their regular patrons and securing a new place to hang out. Lara, Candy Lee, and others were key figures in defending and preserving gay bars as moveable publics while the walls around these places came tumbling down.

In the wake of the eviction, the Front became the scene of homophobic violence, physical intimidation, and property destruction. For three days, a mob of "toughs" swept through the area, vandalizing property and threatening gay bar patrons. They smashed up the Headhunters on the first night, breaking a mirror and a window. The following night, the violent crew descended on 90 Market and "completely ruined the foodstuffs." On the third night, the police apprehended the group of thugs when they returned to harass the patrons at the Headhunters.[18] In a sign of the escalating tensions, a mysterious three-alarm fire broke out the following week at the Ferry Building, damaging the local headquarters of the Alcoholic Beverage Control (ABC).[19] Allegedly started by "transients," the conflagration was likely retaliation by the bar crowd for the "three-day attack by hoods" that "scared a hell of a lot out of people."[20]

Conditions deteriorated even further over the next several months. ABC officials had reassured Stoumen the previous year that they would not interfere if he purchased the former Castaways nightclub at 90 Market. However, ABC administrators reneged on the promise and revived charges against Stoumen for operating a disorderly house at the Black Cat in North Beach.[21] Pending the case's outcome, they also suspended liquor sales at the Talk of the Town, his new club at 90 Market. After a failed attempt to transfer the license to bartender Eddie Paulson, José Sarria welcomed the now twice-displaced crowd from the Ensign Club to turn the nightclub into a late-night, alcohol-free cinema serving coffee, soft drinks, and sandwiches.[22] Sarria greeted the displaced crowd in a ceremonious handover to the new crew: "Promptly at 11:00, José from the Black Cat led the grand march into the Stage Room and the Living Room. With Candy Lee acting as Master of Ceremonies, Sarria was introduced to the assemblage. Many there were not of the general bar crowd and his act came as much of a surprise."[23] The former Ensign Club group renamed their new venue "As a Last Resort." Their late-night "coffee and cokes" club, along with Sarria's Five an Ounce food concession, stayed open for another fifteen months until just before the Redevelopment Agency took possession of the building. The cooperative spirit between Sarria and Candy Lee in creatively managing the displacement of nightlife crowds was indicative of how the LCE-affiliated bar hosts resisted urban renewal. They rallied bar patrons to stick together and secured new places for drinking publics to gather in a rapidly contracting queer world.

By the fall, the operators, staff, and patrons from four waterfront gay bars facing displacement came together under the auspices of the LCE to defend their right to stay put. Billed as the "Michelle International," the fall 1962 fundraiser was the fullest expression of the LCE's efforts to unite and rally the different bar crowds and mobilize against impending displacement. Michelle and her troupe of drag performers organized the two-night fundraiser to benefit the organization's new legal defense fund, the "war chest." They modeled the event on the LCE's first fundraiser, a New Year's Eve farewell party honoring gay bar owner Don Cavallo, who lost his lease for an after-hours place, Coffee Don's, at the end of 1961. At that event, the LCE recognized Cavallo for his efforts in fending off law

enforcement's "attempts to suppress the right of freedom of assembly."²⁴ Four
drag performers cohosted the evening, including Michelle representing the
Jumping Frog, José Sarria from the Black Cat and Talk of the Town, Carlos
Lara from the Headhunters, and Candy Lee from the Ensign Café.²⁵ The
1961 event ended in a police raid and the arrest of Cavallo and four others.
More importantly, however, it unified and emboldened a growing network
of gay bar operators and staff to resist efforts by authorities to shut down,
rather than contain, queer nightlife circuits in the early 1960s.

One year later, drag queens once again took the stage. Under the ban-
ner "Unite to Fight" at the Michelle International fundraiser, the lineup
of performers reflected the rich diversity, working-class origins, and camp
sensibilities of waterfront bars. The show featured five entertainers, each
representing a different waterfront bar facing license revocation proceedings
or eviction as a consequence of the Golden Gateway urban renewal project.
Walter Hart, a well-known female impersonator, had been arrested nearly
thirty years earlier in a raid on the newly opened Finocchio's "pansy" bar.²⁶
He had recently been evicted from his residence in the nearby Bay Hotel
when the Redevelopment Agency acquired the building. At the fundraiser,
Hart represented the Crossroads, a former longshoreman's union hall that
police tagged as a "hangout for homosexuals" in 1955. Roby Landers, the
"Mahalia Jackson of the Embarcadero," represented the Barrel House, a
former longshoremen's tavern that became a gay bar frequented by Black
men in the 1950s. José Sarria appeared on behalf of the Black Cat and sang
his rendition of "What Happened to Baby Jane?" Next in the lineup, Jerry
Knight, an African American femme newcomer to the scene, represented 90
Market. Knight reprised a well-received number from a recent production
of "Gypsy." Representing the Headhunters, Candy Lee walked down the
aisle accompanied by a Black drag queen named Franklin, who handed out
gold-stamped calling cards. Franklin had a running rivalry with Michelle
and was upset about being left out of the official program. Wearing "a gal-
axy of small lights that went on and off," Franklin upstaged the other acts
with a "climax" of "lighted roman candles [that] completely stunned the
crowd." Michelle headlined the show, taking the audience on a tour of her
upcoming European trip. She capped off the show with an homage to gay
cruising at the Embarcadero YMCA. Dressed in a gold lamé bathing suit,
she sang a comic rendition of "I'm Going to Wash That Man Right Out of
My Hair" in a staged shower room scene.²⁷

In addition to being a moment of unity among queer drinking publics
of the waterfront, the two-night fundraiser celebrated the grand opening

of "Jack's Hideaway Room" at the Edgewater Hotel. George Bauman and his staff hoped the new performance space next to the lobby bar would rival the popularity of the old Jack's location, vacated six months earlier. The first night of the fundraiser was a reservation-only private party for LCE-affiliated gay bar owners, staff, and regulars, who got a sneak peek at the place. The second evening was a show for the general public. The LCE later published and sold two thousand souvenir programs that showcased the role of drag performers in promoting circuits of queer nightlife. It also offered readers one of the first printed travel guides to gay bars across the country.[28] In total, the Michelle International event raised over $1,000 for the LCE's legal defense fund.[29]

Just as they had during the first LCE fundraiser in 1961, at Coffee Don's, law enforcement raided the Michelle International event in an effort to intimidate the organizers and participants. As soon as the first advertisement for the festivities appeared in the *LCE News*, ABC agents and local police began undercover surveillance and entrapment operations at Jack's to compile evidence of bartenders and waiters knowingly permitting sexual solicitation among men on the premises. Over two weeks, they kept notes about sexual innuendo and physical contact they observed within earshot or sight of the bartenders. Based on their later testimony, the crowd of roughly one hundred patrons was overwhelmingly white and exclusively male. In their only mention of men of color at Jack's, they described an incident when a "Chinese patron" rejected the sexual advances of a "Negro patron." Most of the men were in their twenties and thirties and reflected a range of occupations and aesthetic sensibilities. Some donned dark Levi's and black boots, while others wore business attire or sportswear.[30] On the eve of the LCE fundraiser, the California Supreme Court accepted the ABC's petition to suspend Bauman's liquor license based on testimony from the undercover agents and a narrow interpretation of his operating permit.

On the afternoon of the benefit, ABC agents seized Bauman's liquor license, claiming that he had extended the floor space of the bar into the new Jack's Hideaway Room without notifying officials.[31] A police sergeant warned Bauman, "If you do not remove all that liquor by midnight I will be back and break every damn bottle!"[32] The LCE benefit proceeded without the sale of alcohol. Nevertheless, the sergeant and four officers returned at 1:00 a.m. and removed the entire stock of liquor from the bar without a court order. Bauman challenged the license seizure, and the unauthorized confiscation of his stock of alcohol, in court. In early January, a municipal judge dismissed the ABC's charges against him for selling alcohol in the

Hideaway Room and ordered police to return the liquor they confiscated from the bar.[33] Although Bauman was exonerated of wrongdoing, the ABC soon permanently revoked his liquor license on separate grounds—for knowingly operating a "resort for sexual perverts" based on evidence collected by undercover agents in the lead-up to the LCE fundraiser.

The closure of Jack's devastated its staff and patrons, including Guy Strait. In January 1962, the staff and invited guests held a private party to reminisce about the end of Jack's and watch a slide show of color images of the Michelle International fundraiser. Strait characterized the mood with a literary allusion to the antiheroes in underworld crime stories:

> It was almost as if Damon Runyon was there . . . Two of the old bartenders from Jacks decided that it was just too much. One still had a key to the place and since the big room in the back still had the liquor stored there, he went into it and poured two drinks. Then he turned the Juke all the way up and they sat there with tears like crocodiles streaming down their faces. When George [Bauman] got to the place to find out what the hell was going on he was told very slobberly that "We are having a wake."[34]

The account of two bartenders mournfully taking one last drink in the empty showroom with the music blaring captured for *News* readers the significance of the short-lived "Jack's Hideaway Room" to queer waterfront drinking publics. Moreover, the two men spoke to the feelings of loss unleashed by the demise not just of Jack's but the entire queer world of the waterfront.[35]

In another major blow to the circuit of gay bars on the Embarcadero, several places that were cosponsors of the Michelle International fundraiser closed abruptly in April 1963.[36] In a one-story building just down the block from the Ensign Café, Filipino drag queen Charles "Carlos" Lara ran the Headhunters bar and an adjoining performance space in a former seamen's bar known as Denny's Barrel House. He hosted regular drag shows with a lineup of African American queens, including Roby Landers, Franklin, and Blotchy Blotter, as well as an Asian American female impersonator known pejoratively as "Chino."[37] Lara was active in the LCE from the start of the organization as a headliner at the first fundraiser, a regular advertiser in the *LCE News*, and a backer of Sarria's candidacy for supervisor. In 1961 and 1962, the Headhunters was also an essential stop for the corps of drag personalities who circulated among LCE-affiliated bars in a parade of rented buses on Halloween. Year-round, Lara and many of the Headhunters crowd dressed in feminine clothes, kept their hair long, and were referred to as "hair fairies" in the *LCE News*. In April 1963, the building owners ejected the diverse crowd, ripped out the stage, and evicted Lara from the premises.[38] After a failed attempt to install new management, the building owners—who also owned the liquor license—sold the property to the city's Parks Department.[39] Lara decamped to the Tenderloin. He opened the Chukker Club with a commemorative Headhunters Room, where he and his patrons continued to be the target of transphobic harassment by the police.[40]

The Crossroads also closed the same month as the Headhunters. The location had a long association with waterfront labor organizing, serving as a social club on the first floor of the ILWU headquarters during the 1934 Waterfront Strike. Operating as the Sea Cow in 1954, the Mattachine Society singled out the bar as a place for "Beer, Wine, and Seamen" in a visitor's guide for homophile activists attending the organization's first convention in the city. The following year, police raided the Sea Cow in an anti-homosexual sweep, leading to the arrest of wealthy crossdresser "Bunny" Breckenridge on vagrancy charges.[41] In 1956, the ABC tagged the Sea Cow, along with the Black Cat and the Paper Doll, as a priority for license revocation proceedings on the basis that it was a "hangout for homosexuals."[42] By the early 1960s, the Crossroads owners, Mel DeBoer and Robert Threlkell, began participating in the emerging queer political culture of the waterfront. They supported Sarria's campaign for supervisor, regularly advertised in the *LCE News*, and participated in the LCE-sponsored fundraisers. Soon after Walter Hart represented the Crossroads at the Michelle International event, the ABC revoked the bar's liquor license.[43]

The Michelle International was a significant moment in forging a new group identity based on community building and collective action embedded in specific place-making projects. Gay and queer drinking publics came together to promote and defend the circuit of waterfront bars either located in buildings slated for redevelopment or viewed by officials as contributing to blight in the area. During the event, bar operators, performers, and patrons saw themselves both as a sexual minority and a political constituency bound together by a shared interest in securing spaces in the city around which to organize their lives. In the wake of the closure of Jack's, the LCE recognized the social significance of the Michelle International event in a formal resolution: "To whom it may concern: On the night of the nineteenth and twentieth of November, the Community of San Francisco presented and received

EDGEWATER HOTEL

Permanent Transient

226 Embarcadero

EXODUS
To The TOOL BOX
399–4th

Figure 5.2 When state officials revoked George Bauman's liquor license in early 1963, the Tool Box welcomed the Jack's crowd with an advertisement in the *LCE News*. This "exodus" was the first in a series of displacements of gay bar publics from the waterfront sparked by land acquisitions in the Golden Gateway. (Advertisement, *LCE News*, January 7, 1963, 7.)

the show Michelle International in a spirit indicative of the feelings of all of us when we say 'Unite to Fight.'"[44] The LCE cast the frustrated attempt to reestablish Jack's in the Edgewater Hotel as a powerful demonstration of solidarity among gay bar publics. The language of community foregrounded the shared identity among drag queens and gay bar patrons at a time when state and local authorities were actively engaged in destroying the places where they gathered.

Following the closure of Jack's at the Edgewater Hotel, Bauman and his staff refocused their energies on running the hotel and tried briefly to make it a hub for LCE activities. The Jack's bar crowd headed to South of Market in an "Exodus" to the Tool Box, the new center of the city's growing gay male leather community (figure 5.2).[45] Bauman teamed up with Don Cavallo to open an all-night charbroiler restaurant, Original Don's, in the former Jack's Hideaway showroom.[46] As discussed earlier, Cavallo had been instrumental in hosting the LCE's first fundraiser when his after-hours gay bar near Nob Hill closed after his landlord evicted him.[47] As the guest of honor at an invitation-only preview party for the new restaurant, Michelle inaugurated the new Michelle Room, a large dining room with dark red walls covered by Toulouse Lautrec–inspired murals and white vinyl floors. Around the same time, Guy Strait moved the offices of the LCE to the Edgewater Hotel and began publishing the *News* out of a room on the second floor.

Bauman's resolve to operate the overtly gay hotel and restaurant faltered in January 1964 after he suffered two broken legs—reputedly as the result of a hit-and-run accident in front of the building. The same month, the LCE began to come apart. Strait was ousted as president over financial improprieties, and he moved out of the building.[48] In the late summer, Bauman and Cavallo closed the Original Don's restaurant. The Don's crowd moved to the Tenderloin, where they revived the Hideaway tavern in the basement of the Jefferson Hotel with the grand opening of "Coffee Don's Celebrity Room."[49] In the fall, Strait announced the closure of the Edgewater Hotel, so he "shed a few more tears for another place has bit the dust."[50] By year's end, the former seamen's hotel that had recently served as an important site of the LCE's efforts to organize gay bar publics became the Kennedy Hotel. The building owner offered a free ninety-day lease to anyone with a liquor license who would open a new nightclub in the "newly remodeled" bar and restaurant adjoining the lobby.[51] The shuttering of the gay hotel and restaurant and the dissolution of the LCE were major victories for the city's pro-growth coalition, which had long championed the transformation of the waterfront.

THE DEATH AND LIFE OF THE ENSIGN CAFÉ, INC.

While state highway officials, the ABC, and local law enforcement all played a role in the demise of Jack's, the Ensign Club and the Broken Drum faced a different threat—commercial eviction at the hands of the San Francisco Redevelopment Agency. Unlike Stoumen, Sarria, Bauman, and other gay bar operators affiliated with the LCE, Mike Caldaralla was a product and beneficiary of an older vice management system. That system rewarded bar operators like Caldaralla, who confined queer nightlife crowds to an underground, captive, exploitative economy of illicit liquor sales. The history and fate of the Broken Drum and Ensign Club during the SFRA's efforts to acquire and raze the building underscores the complex ways queer containment and queer displacement operated on the waterfront until the early 1960s. The destruction of the queer waterfront did not stop with the demolition of well-known places that had an emergent culture of resistance. The Ensign Café also succumbed to the wrecking ball. However, as we shall see, Caldaralla fared much better than his subtenants in the process—which was very much in keeping with the tacit support he enjoyed from local and state authorities in running a queer nightlife complex at the foot of Market Street.

The Redevelopment Agency purchased the Merrimac Building in April 1962 for well below the fair market value specified in its own internal appraisals of the property. The Hihn family of Santa Cruz was the first and only owner of the waterfront parcel created when the state harbor commission reclaimed part of the Bay to construct the Embarcadero complex of piers and wharves.[52] After the Hihns purchased it in 1903, the property remained in the family's real estate trust, the Coast Realty Company, for the next sixty years.[53] SFRA's real estate division negotiated with the Hihns' real estate trust officer over the final purchase price. In 1958, the agency had appraised the property's value at $186,000 and again three years later at $171,400.[54] However, just before the purchase in 1962, agency staff negotiated the sale price of the Merrimac Building down to $157,500—nearly $30,000 below the fair market value estimated in the agency's initial appraisal of the property.[55] The deep discount suggests that law enforcement efforts to steer queer nightlife crowds to lower Market Street in the late 1950s drove down the cost of land acquisitions by depressing property values within the Golden Gateway urban renewal area.

The 1961 appraisal detailed Mike Caldaralla's long-term tenancy at 1 Market and the extent to which he profited from multiple subareas throughout the building as the master tenant. He had paid $700 per month, when all the spaces were occupied, as recently as 1960. In the 1950s, he leased the bar and nightclub on a percentage basis, paying as much as $1,000 per month to the Hihns. He also presumably collected a cut of beer and liquor sales from nightclub promoters, who lined up to fill the space with queer patrons, performers, and bartenders. He likely stayed in business for so long by sharing his profits from queer nightlife crowds not only with liquor and beer distributors, but also the building owners, local law enforcement, and state liquor agents. According to the appraisal, however, Caldaralla's queer nightlife complex at the foot of Market Street was no longer as lively as it once was. It specified that the sublease for the Ensign Club expired in 1960. Although the appraisal claimed that the bar and restaurant space was vacant, it was in fact still operating as a private after-hours club, along with the upstairs nightclub. The report also showed that he pulled in a small amount of rental income from a small barbershop. His largest source of revenue, however, was the Broken Drum, the second-floor nightclub he sublet for $300 a month and supplied with overpriced beer and alcohol.

As part of the terms of the sale of the Merrimac Building to the SFRA, George Carter, the Hihn family's representative, omitted Caldaralla from his inventory of active commercial tenants in the building. Carter certified that Caldaralla's storefronts were vacant while recognizing the right of a small bar, a liquor store, a cigar stand, and a billboard advertiser to stay on the premises after the sale.[56] These businesses had no greater claim to the space than Caldaralla, who had been in the building since 1933. The smaller storefronts paid less rent and operated on a month-to-month basis without a long-term lease. Further invalidating any potential property claims by Caldaralla, Carter associated Caldaralla's primary business address, 1 Market, not with the Ensign Café, Inc., but with the cigar stand at the corner of the building. Most significantly, Carter excluded Caldaralla when he sent a letter to each of the four recognized tenants notifying them of the transfer of ownership of the building to the San Francisco Redevelopment Agency. He explained to them that Coast Realty would prorate their rent for April and he encouraged them to work with the agency "regarding your future tenancy in this property."[57] Carter's actions to sideline Caldaralla were likely part of the unofficial sale terms worked out with SFRA staff. By persuading Carter to deliver Caldaralla's storefronts vacant, at least on paper, the agency would not be obligated to rent to or provide relocation assistance to him or any of his sublessors. In the parlance of urban renewal administrators, the Ensign Café, Inc., and its associated enterprises would not become part of the agency's official "workload."

When the redevelopment agency took possession of the Merrimac Building on April 11, 1962, the site manager for Area E, Virginia Wortman, was surprised to discover that the Broken Drum was not vacant and that Caldaralla was still running the Ensign Café on the first floor. Wortman was responsible for maintaining the property and collecting rent from the remaining occupants. She reached out to Carter to clarify the situation. During the conversation, Carter admitted to discrepancies between the tenancy relationships outlined in his official roster of leases and the actual occupants of the Merrimac Building. He told her that the bank had owned "the greater portion of this property and that space was also being rented by a barber shop, restaurant, and operation called the Broken Drum." Carter acknowledged that the omission was intentional, as "the Broken Drum was some sort of operation which the Bank 'turned their back upon.'" Nevertheless, he admitted that the bank, in fact, collected monthly rental payments for the three areas, totaling $325, from Mike Caldaralla, who was the "Master Tenant." He expressed sympathy for Caldaralla, who had "become involved in a shooting some time back and had lost all of his holdings."[58]

After learning about the Broken Drum, Wortman tried without success to keep the nightclub out of the SFRA's workload by warning the unauthorized, queer nightlife crowd to vacate the building. When the agency took possession of the property, she instructed the on-site maintenance worker to post signs notifying the operators and patrons that the establishment was closed under the authority of the new owner. The following Friday at 9:30 p.m., an orchestra leader called Wortman at home to protest that he lost a two-week engagement due to the closure. He demanded that the agency compensate him for his canceled contract, or he would "take possession of the property" for the duration of the engagement. Wortman directed him to take up the canceled contract with Mike Caldaralla. She then made several attempts to reach Caldaralla, asking him to return the rent he collected from the Broken Drum and to vacate the property. When he finally turned up, Caldaralla told Wortman that "he was unable to vacate these people [at the Broken Drum]."[59] Wortman tried another tactic. She directed the on-site maintenance worker to padlock the door to the second-floor nightclub. Unbowed, the operators of the Broken Drum, Opal Waldo and her husband, showed up with the band leader in tow at the site office and presented rent receipts stamped "Paid to May 4th." They refused to vacate without a formal thirty-day eviction notice from the SFRA. Reluctant to put anything in writing that would legitimize their tenancy, Wortman relented, agreeing to hold off padlocking the nightclub until the end of the rental period. It proved to be an empty threat. Wortman's deadline came and went, and the Broken Drum crowd refused to leave the building.

When Caldaralla and the Broken Drum crowd did not vacate the premises in early May, the SFRA turned to the courts for assistance. The agency filed eviction proceedings against Mike Caldaralla, Opal Waldo, and other subtenants, claiming they were unrecognized occupants running an illegal club in the Merrimac Building.[60] Although neither Caldaralla nor the Broken Drum crowd appeared as tenants in the sale agreement, they argued that they had been ongoing tenants and subtenants in the building. The parties came to a negotiated settlement.[61] The agency agreed to recognize Caldaralla as a legitimate commercial tenant in the building. Under the terms worked out by Caldaralla and the SFRA, the court ordered Waldo to vacate the property by mid-August, pay a prorated rent of $50 per month, and forego a claim for moving expenses. In a win for the SFRA, Wortman was able to leave the Broken Drum out of the agency's official workload, making Waldo ineligible for compensation and ensuring the Broken Drum would not appear in administrative tallies of displaced businesses in Area E. On August 16, five days after the date that Waldo was required to vacate the premises, an agency lawyer dispatched the San Francisco sheriff, Matthew C. Carberry, to remove the Broken Drum's occupants.[62] The eviction of Opal Waldo and the Broken Drum crowd marked the end of more than ten years of operation of the after-hours club.[63] The club ultimately closed, as a consequence not of liquor licensing or law enforcement actions but of land acquisition actions in the Golden Gateway orchestrated by the San Francisco Redevelopment Agency.

As part of its effort to ensure that the Waldos would not become part of the agency's workload, the SFRA excluded their personal property from an inventory of the furnishings and fixtures in the nightclub. Leading up to the court-ordered eviction of the Broken Drum crowd, Wortman compiled an inventory of the furnishings of the Broken Drum to determine the value and ownership of anything for which the agency would be obligated to provide compensation. The list included an assortment of restaurant-grade appliances and a mix of twenty small tables and approximately ninety chairs of various styles. As master tenant, Caldaralla owned the kitchen equipment. Waldo and her husband, who ran the club, claimed two upright pianos, a coin-operated jukebox, and most of the tables and chairs. Wortman was careful never to identify the Waldos by name in the property management records, to ensure they would not be considered part of the agency's official workload. In particular, she specified that the items owned by the "people operating the Broken Drum" would be "moved at the expense of the present tenants," adding that "none of these items would be considered real property." As a result, the agency absolved itself of any obligation to compensate the nightclub operators for moving expenses or for "loss of use" if they opted to leave their furnishings behind. The lengths to which the SFRA went to keep the Broken Drum out of its workload underscores how marginalized groups were viewed as expendable in the planning and implementation of urban renewal projects. As was the case with hotel and apartment dwellers, planning officials lowballed or invalidated what limited property claims queer commercial tenants made during the land acquisition phase of urban renewal.

Soon after the agency evicted Opal Waldo and her husband from the Merrimac Building, they revived the Silver Dollar as a queer after-hours club in the Audiffred Building (100 Embarcadero). The Silver Dollar had moved back and forth between the Tenderloin and the Embarcadero from 1940 to

1961 and had always attracted a mixed crowd. After the new location was listed in several gay nightlife directories, the police repeatedly raided the club, once in May 1963 and twice more in the fall of 1964.[64] In the second raid, officers arrested and hauled away forty-seven "prostitutes, pimps, narcotics addicts, and drunks" for visiting a disorderly house.[65] A month later, undercover officers observed waitresses "slithering with smiles through the smoke-filled room" and spiking coffee mugs with whiskey. They arrested twenty-one "obviously drunken" patrons who had been doing the watusi and stomping the mashed potato at the unlicensed, all-night dance hall.[66]

Remarkably, after the eviction of the Broken Drum crowd, the SFRA recognized Caldaralla as the primary commercial tenant at 1 Market, bringing him into its workload and collecting monthly rent from him.[67] He remained the agency's master tenant in the Merrimac Building for three more years, paying a total of $4,833.40 in rent to the Redevelopment Agency.[68] Local law enforcement and state liquor agents overlooked the return of sex- and gender-transgressive late-night revelers to the Ensign. This revival of the Ensign Club, even after the Redevelopment Agency had purchased the Merrimac Building, speaks to Caldaralla's ability to skillfully manage and profit from the containment of queer drinking publics, with the tacit support, if not direct involvement, of law enforcement.

In its final years, the Ensign Club headlined female impersonators as an after-hours show bar popular with transgender patrons. In a series of print ads and nightlife mentions in the *San Francisco Chronicle*, Caldaralla grew bolder in promoting the nature of the entertainment. In early November 1963, in a small item in his nightlife column, entertainment reporter Hal Schaefer announced: "Last night a new Breakfast Club opened at No. 1 Market called the Ensign Club. They will be open at 10 PM with good food and a floor show and will stay open until 6 AM. It is under the management of Mike Caldaralla."[69] For the club's longtime regulars, Caldaralla's name in the ad signaled that the place was back in the good graces of law enforcement and would again welcome them with overpriced drinks and minimal harassment from authorities. The following month, Caldaralla announced regular appearances by "Kandyman and His Trio," a likely reference to Candy Lee and his drag ensemble.[70] By February 1964, he touted six shows nightly of "America's Foremost Female Impersonators."[71] His turn to the *Chronicle* to advertise suggests that, right until the end, Caldaralla enjoyed the tacit support of law enforcement and state liquor agents. The Ensign's last call in July 1965 marked the end of Mike Caldaralla's nearly thirty-year tenure in the Merrimac Building. At eighty-two years of age, he opted to retire from the bar trade of his own accord as one of the very last commercial tenants to vacate not just the building, but the entire Golden Gateway urban renewal project area.

In his departure from the building, Caldaralla was treated like most of the other business owners displaced by the project. Caldaralla dropped off his final rental payment of $125 at the Redevelopment Agency's site office.[72] Subsequently, the agency followed established internal administrative procedures for disposing of real property in urban renewal areas prior to demolishing condemned buildings. In early August, the agency paid Caldaralla $3,879.32 to satisfy his relocation claim for the loss of use of the equipment and the furnishings left behind.[73] The remaining occupants—3 Market Liquors, Giles's Cigar Store, and Joe's Café—stayed another year before the structure was vacated entirely in early October 1966.[74] The treatment of Caldaralla by the SFRA stands out in sharp contrast to how the agency handled the purchase of 90 Market and resolved the property claims of its primary tenant, Sol Stoumen. The SFRA rewarded Caldaralla for running a managed vice operation that served to perpetuate blight conditions at the foot of Market Street, helping drive down the cost the SFRA ultimately paid for properties in the area. In contrast, Stoumen and his staff attempted to revive 90 Market by setting up and running a legitimate nightclub and restaurant that catered to the city's growing gay population. As the following section documents, Sol Stoumen fared far worse than Mike Caldaralla in his interactions with the SFRA.

LAST CALL AT 90 MARKET

In the early 1960s, state and local officials were particularly punitive in going after the community of queer drinking publics on the waterfront that pushed back against discriminatory policing and liquor licensing practices and supported José Sarria's election campaign. Stoumen's gay bar-restaurant-nightclub at 90 Market, however, was the biggest prize for liquor agents, local law enforcement, and SFRA officials seeking to shut down the circuit of gay bars on the waterfront. The fate of 90 Market was bound up with ongoing revocation proceedings at the Black Cat. Nevertheless, Stoumen faced a final series of administrative and legal actions in 1962 and 1963 that shuttered his entire business enterprise, barred him from the liquor trade, seized his assets, and auctioned off the contents of his nightclub complex.

As with the Ensign and Broken Drum, the SFRA hoped to avoid taking

Sol Stoumen and José Sarria into its workload as commercial tenants. A paper trail, however, documented Stoumen—and Sarria's—financial stake in 90 Market Street. Unlike Caldaralla and his subtenants, Stoumen had signed a long-term lease when he took over the former Castaways nightclub during the gayola trials. He also had a liquor license associated with 90 Market, in addition to the Black Cat license tied up in the appeals process. When he and José Sarria set up the Talk of the Town and the Five an Ounce food concession, they formed the Vend-a-Teria corporation and registered the new business with the State of California. The articles of incorporation enabled Stoumen and Sarria to raise funds from investors, secure a liquor license, and shield themselves personally from charges of violating state liquor laws. The commercial lease, the liquor license, and the corporate entity established Sol Stoumen as the primary commercial tenant at 90 Market. The latter listed José Sarria, for a time, as one of the directors. Taken together, Stoumen's stake in the business and record of occupancy in the building would make it difficult for the agency to justify keeping him out of its workload upon taking possession of the premises.

SFRA Executive Director Justin Herman was aware of the complications Stoumen's lease posed for the agency. In late 1961, he requested a status update from the real estate division on its acquisition of the prime commercial blocks in Area E, reserved for new office towers and the Ferry Building park.[75] The division chief reported that the agency had already purchased or nearly closed on three-quarters of the parcels in the two blocks near the foot of Market Street. However, the owners of seven parcels had not agreed to sell and would require individual condemnation suits. One of the holdouts was Ernest Blumenthal, who owned the building at 84–98 Market Street. The sale was held up by what agency officials characterized as "lease issues." The agency wanted to avoid taking possession of the building in a negotiated sale with Blumenthal while Stoumen and Sarria still ran the large gay nightlife complex out of much of the first floor. Upon taking possession, the agency planned to generate rental income from the current tenants until it found a buyer for the lot, situated on prime commercial block in the Golden Gateway. As with the Ensign, however, the agency faced the uncomfortable prospect of becoming Stoumen and Sarria's landlord. In order to avoid a drawn out eviction, like in the recent Broken Drum case, Herman wanted the primary commercial storefront leased by Stoumen delivered vacant.

By 1961, the SFRA had a baseline understanding of fair market value, tenancy relationships, and the layout of the commercial spaces of the building. Stoumen leased most of the first floor and the basement, while Southern

Pacific had turned the entire second floor into an office annex of its head-quarters located across the street. In addition, a jewelry store and a straight businessmen's tavern occupied two small storefronts next to Stoumen's bar, restaurant, and nightclub space. In July 1960, Sol Stoumen signed a five-year agreement to lease 90 Market at $650 per month, with an option to renew for five more years for $750.[76] The 90 Market space included most of the first floor, nearly all of the basement, and a mezzanine with dressing rooms behind the stage. In total, Stoumen's lease covered nearly 60 percent, or 19,000 square feet, of the available commercial space in the building. In preparation for negotiations over the terms of the sale, agency personnel reviewed a title report for 84–98 Market that included a list of current and former tenants with potential claims to leased spaces or fixtures.[77] The report identified Sol Stoumen, the two men who subleased the Talk of the Town from him, and the former operators of Castaways—Bryan Ray and Norman Tullis—as potential claimants of of real or personal property on the premises.[78]

The SFRA used this information to discriminate against Stoumen and Sarria in the process of acquiring the building from Ernest Blumenthal. First, the SFRA excluded Stoumen's subtenants from consideration for reimbursement for moving expenses or lost property. The 90 Market commercial space was partitioned into three primary subareas, each with a different kind of business and operator. José Sarria ran a lunch counter in the restaurant and kitchen space in the front of the building. One of Stoumen's waiters from the Black Cat managed the adjacent small bar. Two other men ran the showroom and cocktail lounge in the back of the building.[79] Most importantly, the appraiser omitted any reference to Sarria's food concession, effectively excluding him from relocation assistance or other compensation from the agency.

Second, the SFRA deeply devalued the fair market value of the building, citing Stoumen's gay nightclub as the principal reason. After pegging the replacement cost of the building at $319,000, the appraiser estimated that the depreciated value of the structure was a mere $84,000 based on the building's general state of repair, internal layout, and current occupants. In outlining his reasoning for the deep discount, he singled out Stoumen's "gaily decorated" cocktail lounge at the back of the building for a $75,000 deduction, claiming functional and economic obsolescence.[80] He asserted that "the location and *type of patronage* does not warrant a nightclub lay-out."[81] He added that the "outmoded design and layout and excess space" of the club detracted from the commercial value of the structure, reasoning that the owner could collect more rental income by razing the nightclub-lounge portion of the building to create off-street parking for the tenants in the front. His logic sent a clear signal to agency staff negotiating with the building owner: Stoumen's continuing occupancy would have a negative impact on the final sale price.

Finally, the SFRA sought to destroy Stoumen's investment in 90 Market by preventing him from claiming compensation for his possessions. When Stoumen took over Castaways in 1960, he paid $10,000 for all of the furnishings and fixtures at a government auction held to liquidate the assets of the former owners.[82] The appraiser claimed that most of the furnishings and fixtures at 90 Market were the property of the building owner and had already been "evaluated with the real estate." It was a remarkable claim that did not apply to other tenants in the building. In the case of the much smaller straight bar next door, the 98 Club, he classified all fixtures as removable property and estimated the replacement value at $35,000. Stoumen's financial interest in the property was limited to several improvements he made after taking over, totaling $3,000 for a new stage, carpet, and booths in the nightclub space and $8,500 for kitchen and serving equipment in the restaurant area. Even these unfavorable terms, however, were too generous for the head of the SFRA. Agency Executive Director Justin Herman inexplicably reduced Stoumen's financial stake by $900, zeroing out compensation for the "Sandwich Board Refrigerator." It was likely a move to ensure that Sarria would not be eligible for compensation for equipment at his Five an Ounce lunch counter.[83]

In 1963, the SFRA compelled Blumenthal to evict Stoumen from 90 Market in the court-ordered sale of his building to the agency. In January, the agency filed a condemnation suit against Blumenthal and all leaseholders in the building.[84] The negotiations dragged out over ten months.[85] Finally, in early October, the SFRA agreed to pay Blumenthal $240,000 for the property, which was $12,000 over the fair market value set by the agency's own real estate appraisal.[86] In return, Blumenthal agreed to evict Stoumen before the agency took possession of the building on November 1, 1963. Presumably as a reward to Blumenthal for delivering 90 Market vacant, SFRA Executive Director Justin Herman signed off on the higher sale price. The premium Blumenthal received was roughly equivalent to Stoumen's (uncompensated) investment in 90 Market.[87]

The timing of the real estate transfer was devasting to Stoumen's gay bar and nightclub enterprise that stretched from North Beach to lower Market Street. When Stoumen took over 90 Market, he was aware that if the ABC revoked his liquor license at the Black Cat, he would be barred from holding a permit to sell alcoholic beverages anywhere in the state. ABC administrator Feinberg assured Stoumen that he could "safely" invest $10,000 in Castaways, claiming that state agents would not pursue revocation proceedings at the Black Cat, in recognition of his cooperation in the gayola investigation.[88] It proved to be a false promise. For much of 1962 and 1963, Stoumen fought a new set of charges, based on old evidence, of running a disorderly house at the Black Cat. By October 1963, he had exhausted all his appeals in a case designed to put him permanently out of the bar business. The California Supreme Court denied a final review of the case and set midnight, October 31, 1963, for Stoumen to surrender his permit to state liquor agents, effectively ending a nearly fifteen-year battle over the legality of the gay bar trade. The SFRA insisted on scheduling his eviction from 90 Market on the same day, ensuring that when the agency took possession of the building the next day, Stoumen would have no legal claim to the space or its contents.

At midnight on Halloween—during the final pageant of queer costumed revelry—state liquor agents entered the Black Cat and removed Stoumen's license to sell alcoholic beverages from the wall behind the bar. The next day, the San Francisco Redevelopment Agency took possession of Stoumen's vacant commercial space at 90 Market and seized all the furnishings and fixtures. At a minimum, Stoumen lost both his $10,000 investment in purchasing the nightclub and all the kitchen equipment, valued at $8,500, that the agency's own appraiser said belonged to him.[89] In short order, agency staff disposed of Stoumen's property in the aptly named gay restaurant-bar-nightclub complex, As a Last Resort. At a hastily arranged auction, the agency advertised the sale of "$10,000 of Original Oils by old masters including one Rubens," two jukeboxes, a cigarette vending machine, a fully equipped commercial kitchen, an assortment of tables, hundreds of chairs, two thousand sun glow dishes, a George Steck grand piano, and a "rinky tink piano" (see figure 5.3).[90]

In sharp contrast to how the SFRA treated the occupants of 90 Market—which at that time was known simply as the Last Resort—the agency welcomed the other three commercial tenants in the building into their workload and found a new tenant for the vacated gay nightclub. Southern Pacific, which rented the entire second floor and paid $700 per month when the SFRA took possession, but less than a year later, negotiated the rate down to $550. As soon as it disposed of the contents of 90 Market, the agency

AUCTION SALE
THE LAST RESORT
MODERN FULLY EQUIPPED
RESTAURANT—BAR—NIGHT CLUB
90 Market Street, San Francisco
Wednesday Nov. 13th 10 A.M. Sharp!
Buliding being razed for Golden Gateway Expansion

$10,000.00 of Original Oils by old masters including one Rubens to be sold at 12:00 Noon.

Items include 2 juke boxes, cigarette vending machines, fully equipped kitchen has all S. S. Eikington dishwasher with s.s. drain bds., spray unit, garbage disposal, etc. Hot & cold serving counters, pedestal tables, booths, hundreds of chairs, heavy duty stock pots, ss pans, 2000 sun glow dishes, George Stack grand piano, rinky tink piano, 2400-lb. capacity ice cube makers by Frigidaire, 6-ft. s.s. salad case. Gas rotisserie. Much too much to enumerate! Attend this sale.

Inspection Tuesday, November 12, 10:00 A. M. to 4 P. M.
or for detailed brochure contact

B. Levy & Sons Victor Levy · Auctioneer
945 MISSION STREET   EX 2-0160   SAN FRANCISCO, CALIFORNIA
CALIFORNIA'S MOST DYNAMIC LIQUIDATORS AND AUCTIONEERS

Figure 5.3 The San Francisco Redevelopment Agency disposed of the contents of 90 Market at auction soon after taking possession of the building on November 1, 1963. The previous summer, José Sarria had the prescience and camp sensibility to change the name of 90 Market from "Talk of the Town" to "The Last Resort." (Advertisement, *San Francisco Chronicle*, November 10, 1963, 34.)

released the commercial space to August Casazza Wholesale Liquors for $100 a month, which was significantly less than the $650 Stoumen had paid. The new tenants complained of cockroaches in 90 Market and blamed the infestation on Sol Stoumen's tenure in the space. Southern Pacific informed the Redevelopment Agency's property manager that if the situation was not rectified, they would "be forced to vacate as their personnel will not tolerate these conditions."[91] Despite their protestations, the favored tenants stayed put for several years until the agency found a group of private investors, who took advantage of the opportunity to purchase the devalued, state-owned property and redevelop the underlying land for profit.

The compounding losses of the Black Cat liquor license revocation and the 90 Market eviction ruined Stoumen and Sarria financially. In a final plea for leniency in the Black Cat case, Stoumen asked the Supreme Court justices, "What have I been guilty of to deserve this harsh economic punishment which may be likened to a fine of $33,000?"[92] He estimated his liquor license was worth $8,000. The additional $25,000 loss corresponded to the value of Vend-a-Teria, Inc., the corporation that he, Sarria, and others set up when they took over the former Castaways nightclub. By issuing $10 shares to investors in the corporation, Stoumen and Sarria had raised $25,000 to set up the Talk of the Town nightclub and Five an Ounce lunch counter at 90 Market.[93] Stoumen also used the corporation to secure a license to sell alcoholic beverages on the premises.[94] Reasoning that Sarria's participation might jeopardize his relationship with the ABC, Stoumen attempted to put the Vend-a-Teria license solely in his own name.[95] However, the ABC rejected the transfer, citing the pending license revocation proceedings at the Black Cat. When the odds of saving his Black Cat license diminished, Stoumen attempted to transfer the Vend-a-Teria license to Eddie Paulson, one of his bartenders at the Black Cat. Paulson tried to reopen the Talk of the Town as Eddie's 90, but the ABC blocked the transfer and suspended alcohol sales at 90 Market.[96] In the end, Stoumen, Sarria, and an unknown number of investors lost their stake in Vend-a-Teria overnight when the ABC shuttered the Black Cat and the SFRA took possession of 90 Market.

While the ABC's actions ended Stoumen's career in the bar business, the SFRA's efforts to destroy his business enterprise at 90 Market bankrupted him. The agency's relocation staff reported to federal officials that the "controversial bar" discontinued operation because the "owner could not obtain reissuance of license for another location."[97] Remarkably, Sol Stoumen was one of a small number of business operators in all of Area E that did not relocate—and the *only* one that went bankrupt. Of the 426 businesses vacated for the Golden Gateway project by the end of 1963, all but nine had successfully relocated. The nine businesses that "discontinued operations" included five empty storage facilities, a private parking lot, a service station, a billboard advertiser, and Stoumen's nightclub at 90 Market. The latter was the only business in the Golden Gateway that "went bankrupt (through no cause of the agency)."[98] The agency never took responsibility for its role in bankrupting Stoumen, nor did it ever recognize Sarria's lunch counter as a legitimate business displaced by waterfront redevelopment.

The previously unknown story of 90 Market holds the key to understanding the state's multifront effort to put Stoumen and other gay bar operators on the waterfront out of business.[99] Land purchases by government authorities, including SFRA staff, city real estate personnel, and state highway officials, were primarily responsible for dismantling the circuit of gay bars along the Embarcadero. The ABC and local law enforcement played an important supporting role by launching liquor license proceedings against bar owners who operated just outside of the urban renewal project area boundaries. Law enforcement treated Jack's and 90 Market, which formed the nucleus of the League for Civil Education, as "centers of resistance."[100] These bars had a history of challenging corrupt policing practices and discriminatory licensing procedures. As a result, they, along with other LCE-affiliated bars, faced the harshest penalties when state and local authorities ejected them from the waterfront. They were subjected to unlawful property seizures, early evictions, and unchecked physical intimidation. In contrast, the SFRA, the ABC, and local law enforcement gave great deference to the longtime operator of the Ensign Club, who operated within and benefited from the system of queer containment. These differences in treatment underscore how, until the very end, local authorities rewarded nightlife operators who helped advance, rather than threatened, efforts to redevelop the area.

CONCLUSION

DESTRUCTION AND CREATION

This book grew out of an error message that popped up when I tried to generate a map of current and historic queer bars, restaurants, baths, and other sites in San Francisco. I was working with a directory of place names and addresses culled together over several decades by community historians and archivists affiliated with the GLBT Historical Society of Northern California. The places had been mentioned in newspaper articles, oral history transcripts, organizational records, gay press clippings, court proceedings, and commercial guidebooks. Using a mapping program, I attempted to plot the list of roughly three thousand entries onto a map of the city. However, the waterfront hangouts that developed into gay bars in the 1950s were unmappable on the modern street grid, because much of the area was radically altered by urban renewal in the early 1960s. A handful of address-mapping errors pointed to a cluster of places mentioned frequently in oral history transcripts and the *LCE News*. Two of these bars were also mentioned in several scholarly works in connection with the gayola scandal. Another was linked to the emergence of the leather subculture in the city. Before this project, little was known about why these bars became hangouts for gay men or how they fit into the city's postwar urban redevelopment program. The preceding pages reconstruct why and how these particular bars, which served as informal hiring halls for seamen and dockworkers through the 1940s, developed into a politically engaged coalition of working-class gay bars by the early 1960s.

Many of these places—the Sailor Boy, the Sea Cow, Chili's, Lennie's 36, and the Ensign Club—were seamen's hangouts that by the early 1950s served a growing number of queer men excluded from the merchant marines and armed forces (figure 6.1). During this period, growth-oriented business leaders incorporated these so-called homosexual hangouts into an expansive blight declaration encompassing the city's wholesale produce market and adjacent seamen's quarter at the foot of Market Street. By the end of the decade, as plans to raze and rebuild the waterfront took shape, state actors had facilitated the reopening of Jack's Waterfront Hangout and 90 Market as popular gay nightlife spots in the area. In particular, port and highway officials collected commercial rents from Jack's, while law enforcement and state liquor agents extorted protection payments from both places. By exposing this payola system when land acquisitions began in the Golden Gateway, the operators of these places succeeded in postponing eviction for several years. In the early 1960s a handful of other places—the Headhunters, the Barrel House, and the Edgewater Hotel—opened when bar publics displaced by redevelopment reconvened just outside the eastern boundary of the urban renewal project area.

By the mid-1960s, the queer nightlife crowds on the Embarcadero were gone, because government officials acquired and razed the places where they had congregated to make way for the Embarcadero Freeway and Golden Gateway (figure 6.2). This process began in the mid-1950s when highway officials razed the Admiral's Hotel, where the Sailor Boy tavern was located, to make way for a curve in the waterfront freeway. Around the same time, state officials acquired and razed Lennie's to expand a parking lot associated with the Ferry Building. Then, in the early 1960s, highway officials evicted Jack's Waterfront from a building the California Division of Highways owned, to construct an additional set of freeway ramps feeding into the middle of the Golden Gateway urban renewal project. Different components of the Golden Gateway project claimed three other places—the Front, 90 Market, and the Ensign Café. The Front, a lesbian bar that opened in the produce market area around the same time Jack's and 90 Market became gay bars, was incorporated into Sydney G. Walton Square, a park named for a redevelopment agency board member and located in the heart of the residential portion of the Golden Gateway.[1] The Ensign Café became part of a park and plaza complex at the foot of Market Street: Justin Herman Plaza (renamed Embarcadero Plaza in 2017).[2] Finally, 90 Market was razed to build the Embarcadero Center, a complex of office towers, hotel facilities, and shopping amenities located on the prime commercial parcels in the Golden Gateway that stretched from the central business district to the Ferry Building.

The distinct histories and fates of these bars and nightclubs reveal the complex and seemingly paradoxical roles various state actors played in the

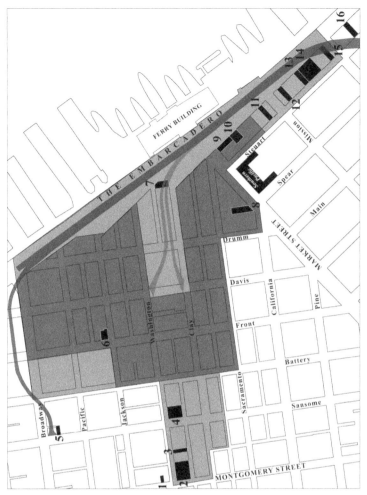

Figure 6.1 Many "homosexual hangouts," gay bars, and other queer spaces in and around Area E were directly or indirectly destroyed by urban redevelopment, including (1) the Black Cat; (2) the Montgomery Block; (3) the Red Lizard and Le Boeuf; (4) Dave's Baths; (5) Gordon's; (6) the Front; (7) Jack's Waterfront Hangout (first location); (8) Castaways, Talk of the Town, and As a Last Resort (also known as the Last Resort); (9) the Ensign Café and Broken Drum; (10) Lennie's 36 Club; (11) the Headhunters showroom at the Barrel House; (12) the Sea Cow Café and Crossroads; (13) Chili's 144 Club and Cove; (14) the Embarcadero YMCA (as an ersatz gay bathhouse); (15) the Admiral and Sailor Boy tavern; and (16) the Edgewater Hotel, Jack's Waterfront (second location), and Original Don's. (Map by the author.)

creation and destruction of queer land uses on the Embarcadero. In the late 1940s and early 1950s, the waterfront became a marginal zone of the city, where queer land uses expanded as a localized consequence of actions by the straight state to identify and persecute suspected homosexuals. In the wake of port screenings and union raids that purged suspected subversives

Figure 6.2 Major urban redevelopment projects transformed the physical, social, and economic fabric of Area E and, in the process, destroyed the queer world of the waterfront that developed out of the city's older maritime and wartime economies. By the early 1970s, few traces of that queer world remained. (Map by the author.)

from the maritime labor force, a growing population of men of all classes, backgrounds, and races sought social and sexual relations with other men in waterfront hangouts. Waterfront redevelopment proponents understood these men and the places they frequented as an indicator of incipient urban blight and a justification for razing and rebuilding blocks of port-related land uses near the foot of Market Street. Periodic bar raids and street sweeps, framed for public consumption in sensationalized crime exposés in city newspapers, did more to stigmatize the waterfront as a problem area than to shut down the queer nightlife scene. The planned destruction and rebuilding of the waterfront hastened the transformation of the informal hiring halls and social clubs of maritime labor unions into a circuit of bars, nightclubs, after-hours "breakfast clubs," and hotel cocktail lounges as the area acquired a more overtly queer and multiracial clientele. Local law enforcement and state liquor agents actually enabled queer nightlife to flourish on the waterfront, by treating it as a vice containment zone. In particular, while redevelopment advocates made a case for the functional obsolescence of maritime and food-wholesaling land uses, state and local officials, including liquor agents, port officials, highway planners, and police officers, quietly worked to steer sexual- and gender-transgressive nightlife crowds to condemned blocks near the foot of Market Street.

Waterfront redevelopment had material consequences for queer subjects. During the 1950s, civic leaders in the public and private sectors reached a consensus on a sweeping redevelopment scheme to transform a twenty-block area into a modern complex of high-rise office buildings and luxury apartment towers. Exposés of gender perversion and sexual danger contributed to a sense of urgency in fast-tracking waterfront redevelopment over competing urban renewal initiatives in other parts of the city. Waterfront redevelopment proponents expanded their map of blighted properties in the core produce-handling blocks to incorporate nearby queer land uses—specifically, a mix of hotels, bars, and nighttime cruising spots popular among men in the late 1940s and 1950s. In the process the same queer land uses that some officials enabled served as a pretext for a series of land clearance and rebuilding proposals. The urban renewal plan that fueled the concentration of queer land uses on the waterfront, when implemented, destroyed them. The end came in a flurry of commercial evictions, liquor license seizures, and auctions that destroyed business enterprises, devalued investments, liquated assets, and ruined livelihoods.

Historian Nan Boyd credited the League for Civil Education with spearheading a novel "political ideology and organizational strategy" that influenced several new gay rights groups that soon followed.[3] A new generation of gay activists and politicians drew inspiration from the queer drinking publics, including many people of color and drag queens, who had been preoccupied with losing their livelihood and performance spaces in the 1960s. As has become clear, the LCE's approach to political mobilization and social organization developed as a response to urban renewal pressures on the waterfront. In the last issue of the *LCE News*, published from the Edgewater Hotel, Strait added a commemorative masthead with the Ferry Building tower to mark the end of the LCE's three-year effort to promote,

10¢   **10¢**

CITIZEN S NEWS

PUBLISHED EVERY TWO WEEKS.   VOLUME III Number 7, 13 January 1964-726 Embarcadero   SAN FRANCISCO,CALIFORNIA.

THE CITIZENS NEWS		BAEDEKER	THE D.O.B.
The News as published by the League for Civil Education suspended publication on the 31st of December 1963. It was felt that the NEWS had accomplished its purpose, to a great extent, and that the urgent need for such a paper did not now exist. Rather than to allow the paper to gradually lose readers because of the militant nature of	suggest that you not buy this paper. Most of all, we hope that THE CITIZENS NEWS provides a method of communication for the Community. How did we choose the name of this newspaper? It was not simple. Wanting a name that expressed both the American heritage and the idea of an independent newspaper, we racked our brains to name this publication. We thought of such titles as "The San Francisco News", but we are national in distribution, we thought of "The Observer", but we want to do more than just observe; we thought of "The National News", but our coverage is not sufficient to warrant that name.	With the approach of summer and the great amount of travel and tourists expected on the highways and skyways of the United States, Strait and Associates are preparing a revision of the Lavender Baedeker, a Guide book to the most interesting places in the United States. Although it was originally planned that the revision would sell for .50¢ along with the original list for $2.00, it has become necessary to in-	A combined Chili Feed-Gab'n Java will be held on Saturday, January 25 in the San Jose-Alum Rock Park area. Sponsored by the DOB,this event is open to women over 21. Menu for the event includes Chili, salad,beer,coffee and soft drinks. Subject of the Gab'n Java will be "Obscenity", moderated by the eminent author, Phyllis Lyon. Starting at 6 PM, the proceeds from this affair will go into the National treasury of the DOB and the

Figure 6.3 When the League for Civil Education moved out of its offices in the Edgewater Hotel, Guy Strait renamed its newspaper the *Citizen's News* and added the Ferry Building to the masthead for the final issue published from the waterfront. (*Citizen's* [formerly *LCE*] *News*, January 27, 1964, 1.)

unify, and defend queer publics on the waterfront (see figure 6.3).[4] The LCE formally disbanded in May 1964 when a group of younger members split off to form the Society for Individual Rights (SIR).[5] SIR prioritized creating a community center rather than promoting drinking establishments as hubs of social organizing. It soon supplanted the LCE, publishing its own newsletter, hosting fundraisers, securing a meeting hall, staging variety shows, and engaging in electoral politics.[6] Similarly, the Tavern Guild, a larger association of gay bar operators that formed around the same time as the LCE, teamed up with the Mattachine Society and Daughters of Bilitis to publish a gay bar newspaper of its own, *Town Talk*. Like the LCE, these new organizations embraced the language of community, emphasized collective action, and relied on print media and public spectacles to secure a new place in the rapidly changing city. In 1973, following in the steps of José Sarria more than a decade later, gay small business owner Harvey Milk ran and won a seat on the San Francisco Board of Supervisors.

When officials pivoted from trying to contain and control queer land uses to devaluing and destroying them, gay bar patrons and operators organized to defend their rights to the city and forged an identity-based, rights-seeking coalition, the League for Civil Education. Queer drinking publics launched a robust legal defense to remain in business, exposed the system of police graft aimed at gay bar operators, and nurtured new forms of cultural expression and political mobilization. When faced with eviction from the waterfront and the loss of a thriving social scene, sex- and gender-transgressive bar-goers organized in fundamentally new ways. Through the LCE, they held voter registration drives and fundraisers to establish a legal defense fund for the benefit of tavern operators and patrons. In addition, they developed a community newspaper complete with business advertisements, a gossip column, and editorials that critiqued urban renewal and called for community activism. In the process of fighting to retain their hold on the Embarcadero, the places where they congregated became more clearly identified as gay bars, and their patrons began to see themselves as members of a persecuted sexual minority.

LOOKING BACK, TEN YEARS LATER

Long after urban renewal destroyed Jack's Waterfront Hangout, 90 Market, the Ensign Café, and other waterfront gay bars, these formative places lived on in the popular imagination of the queer drinking publics who once frequented them. At its fifth annual Coronation Ball in 1971, the Imperial Court of San Francisco, an organization of gay bar hosts and performers founded by José Sarria, produced a comprehensive printed program for the crowning ceremony, which was held at the Jack Tar Hotel. The cloth-bound, seventy-page book was filled with reminiscences of the people, places, and events associated with the city's gay bar culture, dating back to the 1950s. Sarria and other drag performers of the Imperial Court had established a tradition of working with the Tavern Guild, a business association of gay bar operators, to promote the bar trade by staging royalty-themed drag shows, fundraisers, and annual balls.[7] This symbiotic relationship depended on the labor of drag personalities to boost receipts and keep patrons coming back. Sarria's Imperial Court organized the drag queen bar hostesses into a competitive hierarchy of talent, with a taxonomy of aristocratic titles bestowed on the most popular members, who were often associated with particular establishments. The court system gave drag performers some autonomy from the Tavern Guild members who employed them by rewarding community service and political organizing over sales receipts.

The 1971 Coronation Ball marked the fifth anniversary of the Imperial Court system and the tenth anniversary of Sarria's campaign for a seat on the Board of Supervisors. The coronation program opened with a brief history of the Tavern Guild, which had grown dramatically during the early 1960s as San Francisco cemented its status as the "gay capital" of the country.[8] The program then highlighted the foundational story of the Imperial Court: a dramatic standoff at a Tavern Guild–sponsored costume contest, the Beaux Arts Ball, on Halloween 1965.[9] In front of seven hundred revelers, Sarria and his principal rival, Michelle, competed for the award for the best-costumed group at the Winterland Ballroom in the Fillmore District. At midnight, Michelle and her entourage of "Blue Belles" arrived by motorized cable car after appearing at parties at gay bars around town. Later, Sarria and his contingent of Miss Universe pageant contestants "swept in like a United Nations celebration" after visiting the former Black Cat to pay homage to the shuttered bar. When the judges chose Michelle's contingent of Southern debutantes over Sarria's lineup of international beauties, Sarria protested and declared himself "Empress Norton I, Camp Queen of these United States, and Protectress of Mexico." Over the "din and confusion" of the contested costume contest, Sarria seized the moment by announcing the formation of a privy council and plans for his New Year's Eve coronation. Sarria's elevation to empress marked the beginning of the Imperial Court system, which has since grown into an international network of drag performers and nightlife promotors engaged in local fundraising and bar hosting.

Notably, the 1971 souvenir program included a queer photographic archive of the changing sexual geography of the city before the consolidation of distinctive gay neighborhoods and nightlife districts. In the first half of the program, readers were prompted to identify the names of defunct gay bars from recent photographs of each site, annotated with short clues. In the answer key—under the heading "Where Have Our Landmarks Gone?"—the quizmaster included a numbered list of forty-one establishments that had gone out of business. In the second half of the program, the same forty-one photos appeared a second time, this time accompanied by both the name of the landmark and the earlier clue. During his 1961 run for a seat on the Board of Supervisors, Sarria had campaigned in most of the bars included in the quiz. Many of the bars had regularly advertised in the *LCE News* and supported the organization's legal-defense fundraising efforts in the early 1960s. The quiz photos reveal that, by 1971, many of these former queer landmarks were not simply shuttered businesses but sites that had been physically obliterated by urban redevelopment projects. The inclusion of these landmarks in the commemorative program underscores their persistent social significance for the owners, staff, and patrons who ran and frequented them—a depth and type of value that real estate appraisers, redevelopment officials, and state liquor agents willfully ignored.

Figure 6.4 In the mid-1960s, the San Francisco Redevelopment Agency razed the Ensign Café along with much of the rest of the block. The Merrimac Building, occupied by the Ensign Club until the very end, was one of the last buildings demolished in the Golden Gateway project area. On the site, the city built a portion of the long-discussed Embarcadero park and plaza, which officials named after Redevelopment Agency Director Justin Herman. His name was removed in 2017 as part of a reevaluation of his legacy. (1971 Coronation Ball Program, Folder 1, Box 10, Series 3.2, LGBT Collection [AC1146], Courtesy of the Archives Center at the National Museum of American History.)

The 1971 Coronation Ball program reactivated memories of the lost queer world along the Embarcadero before urban renewal. Thirteen of the forty-one landmarks in the quiz had been, or were in the process of being, turned into open lands, parking lots, landscaped parks, freeway ramps, multi-story parking structures, transit facilities, office towers, or high-rise apartment buildings. Seven of the razed landmarks had been located within the boundaries of the twenty-eight-block area declared blighted by the San Francisco Redevelopment Agency in 1955—the Embarcadero–Lower Market Urban Renewal Area E. The agency or highway officials played a direct role in razing the Ensign Café, Jack's Waterfront Hangout, 90 Market, and the Front (see figures 6.4, 6.5, and 6.6). On the Embarcadero, the former Chili's and Sea Cow were still taverns, but queer nightlife crowds had moved on to other parts of the city (see figures 6.7 and 6.8). In the western margins of Area E, the Montgomery Block and an adjacent hotel that housed the Red Lizard gay bar in the early 1950s and later the Le Boeuf restaurant were gone, replaced by the Transamerica Pyramid, a symbol of the Manhattanization of San Francisco.[10]

Figure 6.5 Before this site was cleared, Jack's Waterfront Hangout was located directly in the path of the freeway ramps (out of the frame on the left). In 1962, state highway officials razed a two-block area that included Jack's to create direct automobile access into the heart of the Golden Gateway. The ramps aligned with a large new parking garage topped by the Alcoa Building (center). The integrated office-garage complex was the first structure completed within the urban renewal project area. Occupying the prime commercial parcel in Area E, it soon became a "golden [automobile] gateway" into the city's growing downtown business district. (1971 Coronation Ball Program, Folder 1, Box 10, Series 3.2, LGBT Collection [AC1146], Courtesy of the Archives Center at the National Museum of American History.)

Figure 6.6 On the former site of Castaways and Talk of the Town, a consortium of architects and investors—including John Portman and David Rockefeller—built the fifth building of their office-shopping-hotel development, the Embarcadero Center. The site of José Sarria's lunch counter at 90 Market was incorporated into the footprint of the San Francisco Hyatt Regency, which was seamlessly tied into the adjacent publicly funded park and plaza at the foot of Market Street. (1971 Coronation Ball Program, Folder 1, Box 10, Series 3.2, LGBT Collection [AC1146], Courtesy of the Archives Center at the National Museum of American History.)

Figure 6.7 The Marin Hotel, where Chili ran a bar that catered to queer seamen in the 1950s, was located just outside the boundaries of the Golden Gateway project, which protected it from the bulldozer. By the early 1970s, Chili's was long gone. Its successor, the 144 Club, also known as the Admiral, was a rare holdover of the maritime past. (1971 Coronation Ball Program, Folder 1, Box 10, Series 3.2, LGBT Collection [AC1146], Courtesy of the Archives Center at the National Museum of American History.)

Figure 6.8 The former Sea Cow Café, and later Crossroads, was located outside of the portion of Area E that was razed for the Golden Gateway project. The commercial space, which had been the epicenter of maritime union activism in the 1930s and an important site of gay community organizing in the early 1960s, was a neighborhood Irish bar by the 1970s. (1971 Coronation Ball Program, Folder 1, Box 10, Series 3.2, LGBT Collection [AC1146], Courtesy of the Archives Center at the National Museum of American History.)

Popular narratives of San Francisco's LGBTQ past and its national significance in struggles for civil rights rest on historical amnesia of the pre–urban
renewal queer waterfront, its racially mixed and transgender communities,
and its links to the radical labor politics of the maritime economy.[11] As this
book has shown, maritime union organizing was an important factor in the
emergence of the gay rights movement on the West Coast. Harry Hay, a
cofounder of the Mattachine Society in Los Angeles in 1950, participated
in the 1934 Waterfront Strike in San Francisco as a young man. It was a
formative experience for him, shaping his consciousness about collective
organizing for political rights. As he later recounts, "You couldn't have been
a part of that and not have your life completely changed."[12] The solidarity
among men of color and queens in the Marine Cooks and Stewards Union
must have been particularly impactful, especially given that one of two men
killed by police during the general strike was a marine cook. The purges of
suspected homosexuals from the maritime labor force in West Coast ports in
the late 1940s and early 1950s help explain why sailor bars became so-called
homosexual hangouts by the mid-1950s—and developed into gay bars
by the decade's end. Notably, in many of these bars, José Sarria mobilized
drinking publics to "unite to fight" in the early 1960s under auspices of the
gay bar–based organization he cofounded. The managers, staff, and patrons
he rallied defended their shared interests by flexing their electoral strength
in Sarria's run for public office.

State actors enabled queer nightlife to thrive on the waterfront in ways
that underscore the complicated agendas that animated bar raids, street
sweeps, and roundups of homosexuals during the 1950s. In particular,
policing the city's growing queer nightlife crowds followed a spatial logic
of management and control that advanced plans to rehabilitate some parts
of the city and redevelop others. Street sweeps, homosexual roundups, and
cleanup drives were policing tactics deployed to reclaim areas in the environs
of the central business and downtown shopping districts where sexual- and
gender-transgressive people congregated in the 1950s. However, while law
enforcement officials reined in sexual solicitation in parks, tourist hotels,
public restrooms, and gay cruising strips, they quietly facilitated the growth
of queer nightlife circuits in lower Market Street. The overall effect was to
reverse the encroachment of cruising in public spaces in the core of downtown by permitting queer drinking publics to flourish in marginal maritime
blocks slated for clearance and rebuilding. The gayola scandal exposed the
direct involvement of law enforcement and state liquor agents in steering
queer nightlife crowds to the area in the lead-up to urban redevelopment.

Targeted policing and state intervention in the urban land market, both animated by efforts to advance urban renewal priorities, were at the core of what gay bar publics perceived as periods of relative permissiveness and episodic crackdowns on queer nightlife. When law enforcement and state liquor officials seized the liquor license and bar inventory from Jack's Waterfront Hangout, *LCE News* publisher Guy Strait incredulously asked, "Why?," grasping for a rational explanation for such an uncharacteristic show of force.[13] Based on past experiences, he incorrectly surmised that officials wished to install a more compliant bar manager willing to make payola payments. This time, authorities were not seeking to shake up—or shake down—Jack's. With land acquisitions in the adjacent Golden Gateway nearly finished, the incentive to steer queer nightlife crowds to lower Market Street was over. Authorities permanently closed Jack's, and several nearby gay bars beyond the reach of the redevelopment agency just outside the Golden Gateway boundaries, to prime the area for clearance and sale to private investors for rebuilding. Redevelopment, not reform or regulatory control, was the reason why Jack's closed permanently after nearly five years of tacit support from law enforcement.

The City Aroused has underscored the cultural politics of collective resistance to displacement among queer people in mid-century San Francisco. Self-identified, collectively engaged gay bar patrons and owners responded to urban renewal–induced displacement with a series of place-making cultural spectacles that inscribed a new sexual geography onto the city. At the forefront were drag performers like José Sarria and his contemporaries in the queer nightlife scene on the waterfront, who awakened a collective response among bar patrons to the destruction of sexually permissive zones of the city. For example, on Halloween 1962, the Hairburners of Lower Embarcadero, acting as bar promotors, hired a Gray Line bus and made the rounds to all the costume parties. Similarly, in November, the Michelle International event served as the grand opening party for Jack's Hideaway showroom—the new quarters of the displaced bar crowd from the former Jack's Waterfront Hangout at 111 Embarcadero. Events like these were the direct consequence of the material transformation of urban space. These occasions of performative and material queer placemaking included: drag shows that took on the explicitly political purpose of raising funds or registering voters, street festivals and parades that reflected the growth of a "pink" economy, and opening and closing parties for gay-identified businesses that helped patrons navigate the changing sexual landscape of a city.[14]

Displaced bar operators and their patrons popularized a cultural conception of sexual difference that played an important role in the spatial reordering of urban space. By the mid-1960s, a new, nonstigmatizing vocabulary began to circulate to describe the sociosexual geography of the city. City newspapers that once characterized gay bars as "resorts for perverts" adopted the language of "gay community" from the pages of the *LCE News* when discussing the gay drinking publics and places. As displaced queer businesses relocated to new quarters in neighborhood retail districts and light industrial zones, a new gay/straight binary of sexual difference distinguished previously unmarked heterosexual places from an emergent, expanding "gay" social and sexual geography of the city.[15] This more explicit language for "sexualizing" people and places in San Francisco was, in part, an unintentional by-product of urban renewal. In particular, the Golden Gateway project destroyed a sexual landscape of inference, innuendo, and coded language about sexual desire embedded in the city's maritime past. Only when the state tagged waterfront hangouts for elimination rather than periodic regulation did queer drinking publics adopt a new sexual politics by evoking the language of community and emphasizing the need for sexual minorities to secure rights to the city.

While this history of urban renewal on the San Francisco waterfront strongly suggests that an influx of queer, racially diverse maritime laborers during the Lavender Scare influenced the timing, scope, and approach to redevelopment, the archival sources used in this book have some important limitations. With several notable exceptions, glimpses of an expanding queer world on the San Francisco waterfront during the 1950s primarily come from oral histories with cisgender, white gay men in the 1990s who made fleeting references to the places they visited decades earlier. They were rarely explicit about the sexual subjectivities, gendered presentations, class sensibilities, and racial dynamics of the men congregating in waterfront hangouts. Nevertheless, it is clear that several racially integrated, left-leaning union hangouts developed into gay bars in the wake of purges of suspected homosexuals in the merchant marines and armed forces on the West Coast. This shift is discernible in changing nightlife crowds in seamen's hangouts in lower Market Street. For example, before 90 Market became Castaways, it was a popular jazz club called the Downbeat, where Billie Holiday and a young Johnny Mathis performed in the mid-1950s. Before Jack's became a gay bar, its patrons mirrored the occupational and racial composition of the waterfront labor force—which in the war's final years was nearly one-third African American. Close attention to changing nightlife crowds in other West Coast ports might reveal similar localized impacts of the Lavender Scare, further underscoring how the straight state used anti-homosexual purges to destroy left-leaning maritime labor unions at the onset of the

Korean War. The connection between waterfront redevelopment and sailor-town land uses in other cities also merits further study to draw out the ways Cold War anxieties about sexual deviance and gender subversion influenced urban renewal priorities and projects. *The City Aroused* has laid the historical and methodological groundwork for those studies by unpacking the sexual and social politics of urban renewal.

As this book has documented, urban redevelopment physically remapped the sexual geography of the city in the early 1960s by destroying blocks of residential hotels and queer hangouts on the margins of the central business and shopping districts. The hotel districts and nightlife strips where sexual migrants flooded into the city and put down roots during the Lavender Scare were the precursors to gayborhoods that developed in San Francisco in the late 1960s and 1970s. The queer land uses that developed on the water-front in the 1950s became templates for a range of commercial enterprises that came to define gay neighborhoods in the city. A steady stream of gay migrants fueled the expansion and diversification of LGBTQ-oriented land uses, including bars, restaurants, bookstores, clothing stores, bathhouses, churches, gyms, and social services agencies. By the late 1960s, mixed-use, predominantly gay commercial corridors and residential enclaves developed in neighborhoods left behind by suburbanizing heterosexual families, principally the Haight, Tenderloin, Polk Gulch, South of Market, Mission, and Castro districts.[16]

By establishing, managing, and profiting from their own social enterprises, LGBTQ San Franciscans became an undeniable economic and political force in the city.[17] They revitalized neighborhood commercial districts and reha-bilitated older housing stock into valuable urban real estate.[18] The gay-led gentrification of the 1970s became a viable new model for managing urban development in the 1990s, when it was adopted as public policy across the country to promote "creative cities."[19] This cultural turn in urban governance to affirmatively incorporate homonormative gay-identified land uses—and people—into economic development initiatives has been instrumental in attracting tourists, urban professionals, high-tech investment, and corporate headquarters.[20] While recent scholarship has sought to explain the decline of gayborhoods, or critique the urban entrepreneurialism that made them possible, this project has interrogated the spatial, political, and economic logics that preceded gayborhoods.[21] Those logics were hostile to queer people, animated by heteronormative assumptions about urban life, and operationalized in the management of urban development in homophobic and transphobic ways.

NOTES

ABBREVIATIONS

ABC California Department of Alcoholic Beverage Control
ABCB California Alcoholic Beverage Control Board
AFL American Federation of Labor
AIA American Institute of Architects
ARCV The Internet Archive, http://archive.org
BAC Bay Area Council
BZC Blyth-Zellerbach Committee
CCSF City and County of San Francisco, CA
CIO Congress of Industrial Organizations
CSA California State Archives
CSLL California State Law Library
DOB Daughters of Bilitis
EDA Environmental Design Archives
ELM Embarcadero–Lower Market Urban Renewal Area (legal designation of "Area E")
GG Golden Gateway (redevelopment project that impacted most of Area E)
GLBTHS Gay, Lesbian, Bisexual and Transgender Historical Society of Northern California
ILA International Longshoremen's Association
ILWU International Longshore and Warehouse Union
LCE League for Civil Education
MCSU Marine Cooks and Stewards Union
NCF Newspaper Clippings File (various)
OHC Oral History Collection (GLBTHS)
SBC Scrapbook Collection (SFPD)
SFBOS San Francisco Board of Supervisors
SFCOC San Francisco Chamber of Commerce
SFOAR San Francisco Office of Assessor-Recorder
SFPD San Francisco Police Department
SFPL San Francisco Public Library
SFRA San Francisco Redevelopment Agency
SFRAR San Francisco Redevelopment Agency Records
SHC San Francisco History Center

ARCHIVES AND DIGITAL REPOSITORIES

Archives Center at the National Museum of American History, Smithsonian Institution, Washington, DC
- LGBT Collection, AC1146

California Secretary of State Records, Sacramento, CA
- Business Entities Records, https://bizfileonline.sos.ca.gov/search/business

California State Archives, Sacramento, CA
- Alcoholic Control Board Records, F3718.1-374c
- Alcoholic Beverage Control Board of Appeals Records, F3718.376-464a
- *People v. Caldaralla* (Criminal Case No. 3,393), Case Files, First Appellate Court District, R137, Courts of Appeals Records

California State Law Library, Sacramento, CA
- *Stoumen v. Munro* (Civil Case No. 20,310), Case Files, First Appellate Court District, California Court of Appeals

Environmental Design Archives, University of California, Berkeley, CA
- Ciampi (Mario) Papers, 2007-6
- DeMars (Vernon) Papers, 2005-13

Gay, Lesbian, Bisexual, and Transgender Historical Society of Northern California, San Francisco, CA
- GLBT Historical Sites Database Files (c. 1997), unprocessed
- Lucas (Donald) Papers, 1997-25
- Oral History Collection (partially available online), GLBT-OH
- Sarria (José) Papers, 1996-01
- Tavern Guild of San Francisco Records, 1995-02

The Internet Archive, https://archive.org/about
- San Francisco Public Library Collection, https://archive.org/details /sanfranciscopubliclibrary

McHenry Library, Special Collections and Archives, University of California, Santa Cruz, CA
- Patterson (Noel L.) Papers, Number MS.218

ONE National Gay and Lesbian Archives, Los Angeles, CA
- Maurice & La Monte Papers, 2008–003

OutHistory, https://outhistory.org/about-outhistory

Oviatt Library, Special Collections and Archives, Northridge California State University, Northridge, CA
- Evan (Len) Collection, Number SC.LE

Queer Music Heritage, JD Archives, https://www.queermusicheritage.com

San Francisco Assessor-Recorder's Office, San Francisco, CA

San Francisco History Center, San Francisco Public Library, San Francisco, CA
- George Christopher Papers, SFH 7
- San Francisco Historical Photograph Collection
- San Francisco Police Department Records, SFH 61
- San Francisco Redevelopment Agency Records, SFH 371
- San Francisco Sanborn Fire Insurance Map Collection

San Francisco Planning Department website
- LGBTQ Historic Context Statement project page, https://sfplanning.org/project /lgbtq-historic-context-statement

San Francisco Public Library, San Francisco, CA
  • San Francisco Business Directories Collection
  • *San Francisco Chronicle* Online Historical Database
  • San Francisco Newspapers on Microform Collection
San Francisco Redevelopment Agency Records, Office of Community Investment and
Infrastructure (Successor Agency to the SFRA), San Francisco, CA
  • Administrative Records, Central Records and Archives Division
  • Administrative Records, Community Services Division
  • Administrative Records, Finance and Administration Division
  • Administrative Records, Planning Division
  • Administrative Records, Project Administration Division
  • Administrative Records, Real Estate Division
  • Newspaper Clippings Files
  • Property Records, Acquisition Files
  • Property Records, Business Relocation and Tenant Case Files
  • Property Records, Structure Files
  • Property Records, Tenant Ledgers

INTRODUCTION: EXODUS ON THE EVE OF DESTRUCTION

1. In the early 1960s, Elmer Guy Strait (his given name) was a key figure in early
gay publishing and advertising enterprises in San Francisco, including a newspaper and
a series of travel guides. Martin Meeker, *Contacts Desired: Gay and Lesbian Communications and Community, 1940s–1970s* (Chicago, IL: University of Chicago Press, 2006),
208–217.

2. In her work on the cultural formation of gay male leather communities, anthropologist Gayle Rubin found through ethnographic and archival research that in the early
1950s, gay men clad in black leather motorcycle gear frequented Jack's and other waterfront bars. The city's first dedicated gay leather bar, the Why Not?, opened in the Tenderloin and operated briefly in 1962—the same year the Redevelopment Agency razed Jack's.
See Gayle Rubin, "Elegy for the Valley of the Kings: AIDS and the Leather Community
in San Francisco, 1981–1996," in *In Changing Times: Gay Men and Lesbians Encounter
HIV/AIDS*, ed. Martin P. Levine, Peter M. Nardi, and John H. Gagnon (Chicago, IL:
University of Chicago Press, 1997), 101–144; Gayle Rubin, "The Miracle Mile: South of
Market and Gay Male Leather, 1962–1997," in *Reclaiming San Francisco: History, Politics,
Culture*, ed. James Brook, Chris Carlsson, and Nancy Peters (San Francisco, CA: City
Lights Books, 1998), 247–272.

3. Guy Strait, "Exodus," *LCE News*, April 30, 1962, 1.

4. Christopher Lowen Agee, *The Streets of San Francisco: Policing and the Creation of a
Cosmopolitan Liberal Politics, 1950–72* (Chicago, IL: University of Chicago Press, 2014),
93.

5. "Land Sold for Ramps of Freeway," *San Francisco News*, June 15, 1959, NCF,
SFRAR.

6. Agee, *Streets of San Francisco*, 95.

7. For an excellent analysis of how government policies—including urban redevelopment and suburban housing programs—privileged heterosexual families, see Clayton

Howard, *The Closet and the Cul de Sac: The Politics of Sexual Privacy in Northern California* (Philadelphia: University of Pennsylvania Press, 2019). For a cultural history of suburban perspectives on sex and gender norms and the pervasiveness of a Cold War–era ideology of "domestic containment," see Elaine Tyler May, *Homeward Bound: American Families in the Cold War Era*, 4th ed. (New York: Basic Books, 2017).

8. For a similar argument about the selective deployment and enforcement of liquor laws that highlights opportunities for graft, see Michael Brown and Larry Knopp, "Sex, Drink, and State Anxieties: Governance through the Gay Bar," *Social & Cultural Geography* 17, no. 3 (2016): 335–358.

9. David K. Johnson, *The Lavender Scare: The Cold War Persecution of Gays and Lesbians in the Federal Government* (Chicago, IL: University of Chicago Press, 2004); Margot Canady, *The Straight State: Sexuality and Citizenship in Twentieth-Century America* (Princeton, NJ: Princeton University Press, 2009); Douglas M. Charles, *Hoover's War on Gays: Exposing the FBI's "Sex Deviates" Program* (Lawrence: University of Kansas Press, 2015); Howard, *Closet and the Cul de Sac*.

10. Canady, *Straight State*.

11. Allan Bérubé, *Coming Out under Fire: The History of Gay Men and Women in World War Two* (New York: Free Press, 1990); Johnson, *Lavender Scare*; Eric Cervini, *The Deviant's War: The Homosexual vs. the United States of America* (New York: Farrar, Straus and Giroux, 2020).

12. May, *Homeward Bound*.

13. On urban renewal as a historically specific approach to urban redevelopment, see Jon C. Teaford, *The Rough Road to Renaissance: Urban Revitalization in America, 1940–1985* (Baltimore, MD: Johns Hopkins University Press, 1990); Samuel Zipp, *Manhattan Projects: The Rise and Fall of Urban Renewal in Cold War New York* (New York: Oxford University Press, 2010); Christopher Klemek, *The Transatlantic Collapse of Urban Renewal: Postwar Urbanism from New York to Berlin* (Chicago, IL: University of Chicago, 2011); Samuel Zipp and Michael Carriere, "Introduction: Thinking Through Urban Renewal," *Journal of Urban History* 39, no. 3 (2013): 359–365; Francesca Russello Ammon, *Bulldozer: Demolition and Clearance of the Postwar Landscape* (New Haven, CT: Yale University Press, 2016). Recent works on urban redevelopment in San Francisco foreground the ways local actors participated in and reshaped planning processes and outcomes; see Ocean Howell, *Making the Mission: Planning and Ethnicity in San Francisco* (Chicago, IL: University of Chicago Press, 2015); Alison Isenberg, *Designing San Francisco: Art, Land, and Urban Renewal in the City by the Bay* (Princeton, NJ: Princeton University Press, 2017).

14. On the expanded legal definition and administrative application of "blight" during this era, see Wendell E. Pritchett, "The 'Public Menace' of Blight: Urban Renewal and the Private Uses of Eminent Domain," *Yale Law & Policy Review* 21, no. 1 (2003): 1–52; Colin Gordon, "Blighting the Way: Urban Renewal, Economic Development, and the Elusive Definition of Blight," *Fordham Urban Law Journal* 31, no. 2 (2003): 305–337; Themis Chronopoulos, "Robert Moses and the Visual Dimension of Physical Disorder: Efforts to Demonstrate Urban Blight in the Age of Slum Clearance," *Journal of Planning History* 13, no. 3 (2014): 207–233.

15. Robert D. Bullard, Glenn S. Johnson, and Angel O. Torres, eds., *Highway Robbery: Transportation Racism and New Routes to Equity* (Cambridge, MA: South End Press, 2004); Eric Avila, *The Folklore of the Freeway: Race and Revolt in the Modernist City* (Minneapolis: University of Minnesota Press, 2014).

16. For a selection of works that foreground urban renewal and racial inequity in particular cities, see June Manning Thomas, *Redevelopment and Race: Planning a Finer City in Postwar Detroit* (Baltimore, MD: Johns Hopkins University Press, 1997); Larry Keating, *Atlanta: Race, Class, and Urban Expansion* (Philadelphia, PA: Temple University Press, 2001); Howard Gillette Jr., *Camden after the Fall: Decline and Renewal in a Post-Industrial City* (Philadelphia: University of Pennsylvania Press, 2005); Colin Gordon, *Mapping Decline: St. Louis and the Fate of the American City* (Philadelphia: University of Pennsylvania Press, 2008); Eric Avila and Mark H. Rose, "Race, Culture, Politics, and Urban Renewal: An Introduction," *Journal of Urban History* 35, no. 3 (2009): 335–347.

17. For an excellent synthesis of historical scholarship on race and city planning, see Joseph Heathcott, "Race, Planning, and the American City," *Aggregate*, 2015, http://we-aggregate.org/piece/race-planning-and-the-american-city. Anti-Black racism was deeply embedded in twentieth-century urban planning projects, housing policies, and real estate practices. For examples, see Thomas Sugrue, *The Origins of the Urban Crisis: Race and Inequality in Postwar Detroit* (Princeton, NJ: Princeton University Press, 2005); N. D. B. Connolly, *A World More Concrete: Real Estate and the Remaking of Jim Crow South Florida* (Chicago, IL: University of Chicago Press, 2014); Richard Rothstein, *The Color of Law: A Forgotten History of How Our Government Segregated America* (New York: Liveright Publishing, 2017); Keeanga-Yamahtta Taylor, *Race for Profit: How Banks and the Real Estate Industry Undermined Black Home Ownership* (Chapel Hill: University of North Carolina Press, 2019).

18. Ann Forsyth, "Sexuality and Space: Nonconformist Populations and Planning Practice," *Journal of Planning Literature* 15, no. 3 (2001): 339–358; Michael Frisch, "Planning as a Heterosexist Project," *Journal of Planning Education and Research* 21, no. 3 (2002): 254–266; Leonie Sandercock, ed., *Making the Invisible Visible: A Multicultural Planning History* (Berkeley: University of California Press, 1998); Petra L. Doan, ed., *Queerying Planning: Challenging Heteronormative Assumptions and Reframing Planning Practice* (Burlington, VT: Ashgate Publishing, 2011); Petra L. Doan, ed., *Planning and LGBTQ Communities: The Need for Inclusive Queer Spaces* (New York: Routledge, 2015).

19. May, *Homeward Bound*; Howard, *Closet and the Cul de Sac*.

20. Frisch, "Planning as a Heterosexist Project."

21. Clayton Howard, "Policing and Redeveloping the Queer City," in Howard, *Closet and the Cul de Sac*, 148–181.

22. Rubin, "Miracle Mile"; Samuel R. Delany, *Times Square Red, Times Square Blue* (New York: New York University Press, 1999); Bryant Simon, "New York Avenue: The Life and Death of Gay Spaces in Atlantic City, New Jersey, 1920–1990," *Journal of Urban History* 28, no. 3 (2002): 300–327; Damon Scott, "Before the Creative Class: Blight, Gay Movies, and Family Values in the Haight-Ashbury Neighborhood, 1964," *Journal of Planning History* 14, no. 2 (May 2015): 149–173; Julie A. Podmore, "Queering Discourses of Urban Decline: Representing Montréal's Post–World War II 'Lower Main,'" *Historical Geography*, no. 43 (January 2015): 57–83; Elsa Devienne, "Urban Renewal by the Sea: Reinventing the Beach for the Suburban Age in Postwar Los Angeles," *Journal of Urban History* 45, no. 1 (2019): 99–125.

23. This book enriches and builds on works that critique discourses of urban decline. Alexander J. Reichl, *Reconstructing Times Square: Politics and Culture in Urban Redevelopment* (Lawrence: University Press of Kansas, 1999); Robert A. Beauregard, *Voices of Decline: The Postwar Fate of US Cities*, Revised, 2nd ed. (New York: Routledge, 2002); Podmore, "Queering Discourses of Urban Decline"; Simon, "New York Avenue."

24. Pritchett, "'Public Menace' of Blight"; Daniel M. Abramson, *Obsolescence: An Architectural History* (Chicago, IL: University of Chicago Press, 2016).

25. "The City's Front Need Not Be So Far, Far Behind," *San Francisco News*, July 24, 1954, 3; Mary Ellen Leary, "Ferry Building Plaza Plan Stirs Row," *San Francisco News*, February 11, 1955, 3.

26. For more on how homophile leaders and gay activists influenced urban policies, see Martin Meeker, "The Queerly Disadvantaged and the Making of San Francisco's War on Poverty, 1964–1967," *Pacific Historical Review* 81, no. 1 (2012): 21–59; Ian M. Baldwin, "Family, Housing, and the Political Geography of Gay Liberation in Los Angeles County, 1960–1986" (PhD diss., University of Nevada, Las Vegas, 2016); Timothy Stewart-Winter, *Queer Clout: Chicago and the Rise of Gay Politics* (Philadelphia: University of Pennsylvania Press, 2016). For more on how normative ideologies about sex, sexuality, and gender shaped urban development, see Josh Sides, *Erotic City: Sexual Revolutions and the Making of Modern San Francisco* (New York: Oxford University Press, 2009); Howard, *Closet and the Cul de Sac.*

27. For specific examples, see Gayle Rubin, "Sites, Settlements, and Urban Sex: Archaeology and the Study of Gay Leathermen in San Francisco, 1955–1995," in *Archaeologies of Sexualities*, ed. Robert A. Schmidt and Barbara L. Voss (New York: Routledge, 2000), 62–88; Simon, "New York Avenue"; Petra L. Doan and Harrison Higgins, "The Demise of Queer Space? Resurgent Gentrification and the Assimilation of LGBT Neighborhoods," *Journal of Planning Education and Research* 31, no. 1 (2011): 6–25; Scott, "Before the Creative Class." For powerful articulations of the personal impacts and social implications of the destruction of queer public spaces, see Delany, *Times Square Red.*

28. San Francisco was distinctive among cities with large-scale, federally backed urban renewal projects for its spirited public debates over the design qualities and historic character of new developments, particularly on the northern waterfront. Isenberg, *Designing San Francisco.*

29. Teaford, *Rough Road*, 2.

30. Nancy Olmsted, *The Ferry Building: Witness to a Century of Change, 1898–1998* (San Francisco, CA: Port of San Francisco; Berkeley, CA: Heyday Books, 1998).

31. Samuel Zipp, "The Roots and Routes of Urban Renewal," *Journal of Urban History* 39, no. 3 (2013): 366–391.

32. Andrew M. Shanken, *194X: Architecture, Planning, and Consumer Culture on the American Homefront* (Minneapolis: University of Minnesota Press, 2009); Klemek, *Transatlantic Collapse of Urban Renewal.*

33. Elihu Rubin, *Insuring the City: The Prudential Center and the Postwar Urban Landscape* (New Haven, CT: Yale University Press, 2012); Sara Stevens, *Developing Expertise: Architecture and Real Estate in Metropolitan America* (New Haven, CT: Yale University Press, 2016); Abramson, *Obsolescence.*

34. Ammon, *Bulldozer.*

35. Teaford, *Rough Road*; Lizabeth Cohen, *Saving America's Cities: Ed Logue and the Struggle to Renew Urban America in the Suburban Age* (New York: Farrar, Straus and Giroux, 2019).

36. In the first citywide inventory of blight, the six priority areas for redevelopment were: 1) the "Japtown" section of the Western Addition, 2) a South of Market area of "tenements and flophouses," 3) portions of Chinatown with "the worst housing in the City," 4) "a large, spotty area of blight" in the Mission District, 5) tideland areas that could be reclaimed for industrial use, and 6) the "improperly subdivided" slopes of Twin

Peaks. *The Master Plan of San Francisco: The Redevelopment of Blighted Areas; Report on Conditions Indicative of Blight and Redevelopment Policies* (San Francisco, CA : San Francisco City Planning Commission, 1945), ARCV.

37. San Francisco Redevelopment Agency, *Annual Report to Mayor Elmer E. Robinson for the Fiscal Year Ended June 30, 1955* (San Francisco, 1955).

38. Tadeusz B. Spitzer, *World Trade Center in San Francisco* (San Francisco, CA: Board of State Harbor Commissioners, 1947).

39. For more on the eagerness of city leaders to revert to civilian control, see Roger W. Lotchin, *The Bad City in the Good War: San Francisco, Los Angeles, Oakland, and San Diego* (Bloomington: Indiana University Press, 2003); Frederick M. Wirt, *Power in the City: Decision Making in San Francisco* (Berkeley: University of California Press, 1974).

40. The Housing Act of 1949 grew out of older slum clearance initiatives to raze and rebuild dilapidated residential areas with new housing. Teaford, *Rough Road*, 107.

41. Localities had to have an approved "workable program" in place to request and receive urban renewal funds. Douglas R. Appler, "Changing the Scale of Analysis for Urban Renewal Research," *Journal of Planning History* 16, no. 3 (2017): 200–221.

42. For more on the Chamber of Commerce's involvement in urban redevelopment, see Chester Hartman and Sarah Carnochan, *City for Sale: The Transformation of San Francisco*, rev. and updated ed. (Berkeley: University of California Press, 2002); Howell, *Making the Mission*. The meeting minutes of this working group reveal how its leadership and a changing mix of invited guests expedited waterfront redevelopment over other priorities. "Meeting Announcements and Minutes of the Redevelopment Coordinating Committee of the San Francisco Chamber of Commerce (formerly known as the Special Produce Market Committee and the Coordinating Committee on Produce Market Area Redevelopment), December 2, 1955, to May 6, 1959," SFRAR.

43. For more on the origins of this "booster club," see Hartman and Carnochan, *City for Sale*, 15–43. See also Wirt, *Power in the City*; Stephen J. McGovern, *The Politics of Downtown Development: Dynamic Political Cultures in San Francisco and Washington* (Lexington: University Press of Kentucky, 1998).

44. After changing the trajectory of the city's urban redevelopment program, the BZC took control of a progressive citizen group with roots in the housing reform and slum clearance movement, with an eye toward advancing the city's other priority projects. For more on the BZC and its successor, the San Francisco Planning and Urban Renewal Association (SPUR), see McGovern, *Politics of Downtown Development*; Hartman and Carnochan, *City for Sale*; Howell, *Making the Mission*.

45. The efforts of city leaders to declare the produce market area blighted have been overlooked or treated as a relatively uncontested prelude to the Golden Gateway urban renewal project and the other large redevelopment projects that took off in the early 1960s under the direction of an emboldened San Francisco Redevelopment Agency. For example, see John H. Mollenkopf, *The Contested City* (Princeton, NJ: Princeton University Press, 1983); Hartman and Carnochan, *City for Sale*; Howell, *Making the Mission*; Isenberg, *Designing San Francisco*.

46. At the meetings, a select group of representatives from the city's leading banking, real estate, architecture, construction, and engineering firms, as well as relevant municipal department heads, met to iron out plans to redevelop the produce market area at the foot of Market Street. "Meeting Announcements and Minutes."

47. Marybeth Branaman, *Growth of the San Francisco Bay Area Urban Core* (Berkeley, CA: Real Estate Research Program, Bureau of Business and Economic Research at the University of California, 1956), 52.

48. Branaman, *Growth*, 52–53.

49. Hartman and Carnochan, *City for Sale*, 3.

50. "S.F.'s Population Falling: Alarmed Mayor Set to Request Census Recount," *San Francisco Chronicle*, May 24, 1960.

51. Clayton Howard, "Building a 'Family Friendly' Metropolis: Sexuality, the State, and Postwar Housing Policy," *Journal of Urban History* 39, no. 5 (2013): 933–955; Scott, "Before the Creative Class."

52. The university's Stanford Industrial Park is a prime example—one that had far-reaching effects on the trajectory of regional economic development patterns. Margaret Pugh O'Mara, *Cities of Knowledge: Cold War Knowledge and the Search for the Next Silicon Valley* (Princeton, NJ: Princeton University Press, 2005).

53. Arthur D. Little, *Community Renewal Program: San Francisco Fact Book* (San Francisco, CA: Department of City Planning, 1965), 75.

54. Hartman and Carnochan, *City for Sale*, 3.

55. For more on the history of containerization, see Marc Levinson, *The Box: How the Shipping Container Made the World Smaller and the World Economy Bigger* (Princeton, NJ: Princeton University Press, 2008). For more on the impact of containerization on San Francisco, see Michael R. Corbett, *Port City: the History and Transformation of the Port of San Francisco, 1848–2010* (San Francisco, CA: San Francisco Architectural Heritage, 2010); Jasper Rubin, *A Negotiated Landscape: The Transformation of San Francisco's Waterfront since 1950* (Chicago, IL: Center for American Places at Columbia College, 2011).

56. Mollenkopf, *Contested City*, 143. Quoting from a 1946 pamphlet produced by the California State Reconstruction and Reemployment Commission.

57. Mollenkopf, *Contested City*, 143. Quoting a banker from a 1948 issue of the magazine of the Commonwealth Club of California.

58. John D'Emilio, "Capitalism and Gay Identity," in *The Gender/Sexuality Reader: Culture, History, Political Economy*, ed. Roger N. Lancaster and Micaela di Leonardo (New York: Routledge, 1997), 169–176.

59. George Chauncey, *Gay New York: Gender, Urban Culture, and the Making of the Gay Male World, 1890–1940* (New York: Basic Books, 1994).

60. Elizabeth Lapovsky and Madeline D. Davis Kennedy, *Boots of Leather, Slippers of Gold: The History of a Lesbian Community* (New York: Routledge, 1993); Chauncey, *Gay New York*; Kevin J. Mumford, *Interzones: Black/White Sex Districts in Chicago and New York in the Early Twentieth Century* (New York: Columbia University Press, 1997); Brett Beemyn, *Creating a Place for Ourselves: Lesbian, Gay and Bisexual Community Histories* (New York: Routledge, 1997); Chad Heap, *Slumming: Sexual and Racial Encounters in American Life, 1885–1940* (Chicago, IL: University of Chicago Press, 2009); Julio Capó Jr., *Welcome to Fairyland: Queer Miami before 1940* (Chapel Hill: University of North Carolina Press, 2017).

61. Mumford, *Interzones*.

62. Capó, *Welcome to Fairyland*.

63. John Howard, *Men like That: A Southern Queer History* (Chicago, IL: University of Chicago Press, 1999).

64. Bérubé, *Coming Out under Fire*; Lapovsky and Kennedy, *Boots of Leather*.

65. History Project, comps., *Improper Bostonians: Lesbian and Gay History from the Puritans to Playland* (Boston, MA: Beacon Press, 1998); Kenneth Marlowe, *Mr. Madam: Confessions of a Male Madam* (Los Angeles, CA: Sherbourne Press, 1964); Capó, *Welcome to Fairyland*; Genny Beemyn, *A Queer Capital: A History of Gay Life in Washington D.C.* (New York: Routledge, 2014).

66. Beemyn, *Queer Capital*; Tracy Baim, ed., *Out and Proud in Chicago: An Overview of the City's Gay Community* (Chicago, IL: Surrey Books, 2008); Marc Stein, *City of Sisterly and Brotherly Loves: Lesbian and Gay Philadelphia, 1945–72* (Chicago, IL: University of Chicago Press, 2000); Moira Rachel Kenney, *Mapping Gay L.A.: The Intersection of Place and Politics* (Philadelphia, PA: Temple University Press, 2001); Chauncey, *Gay New York*.

67. History Project, *Improper Bostonians*, 178–180.

68. Capó, *Welcome to Fairyland*, 278–283.

69. Marlowe, *Mr. Madam*.

70. Agee, *Streets of San Francisco*; Nan Alamilla Boyd, *Wide Open Town: A History of Queer San Francisco to 1965* (Berkeley: University of California Press, 2003); Arthur H. Samish and Bob Thomas, *The Secret Boss of California: The Life and High Times of Art Samish* (New York: Crown Publishers, 1971); George Dorsey, *Christopher of San Francisco* (New York: Macmillan, 1962).

71. Johnson, *Lavender Scare*; Charles, *Hoover's War on Gays*.

72. Johnson, *Lavender Scare*; Beemyn, *Queer Capital*; James Kirchick, *Secret City: The Hidden History of Gay Washington* (New York: Henry Holt, 2022).

73. Charles, *Hoover's War on Gays*; Stuart Timmons, *The Trouble with Harry Hay: Founder of the Modern Gay Movement* (Boston, MA: Alyson Publications, 1990).

74. Allan Bérubé, *My Desire for History: Essays in Gay, Community, and Labor History*, ed. John D'Emilio and Estelle Freedman (Chapel Hill: University of North Carolina Press, 2011).

75. John D'Emilio, *Sexual Politics, Sexual Communities: The Making of a Homosexual Minority in the United States, 1940–1970* (Chicago, IL: University of Chicago Press, 1983); Elizabeth A. Armstrong, *Forging Gay Identities: Organizing Sexuality in San Francisco, 1950–1994* (Chicago, IL: University of Chicago Press, 2002); Boyd, *Wide Open Town*; Meeker, *Contacts Desired*; Kwame Holmes, "Chocolate to Rainbow City: The Dialectics of Black and Gay Community Formation in Postwar Washington, D.C., 1946–1978" (PhD diss., University of Illinois at Urbana-Champaign, 2011).

76. For examples of the social history of gay and lesbian bars in other places in this period, see Lapovsky and Kennedy, *Boots of Leather*; History Project, *Improper Bostonians*; Stein, *City of Sisterly and Brotherly Loves*; Baim, *Out and Proud in Chicago*; Beemyn, *Queer Capital*.

77. D'Emilio, *Sexual Politics*.

78. Boyd, *Wide Open Town*, 202.

79. See Martin Meeker, "Assembling a Lavender Baedeker," in *Contacts Desired: Gay and Lesbian Communications and Community, 1940s–1970s* (Chicago, IL: University of Chicago Press, 2006), 201–224.

80. Philip J. Ethington, *The Public City: The Political Construction of Urban Life in San Francisco, 1850–1900* (Berkeley: University of California Press, 2001), 15.

81. Michael Warner, *Publics and Counterpublics* (New York: Zone Books, 2002), 57. For more of "counterpublics" as a feminist critique of Habermas's *The Structural Transformation of the Public Sphere*, see Rita Felski, *Beyond Feminist Aesthetics* (Cambridge, MA: Harvard University Press, 1989); Nancy Fraser, "Rethinking the Public Sphere: A Contribution to the Critique of Actually Existing Democracy," in *Habermas and the Public Sphere*, ed. Craig J. Calhoun (Cambridge, MA: MIT Press, 1992), 109–142.

82. Howard Kimeldorf, "World War II and the Deradicalization of American Labor: The ILWU as a Deviant Case," *Labor History* 33, no. 2 (1992): 248–278; Bérubé, *My*

Desire for History; Albert Morris Bendich, "A History of the Marine Cooks' and Stewards' Union" (master's thesis, University of California, Berkeley, 1953).

83. For accounts of pre–World War II sexual boundary-crossing among men of different racial and class backgrounds, see Chauncey, *Gay New York*; Mumford, *Interzones*; Heap, *Slumming*.

84. Tim Retzloff, "Eliding Trans Latino/a Queer Experience in U.S. LGBT History: José Sarria and Sylvia Rivera Reexamined," *Centro Journal* 19, no. 1 (Spring 2007): 140–161.

85. For a more recent history of queer solidarity and leftist political organizing in the San Francisco Bay Area—from the Vietnam War to the HIV/AIDS public health crisis—see Emily K. Hobson, *Lavender and Red: Liberation and Solidarity in the Gay and Lesbian Left* (Berkeley: University of California Press, 2016).

86. Much of this work considers the dialectics of sexuality and space in the past as embedded in historically contingent social relations. See Mona Domosh, "With 'Stout Boots and a Stout Heart': Historical Methodology and Feminist Geography," in *Thresholds in Feminist Geography: Difference, Methodology, Representation*, ed. John Paul Jones III, Heidi J. Nast, and Susan M. Roberts (New York: Rowman & Littlefield, 1997); Julie A. Podmore and Michael Brown, "Introduction to the Special Issue Historical Geographies of Sexualities?, "*Historical Geography*, no. 43 (2015): 5–16; Podmore, "Queering Discourses of Urban Decline"; Matt Houlbrook, *Queer London: Perils and Pleasures in the Sexual Metropolis, 1918–1957* (Chicago, IL: University of Chicago Press, 2005).

87. See Henri Lefebvre, *The Production of Space*, trans. Donald Nicholson-Smith (Malden, MA: Blackwell, 1991).

88. For earlier works that theorize the relationship between sexual subjectivity and urban development, see Mickey Lauria and Lawrence Knopp, "Toward an Analysis of the Role of Gay Communities in the Urban Renaissance," *Urban Geography* 6, no. 2 (1985): 152–169; Lawrence Knopp, "Sexuality and the Spatial Dynamics of Capitalism," *Environment and Planning D: Society & Space* 10, no. 6 (1992): 651–669; Lawrence Knopp, "Sexuality and Urban Space: A Framework for Analysis," in *Mapping Desire: Geographies of Sexualities*, ed. David Bell and Gill Valentine (New York: Routledge, 1995), 149–161.

89. Max Page, *The Creative Destruction of Manhattan, 1900–1940* (Chicago, IL: University of Chicago Press, 1999).

90. For a similar approach, see Podmore, "Queering Discourses of Urban Decline."

91. For studies of the demise of "maritime quarters" or "sailortowns" composed of a characteristic mix of land uses that served seaman and longshoremen prior to the containerization of the shipping industry, see Stan Hugill, *Sailortown* (New York: E. P. Dutton, 1967); James B. Kenyon, "Land Use Admixture in the Built-Up Urban Waterfront: Extent and Implications," *Economic Geography* 44, no. 2 (1968): 152–177; David Hilling, "Socio-Economic Change in the Maritime Quarter: The Demise of Sailortown," in *Revitalising the Waterfront: International Dimensions of Dockland Redevelopment* (New York: Belhaven Press, 1988), 20–51; Graeme J. Milne, *People, Place and Power in the Nineteenth-Century Waterfront Sailortown* (London: Palgrave Macmillan, 2016).

92. This project grew out of local public history initiatives of the GLBT Historical Society of Northern California and the Friends of 1800. For more, see Damon Scott with Friends of 1800, "Sexing the City: The Development of Sexual Identity Based Subcultures in San Francisco, 1933–1979" (San Francisco, CA: Friends of 1800, 2004), Department of City Planning, https://sfplanning.org/project/lgbtq-historic-context-statement; Donna

J. Graves and Shayne E. Watson, "San Francisco: Placing LGBTQ Histories in the City by the Bay," in *Preservation and Place: Historic Preservation by and of LGBTQ Communities in the United States*, ed. Katherine Crawford-Lackey and Megan E. Springate (New York: Berghahn Books, 2019), 215–254.

93. For more on the methodological, practical, and epistemological issues of using Geographical Information Science (GIS) tools to reconstruct the social and planning history of the waterfront, see Damon Scott, "Queer Cartographies: Urban Redevelopment and the Changing Sexual Geography of Postwar San Francisco," in *Historical Geography, GIScience and Textual Analysis: Landscapes of Time and Place*, ed. Charles Travis, Francis Ludlow, and Ferenc Gyuris (Cham, Switzerland: Springer International Publishing, 2021), 67–84.

94. The GLBT Historical Society collects, transcribes, and preserves a rich collection of oral histories about San Francisco's queer past. I culled most of the personal recollections of the waterfront from these sources, which are cited individually throughout this volume.

95. In the late 1990s, Willie Walker, the managing archivist at the GLBT Historical Society of Northern California, shared with me a compilation of names and addresses of historic queer sites compiled by gay community historians in San Francisco over several decades. I merged Walker's entries with a separate compilation created by Elizabeth A. Armstrong for her book *Forging Gay Identities*. Known as the "Sites Database," this resource has been available to researchers at the GLBT Historical Society since 2002 in the form of a user-friendly FileMaker database with roughly 3,300 entries. I have maintained and updated a separate working copy with additional annotations and sourcing, focused primarily on the origin and fate of waterfront bars from the 1940s to the 1960s. "Queer Bars and Other Establishments in the San Francisco Bay Area," compiled by Willie Walker, Eric Garber, et al. (Microsoft Word files, last modified 1997), personal collection of the author; "San Francisco LGBTQ Businesses and Organizations," compiled by Elizabeth A. Armstrong (Microsoft Access file, last modified 2001), personal collection of the author.

96. "The LCE News," *LCE News*, October 16, 1961. This was the first issue of *LCE News*. For more on Guy Strait and his subsequent publication of the nationwide *Lavender Baedeker* bar guidebook, see Meeker, *Contacts Desired*.

97. On the problematics of locating the sexual and gender subjectivity of historical actors, see Domosh, "With 'Stout Boots and a Stout Heart.'"

98. Jack Loughner, "Tarantino Named Shakedown Artist, Manager of 'Gay' Bar Testifies Defendant Made Personal Call," *San Francisco News*, October 14, 1953, 13.

99. Cultural commentaries and nightlife columns in the *San Francisco Chronicle* in the 1940s and 1950s by Herb Caen and Hal Schaefer frequently used these and other coded terms to differentiate from bars that did not conform to normative heterosexual expectations. The first ethnographic studies of "gay bars" as social institutions appeared in the mid-1950s. See Maurice Leznoff and William A. Westley, "The Homosexual Community," *Social Problems* 3, no. 4 (1956): 257–263; Evelyn Hooker, "A Preliminary Analysis of Group Behavior of Homosexuals," *Journal of Psychology* 42, no. 2 (October 1, 1956): 217–225; Nancy B. Achilles, "The Homosexual Bar" (master's thesis, University of Chicago, 1964). For more on the "discovery" of homosexual social worlds by academics and the public, see Jeffrey Escoffier, *American Homo: Community and Perversity* (Berkeley: University of California Press, 1998); Gayle Rubin, "Studying Sexual Subcultures: The Ethnography of Gay Communities in Urban North America," in *Out in Theory: The*

Emergence of Lesbian and Gay Anthropology, ed. Ellen Lewin and William Leap (Urbana: University of Illinois Press, 2002), 17–68.

100. Meeker, *Contacts Desired*.

101. For an example of the potential of "queer" to differentiate and situate dominant, oppositional, and emergent modes of sexual subjectivity, see Boyd, *Wide Open Town*, 6.

102. See Lauren Berlant and Michael Warner, "Sex in Public," in *Publics and Counterpublics*, ed. Michael Warner (New York: Zone Books, 2002), 203.

103. For examples of this new meaning of "hangouts," see "Three More Bars Placed Off Limits," *San Francisco Chronicle*, November 25, 1954, 14; "State Moves to Shut 4 Gay Bars," *San Francisco Examiner*, August 28, 1956, 27; "State Has Record of 20 Bars as Deviate Hangouts," *San Francisco News–Call Bulletin*, October 13, 1959, SBC, SFPD Records, SFH 61, SHC; "Ruling Is Voided in Bar Closing: Hangout for Homosexuals," *San Francisco Examiner*, December 25, 1959, SBC, SFPD, SHC; "Gayola Hangout Handout Told," *San Francisco News–Call Bulletin*, July 30, 1960, SBC, SFPD, SHC.

CHAPTER 1: THE CHANGING SEXUAL GEOGRAPHY OF THE WATERFRONT

1. Robert, "San Francisco as I See It: Down Memory Lane," *B.A.R.*, September 30, 1976, 19.

2. In 1983, a popular gay bar, Club Dori, held a contest to name the most shuttered gay bars as part of its twenty-first-anniversary celebration. The *San Francisco Sentinel* published the final list, which ran into the hundreds. It included many from the 1940s and 1950s razed to make way for the Golden Gateway and Embarcadero Freeway in the early 1960s. "Club Dori 21st Anniversary," advertisement, *San Francisco Sentinel*, December 8, 1983, 4.

3. Allan Bérubé, *My Desire for History: Essays in Gay, Community, and Labor History*, ed. John D'Emilio and Estelle B. Freedman (Chapel Hill: University of North Carolina Press, 2011); Clayton Howard, *The Closet and the Cul de Sac: The Politics of Sexual Privacy in Northern California* (Philadelphia: University of Pennsylvania Press, 2019), 153–154.

4. Clifford M. Drury, *San Francisco YMCA, 1953–1953: One Hundred Years by the Golden Gate* (Glendale, CA: Arthur H. Clark Company, 1963).

5. Elaine Tyler May, *Homeward Bound: American Families in the Cold War Era*, 4th ed. (New York: Basic Books, 2017); Howard, *Closet and the Cul de Sac*.

6. Margot Canady, *The Straight State: Sexuality and Citizenship in Twentieth-Century America* (Princeton, NJ: Princeton University Press, 2009).

7. David Hilling, "Socio-Economic Change in the Maritime Quarter: The Demise of Sailortown," in *Revitalising the Waterfront: International Dimensions of Dockland Redevelopment* (New York: Belhaven Press, 1988), 23–24.

8. Nancy Olmsted, *The Ferry Building: Witness to a Century of Change, 1898–1998* (San Francisco, CA: Port of San Francisco; Berkeley, CA: Heyday Books, 1998), 110; Jasper Rubin, *A Negotiated Landscape: The Transformation of San Francisco's Waterfront since 1950* (Chicago, IL: Center for American Places at Columbia College, 2011), 32.

9. Olmsted, *The Ferry Building*, 111.

10. Neil Shumsky and Larry M. Springer, "San Francisco Zone of Prostitution, 1880–1934," *Journal of Historical Geography* 7, no. 1 (1981), 71–89.

11. Herbert Asbury, *The Barbary Coast: An Informal History of the San Francisco*

Underworld (New York: Garden City Publishing, 1933); Jack Lait and Lee Mortimer, *U.S.A. Confidential* (New York: Crown, 1952).

12. Graeme J. Milne, *People, Place and Power in the Nineteenth-Century Waterfront Sailortown* (London: Palgrave Macmillan, 2016); James B. Kenyon, "Land Use Admixture in the Built-Up Urban Waterfront: Extent and Implications," *Economic Geography* 44, no. 2 (1968): 152–177; Hilling, "Socio-Economic Change."

13. Michael R. Corbett, *Port City: The History and Transformation of the Port of San Francisco, 1848–2010* (San Francisco, CA: San Francisco Architectural Heritage, 2010), 53; Paul Groth, *Living Downtown: The History of Residential Hotels in the United States* (Berkeley: University of California Press, 1994), 135.

14. Clayton Howard, "Building a 'Family Friendly' Metropolis: Sexuality, the State, and Postwar Housing Policy," *Journal of Urban History* 39, no. 5 (2013): 933–955; Howard, *Closet and the Cul de Sac.*

15. According to the Seamen's Act of 1931, the term "merchant seaman" refers to "anyone employed or engaged to serve in any capacity on board any vessel." Quoted in James C. Healey, *Foc'sle and Glory-Hole: A Study of the Merchant Seaman and His Occupation* (New York: Greenwood Press, 1936), 7. The term is inclusive of personnel in any of the three divisions of the ship's crew: the deck department responsible for general navigation, the engineer's department tasked with tending to the fuel supply and propulsion system, and the steward's department detailed to cater to passengers and other crewmembers. For a more detailed portrait of the occupational structure of merchant marines, see Healey, *Foc'sle and Glory-Hole*, 18–31. Here, and throughout the book, the term "merchant marines" refers to any and all workers aboard commercial vessels. "Sailors" and "seamen" are used interchangeably to refer more generally to both merchant marines in the civilian navy and military servicemen working aboard warships.

16. Marvel Keller, *Decasualization of Longshore Work in San Francisco: Methods and Results for the Control of Dispatching and Hours Worked, 1935–37* (Philadelphia, PA: Works Progress Administration, 1939), 33.

17. See Bruce Nelson, *Workers on the Waterfront: Seamen, Longshoremen, and Unionism in the 1930s* (Urbana: University of Illinois Press, 1990); David F. Selvin, *A Terrible Anger: The 1934 Waterfront Strike and General Strikes in San Francisco* (Detroit, MI: Wayne State University Press, 1996).

18. Keller, *Decasualization of Longshore Work.*

19. Selvin, *Terrible Anger*, 149.

20. Bérubé, *My Desire for History*, 237. This posthumously published collection of Allan Bérubé's essay includes first-person accounts of the extraordinary multiracial and queer solidarity of the MCSU on the San Francisco waterfront from the 1930s to the 1950s. His unpublished monograph holds much promise for an even deeper understanding of the social history of anti-racist, anti-homophobic labor organizing in the maritime trades on the West Coast. For an engaging slide presentation narrated by Bérubé, see "No Red-Baiting! No Race-Baiting! No Queen-Baiting!: The Marine Cooks and Stewards Union from the Depression to the Cold War," OutHistory, 2016, accessed March 8, 2019, http://outhistory.org/exhibits/show/no-baiting/red-race-queen. See also Jane Cassels Record, "The Rise and Fall of a Maritime Union," *Industrial and Labor Relations Review* 10, no. 1 (1956): 81–92.

21. Bérubé, *My Desire for History*, 267.

22. Oceangoing crews are organized into departments based on their primary responsibility, namely navigating and maintaining the vessel, operating the engines, or servicing

the passengers and crew. For more about the nature of queer labor at sea for MCSU members, see Bérubé, *My Desire for History*, 282.

23. A small number of women were able to secure jobs on passenger liners after the war, usually as telephone operators or nurses. Allan Bérubé, "'Queer Work'and Labor History," in Bérubé, *My Desire for History*, 259–269. For more on the gendered division of labor at sea, see Valerie Burton, "The Myth of Bachelor Jack: Masculinity, Patriarchy and Seafaring Labor," in *Jack Tar in History: Essays in the History of Maritime Life and Labour*, ed. Colin Howell and Richard Twomey (Fredericton, New Brunswick: Acadiensis Press, 1991), 179–198.

24. A gay former steward in the MCSU told Bérubé, "I cannot say the stewards were 100 percent gay, but say 65 percent to 70 percent—and everybody knew it!!" Bérubé, *My Desire for History*, 298.

25. Corbett, *Port City*, 69–72.

26. Corbett, *Port City*, 72.

27. Lotchin, *Bad City*, 207.

28. Allan Bérubé, *Coming Out under Fire: The History of Gay Men and Women in World War Two* (New York: Free Press, 1990), 107.

29. Beth Bailey and David Farber, *The First Strange Place: The Alchemy of Race and Sex in World War II Hawaii* (New York: Free Press, 1992); Shumsky and Springer, "San Francisco Zone of Prostitution."

30. John Nichols, "The Way It Was: Gay Life in World War II America," *QQ Magazine* (previously *Queen's Quarterly for Gay Guys*), July/August 1975, 8–11, 51–54.

31. Bérubé, *Coming Out under Fire*; Boyd, *Wide Open Town*.

32. Bérubé, *Coming Out under Fire*. Opened as the Army and Navy YMCA in 1926, the four-hundred-bed facility later became known as the Embarcadero YMCA when merchant marines became the dominant clientele. Drury, *San Francisco YMCA*, 228.

33. Nichols, "Way It Was," 51; Bérubé, *Coming Out under Fire*, 109–110.

34. Bérubé, *Coming Out under Fire*. For more on the longer history of how YMCAs facilitated sexual encounters among men, see George Chauncey, "Christian Brotherhood or Sexual Boundaries in the World War I Era," *Journal of Social History*, no. 9 (Winter 1985): 189–211; George Chauncey, *Gay New York: Gender, Urban Culture, and the Making of the Gay Male World, 1890–1940* (New York: Basic Books, 1994); Nina Mjagkij and Margaret Ann Spratt, eds., *Men and Women Adrift: The YMCA and the YWCA in the City* (New York: New York University Press, 1997); John Donald Gustav-Wrathall, *Take the Young Stranger by the Hand: Same-Sex Relations and the YMCA* (Chicago, IL: University of Chicago Press, 1998).

35. Paul Wonner interviewed by Everett Erlandson, transcript, July 4, 1994, GLBTHS oral history collection, 94–40: GLBT-OHC, GLBTHS, 8–9.

36. Nichols, "Way It Was," 51.

37. Record, "Rise and Fall"; Kimeldorf, "World War II"; Michael Torigian, "National Unity on the Waterfront," *Labor History* 30, no. 3 (Summer 1989): 409–432.

38. Torigian, "National Unity."

39. Kimeldorf, "World War II," 271.

40. Torigian, "National Unity," 424.

41. Bérubé, *My Desire for History*, 246.

42. Bérubé, *My Desire for History*, 282, 314.

43. Bérubé, "No Red-Baiting!"

44. For example, gay diarist Don Vining made several unsuccessful attempts to join

the merchant marines on the East Coast during World War II. As a desk clerk at the Sloane House YMCA in New York, he heard stories of the homosexual subcultures that thrived among sailors in the merchant marines. He also learned that "there were lots of negroes and some Mexicans and many had charges of drunkenness in addition to that of violation of the Selective Service Act" (337). He might have had more success joining in the MCSU in San Francisco, which had a more lax Coast Guard screening process than the National Maritime Union that negotiated labor contracts in eastern ports. See Donald Vining, *A Gay Diary: 1933–1946* (New York: Pepys Press, 1979), 63–64, 77, 82–83, 337.

45. Public morals campaigns targeting sailor bars, and often the lodging rooms frequently connected to them, was neither new nor unique to San Francisco. For more on earlier social reform efforts on the San Francisco waterfront, see Asbury, *Barbary Coast*; Felix Riesenberg, *Golden Gate: The Story of a Harbor* (New York: Alfred A. Knopf, 1940); William Martin Camp, *San Francisco: Port of Gold* (New York: Doubleday, 1947). For similar efforts in other sailortown districts, see Judith Fingard, *Jack in Port: Sailortowns in Eastern Canada* (Toronto: University of Toronto Press, 1982); Milne, *People, Place and Power*.

46. "Program for Seamen on the Beach," *San Francisco Chronicle*, March 6, 1949.

47. Gay men sought out lodgings, social connections, and sex at YMCAs across the country throughout much of the early twentieth century. In the 1940s, New York's Sloan House and the West Side Y were particular well-trafficked counterparts to the Embarcadero Y. See George Chauncey, "Lots of Friends at the YMCA: Rooming Houses, Cafeterias, and Other Gay Social Centers," in *Gay New York: Gender, Urban Culture, and the Making of the Gay Male World, 1890–1940* (New York: Basic Books, 1994), 151–178.

48. Tom Redmon interviewed by Len Evans, transcript, May 17, 1984, GLBTHS oral history collection, 00–03: GLBT-OHC, GLBTHS.

49. Redmon, interview, 22–23.

50. Gerald Fabian interviewed by Bill "Willie" Walker, transcript, November 30, 1989, and January 23, 1990, GLBTHS oral history collection, 94–22: GLBT-OHC, GLBTHS, 93.

51. Justin Spring, *Secret Historian: The Life and Times of Samuel Steward, Professor, Tattoo Artist, and Sexual Renegade* (New York: Farrar, Straus and Giroux, 2010), 173.

52. Spring, *Secret Historian*, 172–177. Quoted from Steward's journals.

53. Spring, *Secret Historian*, 192. Quoted from Steward's journals.

54. "Union Editor in Suicide Attempt," *San Francisco Chronicle*, March 30, 1954, 3.

55. Howard "Allen" Buckley interviewed by Jim Duggins, transcript, October 14, 1994, GLBTHS oral history collection, 94–38: GLBT-OHC, GLBTHS.

56. Buckley, interview, 83–84.

57. Paul Goercke interviewed by Paul Gabriel and Phil Hong, transcript, August 22, 1995, GLBTHS oral history collection, 95–68: GLBT-OHC, GLBTHS, 55.

58. Goercke, interview, 55.

59. Robert Dinsmore interviewed by Jim Duggins, transcript, September 19, 1994, GLBTHS oral history collection, 94–34: GLBT-OHC, GLBTHS, 125.

60. Johnson coined the term "lavender scare" in his history of federal efforts to identify and remove homosexuals from government work at the onset of the Cold War. The Lavender Scare began in 1947 with Republican claims that homosexuals in the State Department undermined national security and dominated federal hiring policies through the 1970s. The nation's second Red Scare paralleled Senator Joseph McCarthy's time in the national spotlight (1950–1954), during which anti-homosexual purges melded with,

but were never completely subsumed by, efforts to remove suspected communists from government employment. David K. Johnson, *The Lavender Scare: The Cold War Persecution of Gays and Lesbians in the Federal Government* (Chicago, IL: University of Chicago Press, 2004), 4.

61. These were the Coast Guard, Navy, and Army. This claim was made in a 1953 policy report on the program. Ralph S. Brown Jr. and John D. Fassett, "Security Test for Maritime Workers: Due Process under the Port Security Program," *Yale Law Journal*, no. 62 (1953): 1163–1208.

62. Brown and Fassett, "Security Test," 1171.

63. Bérubé, *My Desire for History*, 309.

64. Allan Bérubé and John D'Emilio, "The Military and Lesbians during the McCarthy Years," *Signs* 9, no. 4 (July 1984): 759–775; Robert D. Dean, *Imperial Brotherhood: Gender and the Making of Cold War Foreign Policy* (Amherst: University of Massachusetts Press, 2001); Randolph W. Baxter, "'Homo-Hunting' in the Early Cold War: Senator Kenneth Wherry and the Homophobic Side of McCarthyism," *Nebraska History*, no. 84 (2003): 119–132; Johnson, *Lavender Scare*; Canady, *Straight State*; Genny Beemyn, *A Queer Capital: A History of Gay Life in Washington D.C* (New York: Routledge, 2014); Charles, *Hoover's War on Gays*.

65. Torigian, "National Unity," 411.

66. "Ship Unions Won't Extend Contracts," *San Francisco Chronicle*, April 15, 1947, 2.

67. A similarly perceived internal threat to national security—albeit rooted in racism rather than clashing political ideologies and homophobia—led to the removal and internment of nearly 120,000 Japanese Americans from the West Coast during World War II. Craig Robinson, *By Order of the President: FDR and the Internment of Japanese Americans* (Cambridge, MA: Harvard University Press, 2001).

68. Brown and Fassett, "Security Test."

69. "Seamen Loyalty Check: All Sailors on Foreign-Bound Ships Screened to Eliminate 'Subversives,'" *San Francisco Chronicle*, August 1, 1950, 5.

70. "Port Security, All Bay Area Longshoremen to Be Checked by Armed Forces Board," *San Francisco Chronicle*, August 11, 1950.

71. "Water Front Security Check to Start Sept. 5," *San Francisco Chronicle*, August 31, 1950.

72. Exec. Order No. 10,173, 3 C.F.R., 1949–1953 Comp., 356–359.

73. For more on how the FBI concealed its role in compiling and distributing these screening lists—including ordering their eventual destruction—see Charles, *Hoover's War on Gays*; Stuart Timmons, *The Trouble with Harry Hay: Founder of the Modern Gay Movement* (Boston, MA: Alyson Publications, 1990).

74. Bérubé, *My Desire for History*, 316.

75. "Marine Cooks Balk at Security Screening Plan," *San Francisco Chronicle*, August 3, 1950, 11.

76. "65 Stewards Fired over Screening," *San Francisco Chronicle*, August 4, 1950, 17.

77. "Cleveland's Crew Sifted: Nine Marine Cooks Barred as 'Poor Security Risks,'" *San Francisco Chronicle*, August 9, 1950, 1.

78. Johnson, *Lavender Scare*, 105. See also Bérubé, *Coming Out under Fire*, 284–285; Colin J. Williams and Martin S. Weinberg, *Homosexuals and the Military: A Study of Less Than Honorable Discharge* (New York: Harper and Row, 1971); Charles, *Hoover's War on Gays*.

79. Brown and Fassett, "Security Test," 1186.

80. Albert Morris Bendich, "A History of the Marine Cooks' and Stewards' Union" (master's thesis, University of California, Berkeley, 1953), 209.

81. Bendich, "History of the Marine Cooks' and Stewards' Union," 209.

82. Exec. Order No. 10,450, 3 C.F.R. 1949–1953 Comp., 936–940.

83. *Report of the Special Committee on the Federal Loyalty-Security Program of the Association of the Bar of the City of New York* (New York: Dodd, Mead & Co., 1956), 66–67, 221.

84. Williams and Weinberg, *Homosexuals and the Military*, 49.

85. "Bridges Says Stewards Signed Up," *San Francisco Chronicle*, July 31, 1953, 22. The right-wing union was the Sailors' Union of the Pacific, which Bérubé characterized as "antiblack, anticommunist, and antigay." Bérubé, *My Desire for History*, 309.

86. "Union Preference: AFL Stewards Win Coast Schooner Election," *San Francisco Chronicle*, April 21, 1953, 29.

87. Herb Caen, "Herb Caen: It's News to Me," *San Francisco Chronicle*, June 23, 1947, 13.

88. "Negroes Sue over Non-Service," *San Francisco Chronicle*, November 25, 1952, 28.

89. On the social history of slumming, see Chad Heap, *Slumming: Sexual and Racial Encounters in American Life, 1885–1940* (Chicago, IL: University of Chicago Press, 2009).

90. In Sherri Cavan's ethnographic work on gay bars in the city in the early 1960s, she described a subset of them as "homosexual home territory bars," without identifying specific ones. Sherri Cavan, *Liquor License: An Ethnography of Bar Behavior* (Chicago, IL: Aldine Publishing Company, 1966), 208.

91. Larry Howell interviewed by Martin Meeker, transcript, December 17, 1998, to January 14, 1999, GLBTHS oral history collection, 98–040: GLBT-OHC, GLBTHS, 68–17.

92. Howell, interview, 69. The oral history transcript misspelled the names of the four bars as the "Answer Club," "Madam Chilly's," "Sea Cal," and "Lenny's." Based on Howell's description of the location, city directory entries, and newspaper references, he was referring to the Ensign Club, Chili's, the Sea Cow, and Lennie's 36 Club, which were all in operation in the waterfront at the time.

93. Eugene R. Carles interviewed by Jim Duggins, transcript, June 17–20 1994, GLBTHS oral history collection, 94–15: GLBT-OHC, GLBTHS, 49–50.

94. Located at 144 Embarcadero, this place was known as the Embarcadero Café, the 144 Club, or "Chili's" depending on the time and context.

95. Carles, interview, 90.

96. Carles, interview, 90.

97. Gerald Fabian interviewed by Bill "Willie" Walker, transcript, November 20, 1989, and January 23, 1990, GLBTHS oral history collection, 94–22: GLBT-OHC, GLBTHS, 89–90.

98. Glen Price interviewed by Jim Duggins, October 23, 1994, GLBTHS oral history collection, 94–43: GLBT-OHC, GLBTHS, 2–4.

99. Price, interview, 13.

100. Price, interview, 13.

101. Price, interview, 13.

102. Howell, interview, 68–71.

103. Nanette Asimov, "Bob Ross—Pioneering Gay Journalist and Activist," Obituary,

San Francisco Chronicle, December 12, 2003, 29; Bob Ross interviewed by Paul Gabriel, transcript, March 13, 1998, GLBTHS oral history collection, 94–12: GLBT-OHC, GLBTHS.

104. Ross, interview, 80.

105. Ross, interview, 79–80.

106. Selvin, *Terrible Anger*; John Kagel, "The Day the City Stopped," *California History* 63, no. 3 (1984): 212–223.

107. On Bloody Thursday, rioting police officers corralled striking workers onto a stretch of Steuart Street and fired on the crowd, killing two men on the sidewalk around the corner from the ILA headquarters. The event garnered national attention and widespread sympathy strikes that gave the ILA the leverage to set up its own hiring halls. It also galvanized other maritime trades to do the same.

108. Selvin, *Terrible Anger*, 166–167.

109. Eric Marcus, *Making History: The Struggle for Gay and Lesbian Equal Rights, 1945–1990; An Oral History* (New York: HarperCollins, 1992), 68; Martin Meeker, *Contacts Desired: Gay and Lesbian Communications and Community, 1940s–1970s* (Chicago, IL: University of Chicago Press, 2006), 204–205.

110. Community historians at the GLBT Historical Society of Northern California included the sites listed in the Mattachine convention guidebook in a compilation of former gay bars. "Queer Bars and Other Establishments in the San Francisco Bay Area," compiled by Willie Walker, Eric Garber, et al. (Microsoft Word files, last modified 1997), personal collection of the author; "San Francisco LGBTQ Businesses and Organizations," compiled by Elizabeth A. Armstrong (Microsoft Access file, last modified 2001), personal collection of the author.

111. The Mattachine convention guide included this short, campy description of the Sea Cow, which was a social and organizational hub for maritime laborers. Quoted from Walker and Garber, "Queer Bars and Other Establishments."

112. Richard McClure interviewed by Allan Bérubé, transcript, March 12, 1979, World War Two Project, GLBTHS oral history collection, 02–089: GLBT-OHC, GLBTHS, 16.

113. McClure, interview, 16. Although rough trade bars like Jack's contributed to the development of this subculture, the first leather bar in San Francisco was the "Why Not?" bar. For more on San Francisco's early gay male leather culture, see Gayle Rubin, "Valley of the Kings," *San Francisco Sentinel*, September 13, 1984, 10–11; Gayle Rubin, "The Miracle Mile: South of Market and Gay Male Leather, 1962–1997," in *Reclaiming San Francisco: History, Politics, Culture*, ed. James Brook, Chris Carlsson, and Nancy Peters (San Francisco, CA: City Lights Books, 1998), 247–272; Gayle Rubin, "Sites, Settlements, and Urban Sex: Archaeology and the Study of Gay Leathermen in San Francisco, 1955–1995," in *Archaeologies of Sexualities*, ed. Robert A. Schmidt and Barbara L. Voss (New York: Routledge, 2000), 62–88.

114. In November 1954, Mollet bought a liquor license from the former operators of the Silver Dollar to open his 36 Club. For liquor license changes associated with 36 Embarcadero, see "Notice of Intention to Engage in the Sale of Alcoholic Beverages, 36 Embarcadero, On Sale General, Laura Erickson and Agnes Johnson," legal notice, *San Francisco Chronicle*, June 18, 1952, 29; "Notice of Intention to Engage in the Sale of Alcoholic Beverages, 36 Embarcadero, On Sale General, Leonard J. Mollet and Robert R. Bivens," legal notice, *San Francisco Chronicle*, November 23, 1954, 30. According to

city directories, the Silver Dollar had been operated by the Sammon family at that address since 1943. *Polk City Directory*, various years, ARCV.

115. "Three More Bars Placed Off Limits," *San Francisco Chronicle*, November 25, 1954, 14. According to the *Chronicle*, the liquor license was registered to the Silver Dollar at 64 Eddy.

116. Both Larry Howell and Glen Price recalled Mollet operating his club at 36 Embarcadero before a series of subsequent, better-known, commercial enterprises associated with the gay male leather scene. Duggins remembered Mollett as an "old leather queen." Price, interview, 6–7; Howell, interview, 53. Duggins aside quoted in Carles, interview, 87.

117. Ross, interview, 9. Over a forty-year period, Mollet ran "Lennie's 36 Club," 36 Embarcadero (1954–1955); "On the Levee," 987 Embarcadero (1964–1972); and "Off the Levee" at 527 Bryant (1968–1994). Walker and Garber, "Queer Bars and Other Establishments." Mollet was president of the Tavern Guild, an organization of gay bar operators in the 1970s. "Gay Bar Group Elects New Leader," *San Francisco Chronicle*, July 12, 1978, 3.

118. Arch J. Wilson interviewed by Jim Duggins, transcript, July 27 to August 10, 1994, GLBTHS oral history collection, 94–23: GLBT-OHC, GLBTHS.

119. Wilson, interview, 37–38.

120. Jim Kepner interviewed by Allan Bérubé, transcript, June 2, 1981, World War Two Oral History Project, GLBTHS oral history collection, 02–066: GLBT-OHC, GLBTHS, 3–4.

121. "Friendly S. P. May Take Down Its Sign," *San Francisco Chronicle*, August 11, 1961; "A Sign's Last Days," *San Francisco*, April 6, 1963.

122. Jim Duggins personal recollections, June 30, 1995, GLBTHS oral history collection, 95–54: GLBT-OHC, GLBTHS.

123. Quoted from an aside by Duggins during an oral history interview. George Mende interviewed by Jim Duggins, transcript, November 24, 1994, GLBTHS oral history collection, 94–49: GLBT-OHC, GLBTHS, 31.

124. Jim Kirkman interviewed by Jim Duggins, transcript, May 7, 1995, GLBTHS oral history collection, 95–48: GLBT-OHC, GLBTHS, 28.

125. Duggins, interview, 34.

126. David Harrell interviewed by Terence Kissack, transcript, August 13, 2000, GLBTHS oral history collection, 00–004: GLBT-OHC, GLBTHS, 29.

127. Harrell, interview, 29.

CHAPTER 2: THE BIRTHPLACE OF MODERN SAN FRANCISCO

1. Jim Dempsey, "Berkeley Police Brand Aquatic Park Moral Cesspool," *Berkeley Daily Gazette*, February 20, 1958, 1, 2; Jim Dempsey, "Cleanup Begins: City in High Gear to Clean Up Sex Problems in Area," *Berkeley Daily Gazette*, February 21, 1958; "Police Gain in Drive on Aquatic Park Vice," *San Francisco Chronicle*, May 1, 1958, 1, 2. Sex in public park restrooms was common enough to have its own vernacular terminology—the "tearoom trade" in the United States and "cottaging" in the UK. See George Chauncey, *Gay New York: Gender, Urban Culture, and the Making of the Gay Male World, 1890–1940* (New York: Basic Books, 1994).

2. Officials ultimately opted for rehabilitation, police surveillance, undercover

entrapment operations, and brush clearing. Arrests jumped 500 percent. "Police Gain in Drive." Stepped-up policing was ineffective in ending the tearoom trade at Aquatic Park, even as it became more violent. Ten years later, a patrolman shot and killed a man in the process of arresting him for a sex offense at the park. "Homo Death: Group Will Act," *Berkeley Barb*, May 2, 1969, 11.

3. Clayton Howard, "Policing and Redeveloping the Queer City," in Howard, *The Closet and the Cul de Sac: The Politics of Sexual Privacy in Northern California* (Philadelphia: University of Pennsylvania Press, 2019), 148–181.

4. John D'Emilio, *Sexual Politics, Sexual Communities: The Making of a Homosexual Minority in the United States, 1940–1970* (Chicago, IL: University of Chicago Press, 1983); Nan Alamilla Boyd, *Wide Open Town: A History of Queer San Francisco to 1965* (Berkeley: University of California Press, 2003).

5. Crime exposés in national pulp publications underscored and popularized this reputation. For example, see Jack Lait and Lee Mortimer, *U.S.A. Confidential* (New York: Crown, 1952); Eldon Bearden and Terry Hansen, "Don't Call Us 'Queer City,'" *Men*, April 1955. For more on the significance of media representations of the city in growing same-sex social networks, see Meeker, *Contacts Desired: Gay and Lesbian Communications and Community, 1940s–1970s* (Chicago, IL: University of Chicago Press, 2006).

6. Paul Groth, *Living Downtown: The History of Residential Hotels in the United States* (Berkeley: University of California Press, 1994). For more on the close association between gay urban culture and "bachelor" housing in New York, see Chauncey, *Gay New York*.

7. Howard, *Closet and the Cul de Sac*, 180.

8. Harvey Molotch, "The City as Growth Machine," *American Journal of Sociology*, no. 82 (1979): 309–332; Marc A. Weiss, "The Origins and Legacy of Urban Renewal," in *Urban and Regional Planning in an Age of Austerity*, ed. Pierre Clavel, John Forester, and William W. Goldsmith (New York: Pergamon Press, 1980), 53–80; Nancy Kleniewski, "From Industrial to Corporate City: The Role of Urban Renewal," in *Marxism and the Metropolis: New Perspectives in Urban Political Economy*, ed. William K. Tabb and Larry Sawyers (New York: Oxford University Press, 1984), 205–222; Gregory D. Squires, ed., *Unequal Partnerships: The Political Economy of Urban Redevelopment in Postwar America* (New Brunswick, NJ: Rutgers University Press, 1989); John R. Logan, Rachel Bridges Whaley, and Kyle Crowder, "The Character and Consequences of Growth Regimes: An Assessment of 20 Years of Research," *Urban Affairs Review* 32, no. 5 (1997): 603–630; Kevin Fox Gotham, "Growth Machine Up-Links: Urban Renewal and the Rise and Fall of a Pro-Growth Coalition in a U.S. City," *Critical Sociology* 26, no. 3 (2000): 268–300.

9. Mel Scott, *The San Francisco Bay Area: A Metropolis in Perspective*, 2nd ed. (Berkeley: University of California Press, 1985); Chester Hartman and Sarah Carnochan, *City for Sale: The Transformation of San Francisco*, rev. and updated ed. (Berkeley: University of California Press, 2002); Michael R. Corbett, *Port City: The History and Transformation of the Port of San Francisco, 1848–2010* (San Francisco, CA: San Francisco Architectural Heritage, 2010); Jasper Rubin, *A Negotiated Landscape: The Transformation of San Francisco's Waterfront since 1950* (Chicago, IL: Center for American Places at Columbia College, 2011); Alison Isenberg, *Designing San Francisco: Art, Land, and Urban Renewal in the City by the Bay* (Princeton, NJ: Princeton University Press, 2017).

10. A number of works on urban governance in San Francisco highlight the impact of a pro-growth coalition of business leaders in shaping the trajectory of postwar urban development. The origins of the coalition, however, are less clear. John H. Mollenkopf, *The Contested City* (Princeton, NJ: Princeton University Press, 1983); Stephen J.

McGovern, *The Politics of Downtown Development: Dynamic Political Cultures in San Francisco and Washington* (Lexington: University Press of Kentucky, 1998); Chester Hartman and Sarah Carnochan, *City for Sale: The Transformation of San Francisco*, rev. and updated ed. (Berkeley: University of California Press, 2002); Ocean Howell, *Making the Mission: Planning and Ethnicity in San Francisco* (Chicago, IL: University of Chicago Press, 2015).

11. Rubin, *Negotiated Landscape*.

12. "Here Are Whys, Wherefores: Value of Park Told," *San Francisco News*, October 3, 1956, 1. The archives of the San Francisco Redevelopment Agency, maintained by its successor agency, and the GLBT Historical Society of Northern California have been especially useful in reconstructing the impact of urban redevelopment on the queer social history of the waterfront.

13. "Port Security Comes First," *San Francisco Chronicle*, December 28, 1950.

14. For example, see "Three More Bars Placed Off Limits," *San Francisco Chronicle*, November 25, 1954, 14; "State Moves to Shut 4 Gay Bars," *San Francisco Examiner*, August 28, 1956, 27; "State Has Record of 20 Bars as Deviate Hangouts," *San Francisco News–Call Bulletin*, October 13, 1959, SBC, SFPD Records, SFH 61, SHC; "Ruling Is Voided in Bar Closing: Hangout for Homosexuals," *San Francisco Examiner*, December 25, 1959, SBC, SFPD, SHC.

15. Henry Evans, *Bohemian San Francisco* (San Francisco, CA: The Porpoise Bookshop, 1955). The postwar significance of the Black Cat as a key site of queer social and political life, as well as major legal battles over the right of businesses to serve homosexual patrons, is well documented. See D'Emilio, *Sexual Politics*; William N. Eskridge Jr., "Privacy Jurisprudence and the Apartheid of the Closet, 1946–1961," *Florida State University Law Review* 24, no. 4 (1997): 703–839; Boyd, *Wide Open Town*; Christopher Lowen Agee, *The Streets of San Francisco: Policing and the Creation of a Cosmopolitan Liberal Politics, 1950–72* (Chicago, IL: University of Chicago Press, 2014).

16. Gerald Fabian interviewed by Bill "Willie" Walker, transcript, November 20, 1989, and January 23, 1990, GLBTHS oral history collection, 94–22: GLBT-OHC, GLBTHS, 80.

17. "Six Arrested in Black Cat Bar Raid," *San Francisco Chronicle*, September 4, 1947, 12.

18. This shift began in earnest in 1949. Douglas M. Charles, *Hoover's War on Gays: Exposing the FBI's "Sex Deviates" Program* (Lawrence: University of Kansas Press, 2015); David K. Johnson, *The Lavender Scare: The Cold War Persecution of Gays and Lesbians in the Federal Government* (Chicago, IL: University of Chicago Press, 2004).

19. Herb Caen, "Herb Caen: It's News to Me," *San Francisco Chronicle*, November 4, 1947, 13.

20. Herb Caen, "It's News to Me," *San Francisco Chronicle*, June 23, 1947, 13.

21. Evans, *Bohemian San Francisco*, 16.

22. Stuart Loomis interviewed by Allan Bérubé, transcript, March 24, 1980, World War Two Oral History Project, GLBTHS oral history collection, 02–082: GLBT-OHC, GLBTHS, 15.

23. Charles Gilman interviewed by Allan Bérubé, transcript, January 20, 1981, GLBTHS oral history collection, 02–047: GLBT-OHC, GLBTHS, 4.

24. Gilman, interview, 2.

25. "Black Cat Wins Round in Bar Fight," *San Francisco Chronicle*, August 29, 1951, 13.

26. "Homos Invade S.F.!," *The Truth*, July 11, 1949. See also Nan Alamilla Boyd, "'Homos Invade S.F.!': San Francisco's History as a Wide-Open Town," in Brett Beemyn, *Creating a Place for Ourselves* (New York: Routledge, 1997), 73–95; Agee, *Streets of San Francisco*, 84–85.

27. Evans, *Bohemian San Francisco*, 16.

28. Agee, *Streets of San Francisco*, 84–85.

29. Herb Caen, "It's News to Me," *San Francisco Chronicle*, April 4, 1947, 13.

30. "Sad Day on Montgomery St.: Black Cat's License Lifted in Morals Case," *San Francisco Chronicle*, October 15, 1949.

31. Quoted from formal allegation lodged against Stoumen by state liquor agents in "Sad Day on Montgomery."

32. "Recipe for a Restaurant," *San Francisco Chronicle Gourmet Guide*, May 7, 1951, 20.

33. Boyd, *Wide Open Town*, 123.

34. "Police Jail, Warn Sex Deviates in Full Scale Drive; S.F. Meeting Places Hit," *San Francisco Examiner*, June 27, 1954, 1.

35. "Military Aids S.F. Drive on Sex Deviates," *San Francisco Examiner*, July 1, 1954, 1.

36. "Market Street Action on Honkytonks Urged," *San Francisco Examiner*, October 12, 1954, 1.

37. Otto Bremerman interviewed by Everett Erlandson, transcript, November 14, 1994, GLBTHS oral history collection, 94–31: GLBT-OHC, GLBTHS, 50.

38. Allan Bérubé, *Coming Out under Fire: The History of Gay Men and Women in World War Two* (New York: Free Press, 1990); Johnson, *Lavender Scare*; Charles, *Hoover's War on Gays*.

39. Howard, *Closet and the Cul de Sac*.

40. For more on the state liquor licensing reforms, see Nan Alamilla Boyd, "Policing Queers in the 1940s and 1950s: Harrassment, Prosecution, and the Legal Defense of Gay Bars," in *Wide Open Town*, 108–147.

41. "Liquor Board under Study," *San Francisco Examiner*, October 3, 1953, 6; "Weinberger Committee Urges Drastic Changes in State Liquor Control Setup," *San Francisco News*, February 5, 1954, 3.

42. Code quoted in Boyd, *Wide Open Town*, 137.

43. This is corroborated by similar parallels between liquor enforcement and redevelopment priorities in Los Angeles and Sacramento. *California's New Department of Alcoholic Beverage Control: A Report of the Assembly Interim Committee on Government Organization to the California Legislature, February 8, 1957*, Subject Files—Weinberger Committee—1955–1957 folder, F3718:370, ABCB Records, CSA.

44. During its first two years, the Agency took closure action against 9 of the 12 bars along Pacific Street in North Beach, 41 of 155 bars in the Tenderloin, and 36 of 107 bars South of Market. *California's New Department*, Charts 5–10.

45. For more on the roots and impact of this crackdown, see Boyd, "Wide Open Town," 133–146.

46. "Queer Bars and Other Establishments in the San Francisco Bay Area," compiled by Willie Walker, Eric Garber, et al. (Microsoft Word files, last modified 1997), personal collection of the author; "San Francisco LGBTQ Businesses and Organizations," compiled by Elizabeth A. Armstrong (Microsoft Access file, last modified 2001), personal collection of the author.

47. Weinberger withdrew from consideration due to conflicts of interest related to representing property owners in urban renewal project areas. See Hartman and Carnochan, *City for Sale*, 17.

48. "Bunny Breckenridge Arrested as Vagrant," *San Francisco Chronicle*, May 16, 1955, 3; "Vagrancy Charges against 'Bunny' Breckenridge Dropped," *San Francisco Chronicle*, May 27, 1955, 3; Dal McIntire, "Tangents," *ONE Magazine*, August 1955, 11. See also Joanne Meyerowitz, *How Sex Changed America: A History of Transsexuality in America* (Cambridge, MA: Harvard University Press, 2002), 84–85.

49. Chad Heap, *Slumming: Sexual and Racial Encounters in American Life, 1885–1940* (Chicago, IL: University of Chicago Press, 2009); Scott Herring, *Queering the Underworld: Slumming, Literature, and the Undoing of Lesbian and Gay History* (Chicago, IL: University of Chicago Press, 2007); Kevin J. Mumford, *Interzones: Black/White Sex Districts in Chicago and New York in the Early Twentieth Century* (New York: Columbia University Press, 1997).

50. This claim is based on extensive newspaper database searches, police scrapbooks of news clippings, legal proceedings, and oral histories.

51. "Urban Redevelopment Bill Signed by Warren Important to S.F.," *Bay Region Business*, July 19, 1945, ARCV.

52. "Produce Market Site Is Object of Chamber Study," *Bay Region Business*, January 10, 1952, 3, ARCV; Frank Lombardi and Marie Carlberg, *Relocating the San Francisco Wholesale Produce Market* (San Francisco, CA: Department of City Planning, August 1953), ARCV. For more on urban food-market redevelopment initiatives during this era, see Gregory Donofrio, "Attacking Distribution: Obsolescence and Efficiency of Food Markets in the Age of Urban Renewal," *Journal of Planning History* 13, no. 2 (May 1, 2014): 136–159.

53. Jackson Doyle, "State Okays Waterfront Freeway," *San Francisco Chronicle*, August 22, 1952, 1.

54. Tadeusz B. Spitzer, *World Trade Center in San Francisco* (San Francisco, CA: Board of State Harbor Commissioners, 1947).

55. Los Angeles insisted on its own World Trade Center complex, undercutting San Francisco's pitch to prospective tenants. A state agency owned the waterfront land slated for the project and oversaw the financing. State highway engineers had to sign off on new routes.

56. William Richards, "'Frisco's 25 Streets of Sin," *Men*, May 1954, 17.

57. Richards, "'Frisco's 25 Streets," 47.

58. Mel Scott, *Western Addition District: An Exploration of the Possibilities of Replanning and Rebuilding One of San Francisco's Largest Blighted Districts under the California Community Redevelopment Act of 1945* (San Francisco, CA: San Francisco City Planning Commission, 1947), ARCV.

59. Arthur Caylor, "Use State Oil Funds for S.F. Development," *San Francisco News*, April 13, 1954, 13.

60. See Roy Lubove, "The Pittsburgh Renaissance: An Experiment in Public Paternalism," in *Twentieth-Century Pittsburgh: Government, Business, and Environmental Change* (Pittsburgh, PA: University of Pittsburgh Press, 1996), 106–141; John F. Bauman and Edward Muller, *Before Renaissance: Planning in Pittsburgh, 1889–1943* (Pittsburgh, PA: University of Pittsburgh, 2006); Sara Stevens, *Developing Expertise: Architecture and Real Estate in Metropolitan America* (New Haven, CT: Yale University Press, 2016), 113–129.

61. At the time, San Francisco's political influence in Sacramento was waning due to

population growth in Southern California and East Bay cities. This posed a problem for the city's proponents of waterfront redevelopment, because the state owned and managed San Francisco's port facilities.

62. For a comprehensive history and analysis of how this transformation unfolded all along the waterfront during the second half of the twentieth century, see Rubin, *Negotiated Landscape*. With freeway access to the heart of downtown and a modern landscape of office towers and residential complexes, the Golden Gateway transformed the port city into the finance and administrative hub of an expanding metropolitan region in the 1960s.

63. Caylor, "Use State Oil Funds."

64. Frank R. Ford, "Caylor's New Dream," *San Francisco News*, April 14, 1954, 22.

65. Ford, "Caylor's New Dream."

66. "The City's Front Need Not Be So Far, Far Behind," *San Francisco News*, July 24, 1954, 3.

67. Mary Ellen Leary, "Port Director Supports Plan to Beautify Embarcadero," *San Francisco News*, August 24, 1954, 3.

68. "California Ports Linked to Defense," *New York Times*, April 21, 1948, 55; "Gen. Robert Wylie, Headed Coast Ports," *New York Times*, January 4, 1964, 23.

69. "Dr. Sox Tells Produce Market It's Time to Clean Up—Or Else," *San Francisco Chronicle*, September 8, 1954, 14.

70. "Store Is Ordered Out of the Building; Sox Acts after Inspector Reports 'Sinking in the Middle,'" *San Francisco News*, April 8, 1954, 3; "Dr. Sox Tells Produce Market It's Time"; Richard Reinhardt, "Produce Mart Sanitation Report Asked," *San Francisco Chronicle*, September 9, 1954, 1, 6.

71. Handwritten note, "list for fiscal" of demolished hotel rooms, February 8, 1963, box CSR-483, "Relocation Payments G.G." folder, Central Records and Archives Division Records, SFRAR.

72. Arthur Caylor, "Arthur Caylor," *San Francisco News*, December 21, 1954, newspaper clippings files, SFRAR.

73. For more on the planning and design history of urban food-market redevelopment initiatives during this period, see Donofrio, "Attacking Distribution."

74. "40-Story World Trade Center Urged for Ferry Building Site: Substitute Location, Authority Approves Study of $15,000,000 Structure at Foot of Market Street," *San Francisco Chronicle*, January 22, 1948, 1, 12.

75. "San Francisco World Trade Center: A Progress Report," *City-County Record*, May 1952, ARCV; "The Ferry Building Will House the World Trade Center," *San Francisco Chronicle*, December 19, 1952, 3; "'Indifference' Perils World Trade Center," *San Francisco Chronicle*, September 15, 1955, 1.

76. "'Indifference' Perils World Trade Center."

77. Peter Trimble, "Jurisdictional War Breaks Out on the Waterfront: Curran Opens CIO Drive to Organize Marine Cooks," *San Francisco Chronicle*, January 13, 1951; Albert Morris Bendich, "A History of the Marine Cooks' and Stewards' Union" (master's thesis, University of California, Berkeley, 1953), 209.

78. Dick Nolan, "Slum Law Aid Asked in Produce Area Shift," *San Francisco Examiner*, September 24, 1954; "Mayor Back from D.C.—'Slum Plan Aid Likely,'" *San Francisco Chronicle*, September 28, 1954.

79. Paul Oppermann to John McGrath, staff report from city planning director to Board of Supervisors clerk, "Wholesale Produce Market Area, South Basin Housing

Project Area, A Report Recommending Designation of Two Redevelopment Areas under Provisions of the California Community Redevelopment Act," December 2, 1954, "Golden Gateway" folder, box PLN-778, Planning Division Records, SFRAR.

80. Oppermann, "Wholesale Produce Market Area," 5.

81. Dick Nolan, "Board Votes Shift of Produce Market, Area Termed Blighted," *San Francisco Examiner*, February 22, 1955, 1, 9; Dick Chase, "Produce Market Called 'Blighted,' Supervisors Act on 28-Block Area," *San Francisco News*, February 22, 1955, newspaper clippings files, SFRAR.

82. Oppermann, "Wholesale Produce Market Area," 5.

83. Boyd, *Wide Open Town*.

84. "Remove Blighted Housing in South Basin, RA Urges," *San Francisco News*, August 1, 1956, NCF, SFRAR.

85. The mayor declared "war" on the produce market in the summer of 1956 in an unsuccessful attempt to use strict code enforcement to persuade merchants to voluntarily build and relocate to a new purpose-built wholesale produce district. See "Strict Law Enforcement, City Crackdown Set on Produce Sellers," *San Francisco Chronicle*, July 11, 1956, 2; "Produce Crackdown May Widen," *San Francisco Chronicle*, July 12, 1956, NCF, SFRAR; "Produce Man Warns of Market Problem," *San Francisco News*, July 12, 1956, NCF, SFRAR; "Push Produce Mart Shift; Survey OK'd," *San Francisco Call–Bulletin*, August 3, 1956, 5; "Holdouts to New Produce Area Relent: Merchants Group Will Study Proposed Sites," *San Francisco Examiner*, August 3, 1956, NCF, SFRAR.

86. Hartman and Carnochan, *City for Sale*.

87. Hartman and Carnochan, *City for Sale*, 8–10.

88. De Leuw Cather & Company and Ladislas Segoe Associates, *Report to the San Francisco Planning Commission on a Transportation Plan for San Francisco* (San Francisco, CA: San Francisco Planning Commission, November 1948), ARCV. According to the *San Francisco Chronicle*, the consultants anticipated that "traffic along the northern end of the Embarcadero would not warrant this construction for another 25 years." "Six Freeways Included in Transit Plan," *San Francisco Chronicle*, August 13, 1948.

89. The Council was underwritten by six Bay Area firms that endorsed regional cooperation among San Francisco–area governments and businesses in an effort to successfully compete against Los Angeles and Seattle for new plant locations and trade activity. Those firms were: Pacific Gas & Electric, Bechtel Construction, Bank of America, Columbia Company of the U.S. Steel Corporation, American Trust Company, and Standard Oil Company of California. On the BAC's interest in the Embarcadero Freeway, see Letter from BAC General Manager Frank Marsh, reproduced in full as part of front matter of Ralph A. Tudor, *A Preliminary Report to Department of Public Works on Alterations & Approaches to the San Francisco–Oakland Bay Bridge as Suggested by the San Francisco Bay Area Council, Inc. to the California Toll Bridge Authority on October 17, 1949* (San Francisco, CA: Division of Bay Toll Crossings, 1949), HATHIDigital Library.

90. "Embarcadero Freeway Hearing to Be Held January 20," *San Francisco Chronicle*, December 19, 1952; "Embarcadero Freeway Plans Set," *San Francisco Chronicle*, January 21, 1953.

91. "Embarcadero Freeway Plans Set."

92. "Chamber Urges Approval of Embarcadero Freeway," *Bay Region Business*, January 22, 1953, ARCV.

93. "Approving Freeway Agreement Declaring Certain Sections of State Highway

Route No. 224 to Be a Freeway, and Authorizing Chief Administrative Officer and Director of Public Works to Execute Said Document," *Journal of Proceedings of the Board of Supervisors, City and County of San Francisco* 48, no. 21 (May 18, 1953): 411–412, ARCV.

94. "Highway Program Presented Today," *Bay Area Region*, August 20, 1953; "Recommendations: San Francisco and Alameda Counties Submit Projects to Highway Commission," *California Highways and Public Works*, September/October 1953, ARCV.

95. "Recommendations," 45.

96. B. W. Booker, "Bay Area Freeways: Multi-Million Dollar Program of Construction under Way," *California Highways and Public Works*, no. 33 (March–April 1954): 15, ARCV.

97. The text of this Board resolution to fund a feasibility study for the State Ferry Building Park (Resolution 15,314) was reproduced in the first design proposal for the project. *Joint Committee of the Northern California Chapter of the AIA and the California Association of Landscape Architects, Ferry Building State Park: A Proposal for a State Park at San Francisco's Historic Ferry Building, Submitted to the California State Park Commission* (San Francisco, CA: Citizen's Committee for a Ferry Building State Park, 1955).

98. For more on this early set of design proposals to beautify the Embarcadero Freeway, see Vernon DeMars, "The Embarcadero Freeway vs. The Ferry Building Park, Selected Correspondence and News Clippings from August 1955 to December 1957," annotated clippings file, Vernon DeMars Collection, EDA.

99. *Joint Committee.* At the meeting, the business community was represented by Jerd Sullivan, president of the Crocker First National Bank, and Thomas Mellon, president of the San Francisco Chamber of Commerce. The Committee also included Cyril Magnin, president of the State Board of Harbor Commissioners; Edward V. Mills, president of the Downtown Association; William G. Merchant, architect; Eugene Riordan, executive director of the San Francisco Redevelopment Agency; Paul Opperman, director of the City Planning Department; and Benjamin Swig, hotelier and real estate developer.

100. The Commission's role was to vet local proposals for investing tidelands funds in shoreline improvements throughout the state and make funding recommendations to the governor and state legislature.

101. Vernon DeMars, representing the Northern California Chapter of the AIA, headed the committee of consulting architects that also included William G. Merchant, who had proposed plans for an adjacent world trade center complex. Theodore Osmundson, of the California Institute of Landscape Architects, headed the landscape architecture group.

102. This proposal ultimately won $200,000 in preliminary planning funds in 1955 and $2,000,000 the following year for what became the San Francisco Maritime State Historical Monument in 1958. Isenberg, *Designing San Francisco*, 51–52.

103. *Joint Committee.*

104. Although the revocation attempt received lots of coverage, the Ensign Café continued to operate as a multi-story queer nightlife complex, largely unchecked and under the same management, for ten more years. Jackson Doyle, "Liquor Policy Gets Severe: Revocation of 2 S.F. Bar Permits Asked," *San Francisco Chronicle*, March 11, 1953, 4; "State Board Gets Tough with Bars: 4 Licenses Revoked; 82 Suspended," *San Francisco Chronicle*, March 13, 1953, 1, 12; Jackson Doyle, "Two S.F. Bars Are Closed by State, Licenses Revoked (for Good)," *San Francisco Chronicle*, April 3, 1953, 1, 8.

105. "Notice of Intention to Engage in the Sale of Alcoholic Beverages, 36 Embarcadero, on Sale General, Leonard J. Mollet and Robert R. Bivens," legal notice, *San Francisco Chronicle*, November 23, 1954, 30.

106. "Armed Forces Lift Ban on Four Clubs," *San Francisco Chronicle*, October 28, 1955.

107. Bearden and Hansen, "Don't Call Us 'Queer City,'" 11–13, 60–63. The story was related by Bearden to Terry Hansen during a ride-along tour of policing activities.

108. DeMars, "Embarcadero Freeway."

109. Quitclaim deed, "L. J. Mollet, a Single Man, to the State of California," recorded December 23, 1955, book 6759, page 213, CCSF, SFOAR.

110. George Dorsey, *Christopher of San Francisco* (New York: Macmillan, 1962).

111. "City Opens Its Produce Mart 'War,'" *San Francisco News*, April 4, 1956, newspaper clippings files, SFRAR; "Police Assail Produce Mart, Law Violations Cited in Report," *San Francisco News*, May 31, 1956, newspaper clippings files, SFRAR; "Strict Law Enforcement, City Crackdown"; Russ Cone, "Mayor Opens War on Produce Area; Police Action Set, Merchants Face Code Crackdown Wednesday," *San Francisco Examiner*, August 11, 1956, 1, 6; Richard Reinhardt, "All-Out War Declared on Produce Area," *San Francisco Chronicle*, August 11, 1956, newspaper clippings files, SFRAR.

112. "Nonproduce Group Raps 'Blight' Label," *San Francisco Examiner*, September 1, 1956, newspaper clippings files, SFRAR.

113. State redevelopment laws would ensure more local control over the acquisition and disposition of land, as well as the financing mechanism. Local bankers preferred a revolving fund using municipal bonds, rather than federal loans and grants that came with lots of conditions and oversight. "Alioto Says U.S. Rejected His Offer to Quit S.F. Agency Post," *San Francisco Examiner*, April 11, 1956, newspaper clippings files, SFRAR; Michael Harris, "Mayor Defends Produce Area Plan, Takes Dig at Alioto," *San Francisco Chronicle*, November 7, 1956, 16.

114. Dorsey, *Christopher of San Francisco*, 166–174.

115. "Meeting Announcements and Minutes of the Redevelopment Coordinating Committee of the San Francisco Chamber of Commerce (formerly known as the Special Produce Market Committee and the Coordinating Committee on Produce Market Area Redevelopment), December 2, 1955, to May 6, 1959," SFRAR.

116. For more on the impact of the Blyth-Zellerbach Committee on early urban redevelopment initiatives, see Hartman and Carnochan, *City for Sale*. See also "New Shape," *Time*, September 7, 1959.

117. "Freeway Tunnel in Front of Ferry May Bring City a $2 Million Bonus," *San Francisco Chronicle*, August 15, 1956, 20; "Plan Fans Hopes for Ferry Bldg.," *San Francisco Chronicle*, July 31, 1956, 14.

118. Dick Nolan, "Supervisors Hit Use of Tolls to Remove Key Rails," *San Francisco Examiner*, May 29, 1956; "Ferry Bldg. Freeway Delay for Sake of Park Denied," *San Francisco Chronicle*, June 9, 1956, 2; Mary Ellen Leary, "Architect Works on Co-Ordinated Park-Freeway Plan," *San Francisco News* (San Francisco), May 20, 1957, n.p., NCF, Ciampi Papers, EDA. A second "gift" was earmarked for a market analysis of potential new land uses for lower Market Street. Real Estate Research Corporation, *Market Analysis of Redevelopment Area "E,"* San Francisco, California, Prepared for the San Francisco City Planning Commission, 1956, ARCV.

119. Leary, "Architect Works on Co-Ordinated Park-Freeway Plan"; Francis B.

O'Gara, "$2,000,000 State Funds Refused for Ferry Park," *San Francisco Examiner*, August 24, 1957, 1, 6, NCF, Ciampi Papers, EDA; "Fifth Annual Design Awards Program 1958: Planning Award Citation for Ferry Park Project," *Progressive Architecture* 34, no. 1 (January 1958): 124.

120. The Committee members were Harold L. Zellerbach (chair); Alan K. Browne (cochair), Lawrence Lackey (cochair), Albert E. Schlesinger (cochair), Walter A. Haas (treasurer). Zellerbach to Mayor George Christopher, "Complete Report of Campaign Activities on Behalf of Proposition C . . . ," November 13, 1958, letter, box 5, folder 3, George Christopher Papers, SHC.

121. "Golden Gateway, Ferry Bldg. Bond Rally," *San Francisco Call-Bulletin*, October 22, 1958, 14.

122. Zellerbach, "Complete Report of Campaign Activities," 1.

123. "Call-Bulletin Recommendations," *Call-Bulletin*, October 24, 1958, 1.

124. This local chapter was a successor to the more radical MCSU that had been destroyed by the port screening program and right-wing reorganization campaign five years earlier. Mayor Christopher marked up a draft press release with "should have at least one labor man on committee for publicity . . . the names being reported are too downtown." Memo and Edits to "Suggested Draft of Mayor's Statement and Press Release" from Mayor Christopher to Joseph Paul, August 1959, San Francisco History Center, San Francisco Public Library.

125. The BZC featured Born's sketches in its history of urban planning in San Francisco, published to coincide with the completion of the Crown Zellerbach Building, the city's first new office tower since the 1930s. Steven Warshaw, *The City of Gold: The Story of City Planning in San Francisco* (San Francisco, CA: Crown Zellerbach Corporation, 1960).

126. "500 Expected to Join Campaign to Build Market Street 4-Acre Park," *San Francisco Examiner*, September 9, 1959, 4.

127. Joseph Paul, press release for Ferry Park bonds, August 18, 1959, box 5, folder 3, George Christopher Papers, SHC.

128. San Francisco had a series of nationally recognized freeway revolts in the late 1950s in which local leaders blocked planned highway routes and rejected state and federal roadbuilding funds. The extension of the Embarcadero Freeway past Broadway was stopped soon after the first leg opened in 1958. Tom Mathews, "Bitter Fight Brews over City Freeways," *San Francisco Chronicle*, March 16, 1955, 6; "Legislative Response: S.F. May Lose $377 Million by Freeway Action," *San Francisco Chronicle*, January 28, 1959, 1; Jack Burby, "Unanimous Action: Board Kills Plans for 6 S.F. Freeways," *San Francisco Chronicle*, January 27, 1959, 1; "Fury over the Freeways," *Newsweek*, February 16, 1959. For more on San Francisco's freeway revolts, see William H. Lathrop, "San Francisco Freeway Revolt," *Transportation Engineering Journal: Proceedings of the American Society of Civil Engineers* 97, no. TE1 (February 1971): 133–143; William Issel, "'Land Values, Human Values, and the Preservation of the City's Treasured Appearance': Environmentalism, Politics and the San Francisco Freeway Revolt," *Pacific Historical Review* 68, no. 4 (November 1999): 612–643; Katherine M. Johnson, "Captain Blake versus the Highwaymen: Or, How San Francisco Won the Freeway Revolt," *Journal of Planning History* 8, no. 1 (2009): 56–83.

129. San Francisco Redevelopment Agency, *San Francisco Redevelopment Agency Annual Report, 1959–60* (San Francisco, 1959), ARCV.

130. "City's Front."

131. "City's Front."

132. Frederick M. Wirt, *Power in the City: Decision Making in San Francisco* (Berkeley: University of California Press, 1974), 297; McGovern, *Politics of Downtown Development*; Hartman and Carnochan, *City for Sale*, 10–11.

133. Michael Robert Gorman, *The Empress Is a Man: Stories from the Life of José Sarria* (New York: Harrington Park Press, 1998), 204–206.

CHAPTER 3: HANGING OUT AT THE ENSIGN CAFÉ

1. Strait did not identify these bars by name, to protect them from further policing from "Big Brother up in Sacramento." The descriptions of the bars indicate that Strait was referencing the Ensign Café and the lobby bar in the Edgewater Hotel. The latter had been the second location of Jack's Waterfront Hangout, run by George Bauman, who took over the hotel in April 1962. At the time of the essay, "Original Don's" was a restaurant and after-hours club in the same space that Strait frequently featured in his gay nightlife column.

2. Guy Strait, "What Is a Gay Bar?," *LCE News*, December 21, 1964, 6. For more on the usage and meaning of "gay bar" as a distinctive kind of drinking establishment in the early 1950s, see Nan Alamilla Boyd, *Wide Open Town: A History of Queer San Francisco to 1965* (Berkeley: University of California Press, 2003), 125–127, 209.

3. The Merrimac Building was a two-story commercial building built in 1910 on the southeast corner of the intersection of Market Street and the Embarcadero that was razed in the mid-1960s to make way for a park at the foot of Market Street. When it was built by Santa Cruz real estate investor Frederick A. Hihn, it contained eight storefronts on the first floor and offices on the second that, by the 1930s, had been reconfigured to cater primarily to commuters and travelers arriving and leaving the city through the Ferry Building across the street.

4. The local press only once characterized the Ensign as a "gay bar." "No Dancing: 'Gay' Bar Loses Appeal," *San Francisco Examiner*, September 15, 1960, 15.

5. Bill Plath interviewed by Paul Gabriel, transcript, April 18, 1997, GLBTHS oral history collection, 97–24: GLBT-OHC, GLBTHS, 29; Cynthia Laird, "Gay Pioneer Bill Plath Dies at 77," *Bay Area Reporter*, July 25, 2002, 1, 17.

6. For more on vice containment practices and "open town" policing policies in San Francisco, see Neil Shumsky and Larry M. Springer, "San Francisco Zone of Prostitution, 1880–1934," *Journal of Historical Geography* 7, no. 1 (1981), 71–89; Josh Sides, "Excavating the Postwar Sex District in San Francisco," *Journal of Urban History* 32, no. 3 (2006): 355–379; Boyd, *Wide Open Town*.

7. Michael Brown and Larry Knopp, "Sex, Drink, and State Anxieties: Governance through the Gay Bar," *Social & Cultural Geography* 17, no. 3 (2016): 335–358.

8. Martin Duberman, *Stonewall* (New York: Plume, 1994), 181–187; Marc Stein, *The Stonewall Riots: A Documentary History* (New York: New York University Press, 2019), 48, 123–125.

9. On how the Stonewall Riots became central to commemorating the achievements of the gay liberation movement over other similar events, see Elizabeth A. Armstrong and Suzanna M. Crage, "Movements and Memory: The Making of the Stonewall Myth," *American Sociological Review* 71, no. 5 (2006): 724–751.

10. On the legal history of gay bars, see William N. Eskridge Jr., "Privacy Jurisprudence and the Apartheid of the Closet, 1946–1961," *Florida State University Law Review* 24, no. 4 (1997): 703–839.

11. "Dance Halls Selling Liquor, Police Charge," *San Francisco Chronicle*, April 25, 1915. In 1921, the same "resort," a dance hall known as the Dragon, was raided in a two-night police sweep through the nightlife district. Law enforcement arrested 158 women as part of a systematic effort to shut down the district. "Barbary Coast Raids Continue," *San Francisco Chronicle*, November 11, 1921.

12. "Hotel Afire, Guests Flee in Night Robes," *San Francisco Chronicle*, January 29, 1921; "Owner of Wrecked Distillery Sought," *San Francisco Chronicle*, May 27, 1926.

13. According to the San Francisco Polk business directories, Caldaralla operated a series of legitimate businesses during Prohibition years. Caldaralla was listed as the operator of 533 Pacific in the city directories of 1918 and 1919, while his wife, Claudia, continued to operate the nearby hotel on Columbus Avenue. In 1920 and 1921, he was a furniture dealer at 842 Kearny. After that operation was disrupted by a fire, he represented himself as an automotive repair operator located at 83 Broadway. *Polk City Directory*, various years, ARCV.

14. "Owner of Wrecked Distillery Sought."

15. "Police Hunt S.F. Bootlegging Gangster in Sacramento Street Murder: Fifth Killing in Year Laid to Rum Feud," *San Francisco Chronicle*, December 15, 1928; "Avengers Kill 2 S.F. Gunmen, Carry Feud to Sacramento," *San Francisco Chronicle*, December 20, 1928.

16. As time passed, the details in press reports of the incident changed. Initially, the murder scene was identified as an unnamed basement café at 28 Sacramento. Later, the murder was reported to have occurred at the Broken Drum Café at 18 Sacramento. Federal prosecutors charged John Martini as the proprietor of the Broken Drum Café at 18 Sacramento. Both addresses are associated with the Bay Hotel—which had several first-floor storefronts and a basement with various addresses.

17. "Cafe Murder Clue Found in Rum Raid," *San Francisco Chronicle*, June 19, 1930; "Avengers Kill 2 S.F. Gunmen"; "Police Hunt S.F. Bootlegging Gangster"; "Grand Jury Again Indicts Hogesberg," *San Francisco Chronicle*, April 25, 1929; "Cafe Man Sentenced for Selling Liquor," *San Francisco Chronicle*, August 11, 1929.

18. "Bartender, Shot 5 Times, Still on Critical List," *San Francisco Chronicle*, June 24, 1956; "Bartender Shot in Scrape at Cafe; Owner Gets Bail," *San Francisco Examiner*, June 24, 1956, 20.

19. "$2,000,000 S.F. Property in Padlock Suits: Federal Drys File Abatement Pleas against Twenty Places in City, Apartments and Hotels, Owners and Alleged Operators Listed by U.S.," *San Francisco Chronicle*, September 23, 1931.

20. "Still Charges Naming Grape Dealer Dropped," *San Francisco Chronicle*, March 29, 1932.

21. In 1934, Caldaralla was a sales agent for Golden Gate Beverage Distribution Co., Inc., Eastside Brewery, and the Golden Gate Grape & Juice Company. 1934 *Polk City Directory*.

22. An "Ensign saloon" had stood at Embarcadero and Market Street since 1870, when a seawall fixed the location of the waterfront and created space for both the Embarcadero roadway and the city's first ferry building. After the 1906 earthquake destroyed the seamen's hotel that housed the original Ensign, new property owners built the Merrimac Building on the site, a mixed-use commercial building with ground-floor storefronts

and offices on the second level. By 1914, "The Ensign" was back in business on the same site, operating at 1 Market. "Henry Schwartz Dies at His Alameda Home," *San Francisco Chronicle*, May 3, 1910; 1914 San Francisco City Directory.

23. "California's Greeting to a Favorite Son, Frank N. Belgrano, National Commander-American Legion, Courtesy of M. A. Caldaralla, Distributor, Eastside Beer, Eastside Gingerale," advertisement, *San Francisco Chronicle*, December 22, 1934; 1934 *Polk City Directory*; and "Market Street, near the Ferry Building," July 23, 1934, digitized b/w photographic print, number AAB-6312, San Francisco Historical Photograph Collection, SHC.

24. Beginning with the 1940 directory, he was periodically listed as a "pres," "manager," "bartender," "restwkr," or "liquor dealer" at either 1 Market or the Ensign until 1958.

25. Ensign Café, Inc., "Turkey Sandwiches Are Our Specialty," advertisement, *San Francisco Chronicle*, October 4, 1938.

26. Caldaralla's nephew, Vic Orlando, operated an unnamed second-floor "restaurant" in the Merrimac Building in 1937. Vic's brother Samuel ran the same place—at least on paper—as president of the Ensign Café, Inc in 1945. 1937 *Polk City Directory*; 1945 *Polk City Directory*; Ancestry.com.

27. Caldaralla also used the same incorporated business entity to secure licenses to sell alcoholic beverages at other locations in the area. See "Notice of Intention to Engage in the Sale of Alcoholic Beverages: Evans Tavern, 85 Broadway, M. A., Caldaralla, Sec.-Tr., Ensign Cafe, Inc.," legal notice, *San Francisco Chronicle*, July 25, 1940; "Notice of Intention to Engage in the Sale of Alcoholic Beverages: Jockey Club, 77 Broadway, Ensign Cafe, Inc.," legal notice, *San Francisco Chronicle*, January 20, 1942.

28. The shifting and varied locations of the businesses Caldaralla controlled through the "Ensign Café, Inc." corporation included the "Ensign Liquor Store," the "Ensign Café" tavern, the "Ensign Café" restaurant, the "Ensign Club Room," and the "Ensign Club." He also managed the second-floor nightclub known as the Broken Drum, named after the basement speakeasy he ran in the Bay Hotel in the early 1920s. State agents responsible for regulating alcoholic beverage sales were aware that Caldaralla controlled the corporation in all but a legal sense. In the late 1950s, the supervising state liquor control officer for the San Francisco District of the ABC confirmed that, since 1938, "the [liquor] license at the Ensign Café was never held in the name of [Caldaralla], but held in the name of a corporation [Ensign, Café, Inc.] . . . [and that] 98 percent of the stock belonged to [Caldaralla's] wife and 2 percent to outside people." Cross-examination of defense witness (Thomas Gasland), Reporter's Transcript, Superior Court of San Francisco, Criminal Case 52,628, vol. 1, page 114, February 14, 1957. For this courtroom transcription of a murder trial against Caldaralla, see *People v. Mike Caldaralla*, Criminal Case No. 3,393, First Appellate District, California Court of Appeals Records, CSA.

29. Two real estate appraisals—one from 1958 and another from 1961—described the layout and fixtures of the basement of the Merrimac Building. George H. Thomas, *Appraisal [of] Land and Improvements, Lower Market–Embarcadero Redevelopment Area E, San Francisco, California, as of January 10, 1958 for [the] Redevelopment Agency of the City and County of San Francisco*, box RED-01031, Real Estate Division Records, SFRAR; Eling and Hyman, real estate appraisal, 1961, microfiche, Block 3714, Lot 1, ELM drawer, Acquisition Files, SFRAR.

30. While this is purely speculative, it is in line with the use of "backrooms" in other gay bars. Eling and Hyman.

31. "Notice of Intention to Engage in the Sale of Alcoholic Beverages: Ensign Cafe, 10 Embarcadero, on Sale: Beer and Wine and on Sale: Distilled Spirits, William J. Phillips," legal notice, *San Francisco Chronicle*, December 27, 1941, 18.

32. Three other spots that were raided, the Silver Rail, the Pirates Cave, and the Old Crow, were known to attract gay men both in and out of uniform. "S.F. Taverns: State Food Law Violated, Police Charge," *San Francisco Chronicle*, June 23, 1942; "Taverns: Board of Equalization to Consider 29 Charges of Disorderliness Next Week," *San Francisco Chronicle*, July 30, 1942. See also Allan Bérubé, *Coming Out under Fire: The History of Gay Men and Women in World War Two* (New York: Free Press, 1990), 125.

33. The Ensign was likely a popular gay cruising spot with an active tearoom trade even earlier, given its proximity to both the waterfront strip of sailor hotels and the Ferry terminal with its large flow of daily commuters. The pre–World War II commercial and sexual history of the Ensign, however, is impossible to verify from existing sources. Caldaralla's connection to the Ensign going back to the 1930s makes it a distinct possibility that queer nightlife was tolerated, if not encouraged, in the waterfront bar before the war.

34. Charlotte Coleman interviewed by Paul Gabriel, transcript, 1997, GLBTHS oral history collection, 97–23: GLBT-OHC, GLBTHS, 67.

35. John Nichols, "The Way It Was: Gay Life in World War II America," *QQ Magazine* (previously *Queen's Quarterly for Gay Guys*), July/August 1975, 9, 51.

36. John D'Emilio, *Sexual Politics, Sexual Communities: The Making of a Homosexual Minority in the United States, 1940–1970* (Chicago, IL: University of Chicago Press, 1983); Bérubé, *Coming Out under Fire*; George Chauncey, *Gay New York: Gender, Urban Culture, and the Making of the Gay Male World, 1890–1940* (New York: Basic Books, 1994). See also History Project, comps., *Improper Bostonians: Lesbian and Gay History from the Puritans to Playland* (Boston, MA: Beacon Press, 1998); Tracy Baim, ed., *Out and Proud in Chicago: An Overview of the City's Gay Community* (Chicago, IL: Surrey Books); Genny Beemyn, *A Queer Capital: A History of Gay Life in Washington D.C.* (New York: Routledge, 2014).

37. These "gay worlds" had a long history in major cities and were rooted in the same kinds of commercial, residential, and leisure urban land uses that saw an uptick in sexual and social encounters among men during the war—even as their particular locations shifted. Chauncey, *Gay New York*.

38. Nichols, "Way It Was," 51. While the Ensign was the closest tearoom to the Ferry terminal, the Lankershim Hotel was near the city's main long-distance bus station. The basement bathroom below its lobby coffee shop had a reputation similar to the Ensign's for cruising. In 1948, Gerald Fabian, a retail clerk at Gump's, was arrested there on his lunch hour for soliciting sex. See Gerald Fabian interviewed by Bill "Willie" Walker, transcript, November 30, 1989, and January 23, 1990, GLBTHS oral history collection, 94–22: GLBT-OHC, GLBTHS, 62.

39. Nichols, "Way It Was," 11.

40. Ensign Café, Inc., advertisement, *Police and Peace Officers' Journal of the State of California*, February 1946, 60, ARCV.

41. Ensign Café, Inc., advertisement, *Police and Peace Officers' Journal of the State of California*, October 1946, 69, ARCV; Ensign Café, Inc., advertisement, *Police and Peace Officers' Journal of the State of California*, September 1947, 48, ARCV.

42. Reporter's Transcript, 112–116.

43. Coleman interview, 94.

44. Stuart Loomis interviewed by Randy Alfred, radio broadcast, *The Gay Life*, KSAN

radio, March 15, 1980 (rebroadcast April 25, 1982), Randy Alfred subject files and sound recordings, 1991–24, GLBTHS Audio Collection, ARCV. Roughly fifteen and a half minutes into the broadcast, Loomis called for "a very careful study of remarks of [Herb] Caen" to reconstruct the history of gay life in the city.

45. The composite profile of the ages, occupations, and subsequent business activities of the initial directors came from public records found on Ancestry.com. The serving directors of a new business enterprise registered at 1 Market, John Hallquist, Maurice Maggiora, Silvio Vario, Louis Fiora, and Leo Breschi, created a tax-exempt nonprofit corporation to operate a private club on the premises. Ensign Club, Inc., "Articles of Incorporation," December 27, 1948, Business entity number C0233212, Business Entities Database, California Secretary of State, https://businesssearch.sos.ca.gov/.

46. "40-Story World Trade Center Urged for Ferry Building Site: Substitute Location, Authority Approves Study of $15,000,000 Structure at Foot of Market Street," *San Francisco Chronicle*, January 22, 1948, 1, 12.

47. Caldaralla expanded the "Ensign Café, Inc." by subdividing a large, irregular, L-shaped space on the first floor that prior to partitioning had entrances at both 3 Market and 14 Embarcadero. A comparison of Sanborn maps from 1950 and 1956, as well as city directories, shows that he separated 3 Market from 14 Embarcadero in about 1951. The overall effect was to increase the first-floor footage of the "Ensign Café, Inc." and reorient the commercial spaces he controlled away from Market Street and toward the Embarcadero.

48. "Now Broken Drum, #1 Market Street, Across from the Ferry Building," advertisement, *San Francisco Chronicle*, January 27, 1951, 2.

49. In the 1960s, the famous Stonewall Inn in New York City was known for this practice. See Duberman, *Stonewall*, 183–184.

50. Fabian, interview, 90–92.

51. Fabian, interview, 91.

52. For a social history of slumming as a form of racial and sexual boundary-crossing, see Chad Heap, *Slumming: Sexual and Racial Encounters in American Life, 1885–1940* (Chicago, IL: University of Chicago Press, 2009).

53. Fabian, interview, 91.

54. Eugene R. Carles interviewed by Jim Duggins, transcript, June 17–20, 1994, GLBTHS oral history collection, 94–15: GLBT-OHC, GLBTHS, 91.

55. Carles, interview, 92.

56. Jim Duggins, transcript of self-recorded audio, June 30, 1995, GLBTHS oral history collection, 95–54: GLBT-OHC, GLBTHS, 69.

57. Bob Ross interviewed by Paul Gabriel, transcript, March 13, 1998, GLBTHS oral history collection, 98–12: GLBT-OHC, GLBTHS, 10.

58. Arch J. Wilson interviewed by Jim Duggins, transcript, July 27 to August 10, 1994, GLBTHS oral history collection, 94–23: GLBT-OHC, GLBTHS, 43–44.

59. For a discussion of B-girls and the policing of San Francisco bars in the 1950s, see Amanda Littauer, "The B-Girl Evil: Bureaucracy, Sexuality and the Menace of Barroom Vice in Postwar California," *Journal of the History of Sexuality* 12, no. 2 (2003): 171–204.

60. Orvis Bryant interviewed by Jim Duggins, transcript, August 15, 1994, GLBTHS oral history collection, 94–30: GLBT-OHC, GLBTHS, 10–11.

61. Glen Price interviewed by Jim Duggins, October 23, 1994, GLBTHS oral history collection, 94–43: GLBT-OHC, GLBTHS, 1–2.

62. Larry Howell interviewed by Martin Meeker, December 17, 1998, and January 14, 1999, Go West Migration Project, GLBTHS oral history collection, 98–40: GLBT-OHC, GLBTHS, 56–57.

63. "Notice of Intention to Engage in the Sale of Alcoholic Beverages, Cherryland, 1650 Post, Beer, Wine and Liquor, Tamotsu Kikugowa," legal notice, *San Francisco Chronicle*, August 4, 1938, 23.

64. "California Theatre Club, 1650 Post, Sunday Afternoon Jam Session, Gene Krupa, Guest Artist, Sponsored by the San Francisco Jazz Foundation," advertisement, *San Francisco Chronicle*, March 3, 1946, 16; "Flash! Grand Opening California Theater, Theatrical Breakfast Club, Tonight," advertisement, *San Francisco Chronicle*, July 30, 1948, 4; "3 Liquor Licenses Taken Away," *San Francisco Chronicle*, December 18, 1948, 17; "Two Breakfast Clubs Raided; Four Arrested," *San Francisco Chronicle*, May 14, 1950, 14.

65. Robert, "San Francisco as I See It: Down Memory Lane," *B.A.R.*, September 30, 1976, 19.

66. "State Raids After-Hours Spots Here," *San Francisco Chronicle*, January 25, 1953, 1, 16; "State Board Gets Tough with Bars: 4 Licenses Revoked; 82 Suspended," *San Francisco Chronicle*, March 13, 1953, 1, 12; "8 Arrested in New S.F. Club Raid," *San Francisco Chronicle*, March 29, 1953, 14.

67. Sam Whiting, "Aleshia Brevard (1937–2017) Finocchio's Drag Star, Transgender Pioneer," *San Francisco Chronicle* (online edition, SFchronicle.com), July 25, 2017, C1; Aleshia Brevard Crenshaw interviewed by Susan Stryker with Joanne Meyerowitz, transcript, August 2, 1997, GLBTHS oral history collection, 97–40: GLBT-OHC, GLBTHS, 9–10.

68. Fred D. Prakel, *Appraisal Report of Property Known as 84–98 Market Street*, real estate appraisal, 1961, microfiche, Block 234, Lot 9, ELM drawer, Acquisition Files, SFRAR.

69. For more on the publisher of *Transvestia*, Virginia Prince, who coined the term "transgender" and popularized "hose and heels" clubs across the country, see Richard Ekins and Dave King, eds., *Virginia Prince: Pioneer of Transgendering* (Binghamton, NY: Haworth Medical Press, 2005). For more on Prince's role in the early transgender political movement, see Susan Stryker, *Transgender History* (Berkeley, CA: Seal Press, 2008).

70. "News and Notes: Impersonator Shows," *Transvestia*, 1961.

71. "Ensign Club Presents Mr. Rudi Del Rio, Internationally Famous Female Impersonator, also Mr. Bobbi St. Clair, Pantomimist," advertisement, *San Francisco Chronicle*, March 24, 1962, 14.

72. "S.F. Dancer in 'Cowgirl' Holdup," *San Francisco Chronicle*, January 14, 1961, 4.

73. "State Raids After-Hours Spots Here"; Jackson Doyle, "Liquor Policy Gets Severe: Revocation of 2 S.F. Bar Permits Asked," *San Francisco Chronicle*, March 11, 1953, 4; "State Board Gets Tough."

74. "Two S.F. Bars Are Closed by State, Licenses Revoked (For Good)," *San Francisco Chronicle*, April 3, 1953, 1, 8.

75. "Notice of Intention to Engage in the Sale of Alcoholic Beverages, Ensign Cafe, 10 Embarcadero, on Sale: Beer and Wine and on Sale: Distilled Spirits, William J. Phillips," legal notice, *San Francisco Chronicle*, December 27, 1941, 18.

76. This interpretation of changing commercial and legal arrangements in the Merrimac Building is based on Caldaralla's pattern of doing business, city directory entries, and

legal notices of license changes posted in the city's newspaper of record. See "Notice of Intention to Engage in the Sale of Alcoholic Beverages, Broken Drum, 10 Embarcadero, on Sale: Beer Only, Clarke W. Johnson and Elmer Louis Dense," legal notice, *San Francisco Chronicle*, September 3, 1953, 25; "Notice of Intention to Engage in the Sale of Alcoholic Beverages, Ensign Cafe, 10 Embarcadero, on Sale: Beer and Wine and on Sale: Distilled Spirits, William J. Phillips," legal notice, *San Francisco Chronicle*, December 27, 1941, 18.

77. "Notice of Intention to Engage in the Sale of Alcoholic Beverages, Broken Drum, 10 Embarcadero, on Sale: Beer Only, Clarke W. Johnson and Elmer Louis Dense," legal notice, *San Francisco Chronicle*, September 3, 1953, 25.

78. Ancestry.com.

79. Richard McClure interviewed by Allan Bérubé, transcript, March 12, 1979, World War Two Project, GLBTHS oral history collection, 02–089: GLBT-OHC, GLBTHS, 16.

80. Charles Raudebaugh, "8 After-Hours Clubs Face Crackdown," *San Francisco Chronicle*, July 1, 1954, 1, 8.

81. "Bartender Shot in Scrape at Cafe"; "Bartender, Shot 5 Times."

82. Charles Raudebaugh, "Bar Shooting Case: Ahern Probes Role of 5 Witnesses," *San Francisco Chronicle*, February 20, 1957, 2; Charles Raudebaugh, "Testimony of Five Policemen Studied," *San Francisco Chronicle*, February 21, 1957, 3. See also George Dorsey, *Christopher of San Francisco* (New York: Macmillan, 1962), 106–120.

83. Reporter's Transcript, 121–122.

84. "Ex-Champ Charged with Assault," *San Francisco Chronicle*, January 18, 1959, 3.

85. San Francisco police and state liquor agents considered protection payments they extorted from gay bar owners a "gift." See Christopher Agee, "Gayola: Police Professionalization and the Politics of San Francisco Gay Bars, 1950–1968," *Journal of the History of Sexuality* 15, no. 3 (July 2006): 462–489.

86. Raudebaugh, "8 After-Hours Clubs."

87. "The City's Front Need Not Be So Far, Far Behind," *San Francisco News*, July 24, 1954, 3.

88. Mary Ellen Leary, "Ferry Building Plaza Plan Stirs Row," *San Francisco News*, February 11, 1955, 3.

89. Joint Committee of the Northern California Chapter of the AIA and the California Association of Landscape Architects, *Ferry Building State Park: A Proposal for a State Park at San Francisco's Historic Ferry Building, Submitted to the California State Park Commission* (San Francisco, CA: Citizen's Committee for a Ferry Building State Park, 1955), 14–15.

90. Joint Committee, *Ferry Building State Park*, 13–14.

91. "Liquor Licenses of 2 S.F. Spots Are Threatened," *San Francisco Chronicle*, December 4, 1959, 36.

92. The four late-night spots raided were the Broken Drum, the 181 Club, Coffee Don's, and Jimbo's Bop City. The first three were well-known queer clubs. The fourth was a popular jazz club in the predominantly African American Fillmore District—which, like the Broken Drum, was also slated for urban renewal. The 181 Club and Coffee Don's were in the Tenderloin and considered a drag on the downtown shopping district. "After-Hours Clubs Raided by T-Men," *San Francisco Chronicle*, March 13, 1960, 1–2.

93. "Ex-Boss of After-Hours Club Fined," *San Francisco Chronicle*, May 14, 1960, 18; "Liquor Violation," *San Francisco Chronicle*, May 19, 1960, 28.

94. "Bar Ordered Closed—'Lewd Acts,'" *San Francisco Chronicle*, May 21, 1960, 2.

95. Hal Schaefer, "The Owl Steps Out," *San Francisco Chronicle*, September 3, 1960, 8.

96. "No Dancing."

97. Ensign Club Room, advertisement, *San Francisco Chronicle*, October 8, 1960, 7.

98. Rod Geddes interviewed by Jim Duggins, transcript, June 13, 1995, GLBTHS oral history collection, 94–52: GLBT-OHC, GLBTHS, 127–130.

99. Martin Meeker, "Assembling a Lavender Baedeker," in *Contacts Desired: Gay and Lesbian Communications and Community, 1940s–1970s* (Chicago, IL: University of Chicago Press, 2006), 201–224; Larry Knopp and Michael Brown, "Travel Guides, Urban Spatial Imaginaries and LGBTQ+ Activism: The Case of *Damron* Guides," *Urban Studies* 58, no. 7 (2021): 1380–1396.

100. Geddes, interview, 128.

101. Strait, "What Is a Gay Bar?"

102. "Ensign Club Presents."

103. Ensign Club, advertisement, *San Francisco Chronicle*, November 9, 1963, 29; Ensign Club, "Kandyman and His Trio," advertisement, *San Francisco Chronicle*, December 14, 1963, 30. The Ensign was not included in the first *Lavender Baedeker*, published by Guy Strait in 1963.

CHAPTER 4: A QUEER HISTORY OF 90 MARKET STREET

1. José Sarria, undated announcement, "A Meeting Will Be Held at 90 Market on the 21st of March at 8 PM Sponsored by This Organization," League for Civil Education folder, José Sarria Papers, GLBTHS; José Sarria, undated newsletter, "The League for Civil Education Held a Meeting at 90 Market Last Tuesday [21 March 1961]," League for Civil Education folder, José Sarria Papers, GLBTHS.

2. "Report to the Membership," *LCE News*, April 29, 1963, 1.

3. "Report to the Membership."

4. José Sarria, flyer, "The L.C.E. Story," League for Civil Education folder, José Sarria Papers, GLBTHS.

5. In offering the most complete assessment of the group, she emphasized the LCE's influence on subsequent homophile activism in the city. Nan Alamilla Boyd, *Wide Open Town: A History of Queer San Francisco to 1965* (Berkeley: University of California Press, 2003), 220. See also John D'Emilio, *Sexual Politics, Sexual Communities: The Making of a Homosexual Minority in the United States, 1940–1970* (Chicago, IL: University of Chicago Press, 1983), 188–189; Susan Stryker and Jim Van Buskirk, *Gay by the Bay: A History of Queer Culture in the San Francisco Bay Area* (San Francisco, CA: Chronicle Books, 1996), 43; Martin Meeker, *Contacts Desired: Gay and Lesbian Communications and Community, 1940s–1970s* (Chicago, IL: University of Chicago Press, 2006), 208–209.

6. From the beginning, Guy Strait was the president of the LCE. After an irregular run of news bulletins penned by José Sarria, Strait took over as editor and publisher of the newspaper (identified as the *LCE News* throughout this volume). The name of the publication had minor variations between October 1961 and December 1963, including *The L.C.E. News* and *The News*. After he was ousted as president of the LCE, he renamed the paper the *Citizen's News*, moved to South of Market, and continued publishing the paper for several more years, including as the *Cruise News and World Report*. Boyd, *Wide*

Open Town, 222–223. For more on Strait and his role publishing early gay travel guides, see Meeker, *Contacts Desired*, 208–217. For drafts of Sarria's early news bulletins, often printed on LCE letterhead, see "LCE" folder, Sarria Papers, GBLTHS.

7. Meeker, *Contacts Desired*, 214.

8. Clayton Howard, *The Closet and the Cul de Sac: The Politics of Sexual Privacy in Northern California* (Philadelphia: University of Pennsylvania Press, 2019), 155.

9. Boyd, *Wide Open Town*, 62.

10. Boyd, *Wide Open Town*, 202.

11. Histories of gay community formation point to the 1959 election as a key turning point in opening up public discussions about homosexuality in San Francisco, sparking a widening social movement for civil rights. See John D'Emilio, "The Movement and Subculture Converge: San Francisco during the Early 1960s," in *Sexual Politics*, 176–195; Elizabeth A. Armstrong, "Beginnings: Homosexual Politics and Organizations, 1950–1968," in *Forging Gay Identities: Organizing Sexuality in San Francisco, 1950–1994* (Chicago, IL: University of Chicago Press, 2002), 31–55; Nan Alamilla Boyd, "Queer Cooperation and Resistence: A Gay and Lesbian Movement Comes Together in the 1960s," in *Wide Open Town*, 200–242; Meeker, *Contacts Desired*, 209.

12. For a cultural analysis of Sarria's drag performances as a form of political organizing, see Boyd, *Wide Open Town*, 56–63, 210–212. Sarria, along with Stonewall rioter Sylvia Rivera, were leading queer and trans Latino/a civil rights activists whose legacies have been flattened in popular narratives of their life and political organizing. See Tim Retzloff, "Eliding Trans Latino/a Queer Experience in U.S. LGBT History: José Sarria and Sylvia Rivera Reexamined," *Centro Journal* 19, no. 1 (Spring 2007): 140–161. For Sarria's personal recollections, see Michael Robert Gorman, *The Empress Is a Man: Stories from the Life of José Sarria* (New York: Harrington Park Press, 1998).

13. For more on the 1959 San Francisco mayor's race, see D'Emilio, *Sexual Politics*, 121–122, 182; Boyd, *Wide Open Town*, 204–206; Meeker, *Contacts Desired*, 63–66; Christopher Lowen Agee, *The Streets of San Francisco: Policing and the Creation of a Cosmopolitan Liberal Politics, 1950–72* (Chicago, IL: University of Chicago Press, 2014), 90–91; Howard, *Closet and the Cul de Sac*, 167–168.

14. Herb Caen, "It's News to Me," *San Francisco Chronicle*, June 22, 1958.

15. Herb Caen, "It's News to Me," *San Francisco Chronicle*, January 29, 1959.

16. Jim Kirkman interviewed by Jim Duggins, transcript, May 7, 1995, GLBTHS oral history collection, 95–48: GLBT-OHC, GLBTHS, 29; Arch J. Wilson interviewed by Jim Duggins, transcript, July 27 to August 10, 1994, GLBTHS oral history collection, 94–23: GLBT-OHC, GLBTHS, 38.

17. Hal Schaefer, "The Owl Steps Out," *San Francisco Chronicle*, September 3, 1960, 8; "3 Days Celebration—Oct 3–4–5 Grand Opening, Jack's Waterfront Hangout, under New Ownership of George Bauman and Mary E. Brown, Featuring Waterfront Entertainment after Dark, Open from 11 A.M. to 2 A.M., 111 Embarcadero, Showtime 10 P.M., 11:30, 1:00," advertisement, *San Francisco Chronicle*, September 28, 1957, 7.

18. "Gayola Hangout Handout Told," *San Francisco News–Call Bulletin*, July 30, 1960, SBC, SFPD, SHC.

19. "Cops Target of Gay Bars, Says Atty." *San Francisco Call-Bulletin*, July 25, 1960, 1, 4, SBC, SFPD, SHC.

20. Peter Hann, "Woman Tells of Paying Cops at Bar," *San Francisco Chronicle*, July 31, 1960.

21. Ernest Lenn, "Cop Out, More Face Bribe Quiz," *San Francisco Examiner*, May 7, 1960.

22. "2nd Barman Tells of Gayola Payoff," *San Francisco News–Call Bulletin*, August 1, 1960. According to the paper, both "had a following among the gay crowd."

23. Bob Ross interviewed by Paul Gabriel, transcript, March 13, 1994, GLBTHS oral history collection, 98–12: GLBT-OHC, GLBTHS, 50.

24. "The Castaways Presents Maurice & La Mont [*sic*], Cass & Bea," advertisement, *San Francisco Chronicle*, August 8, 1959, 8; "The Castaways Presents Maurice & La Monte, Record Pantomine, Cass & Bea," advertisement, *San Francisco Chronicle*, August 15, 1959, 10. See also Maurice & La Monte Papers, Collection 2008–003, ONE National Gay and Lesbian Archives, Los Angeles, CA.

25. Ernest Lenn, "Suspended Cop Accused Again," *San Francisco Examiner*, May 19, 1960, 1; "Bar Bribery Story Tagged 'Lieutenant,'" *San Francisco Chronicle*, June 7, 1960, 1; "Jury Report Links 2 More Cops to Payoff," *San Francisco Examiner*, June 7, 1960, 3.

26. "Another Bar Involved, We Paid Off Cops, 2 More Testify," *San Francisco Examiner*, August 2, 1960.

27. "Jury Report Links 2 More Cops to Payoff."

28. "6 Bars Charged in Homosexual Drive," *San Francisco Chronicle*, May 6, 1959.

29. "Statement from Wolden: How Freeways Will Cut City Tax Rolls," *San Francisco Chronicle*, July 20, 1956, newspaper clippings files, SFRAR; Dick Nolan, "Wolden Joins Freeway Row, Estimates Property Tax Loss," *San Francisco Examiner*, July 20, 1956, newspaper clippings files, SFRAR.

30. George Dorsey, *Christopher of San Francisco* (New York: Macmillan, 1962), 166–174, 179–187.

31. Ron Johnson, "Wolden in 'Smear' Campaign, Charges Spiked by Christopher," *San Francisco Examiner*, October 8, 1959.

32. Brandhove's involvement in politically motivated smear campaigns stretched back to the beginning of the Red and Lavender Scares, rooted in the interrelated anti-communist and anti-homosexual drive to reorganize the maritime labor force. In the 1940s, Brandhove joined anti-communist raids on waterfront union membership rolls after a California Senate investigative subcommittee of "un-American" political activity tagged him as a suspected homosexual. Campaign flyer, "William Patrick Brandhove, Christopher Desperate!," 1959, Wolden Campaign Libel Suit folder, Don Lucas Papers, box 7, folder 7, GLBTHS.

33. Founded in Los Angeles in 1951, the Mattachine Society was organized in a hierarchical network of closed cells that grew into a network of local chapters in different cities. During the Lavender and Red Scares, the California chapters split the organization along ideological and regional lines. By the late 1950s, San Francisco had emerged as the national headquarters, with an active publishing program. The Daughters of Bilitis, a national organization with local chapters across the country, was founded in San Francisco in 1955. Meeker, *Contacts Desired*, 52–53, 77–80.

34. Wolden Campaign Libel Suit folder, 1959, Don Lucas Papers, Box 7, Folders 6 and 7: San Francisco.

35. Russell Wolden, speech transcript, "The Truth about the Mayor's 'Clean' City, a Radio Speech by Russell L. Wolden, October 7, 1959, 6:45 PM, KNBC," Wolden Campaign Libel Suit folder, Don Lucas Papers, box 7, folder 7, GLBTHS.

36. Wolden, "Truth about the Mayor's 'Clean' City."

37. "Gay Bar Manager Tells of Payoffs," *San Francisco Chronicle*, August 2, 1960, 3.

38. "2nd Barman Tells of Gayola Payoff."

39. Ernest Lenn, "Jury Hears 2 Tell of Bar Payoff," *San Francisco Examiner*, May 24, 1960, 1, 14.

40. "Bar Owners Met during Bribe Probe," *San Francisco Chronicle*, July 27, 1960, 1, 8.

41. "Land Sold for Ramps of Freeway," *San Francisco News*, June 15, 1959, NCF, SFRAR.

42. George Draper, "Sex in Mayoral Campaign, Vice Charges by Wolden Backfire—Hoax Revealed, Praise of Mayor's Policy on Deviates Engineered by Ex–Police Informer," *San Francisco Chronicle*, October 9, 1959; "Unforgiveable Slur on San Francisco, an Editorial," *San Francisco Examiner*, October 9, 1959; "Wolden Aide Admits: Vice Story Planned, Smear Try Backfires in Mayor Race," *San Francisco News–Call Bulletin*, October 9, 1959; "City Insulted by Wolden, Cahill Says, Chief Assails Campaign Shift to Smear Tactics," *San Francisco Examiner*, October 11, 1959.

43. Meeker, *Contacts Desired*, 59–63.

44. D'Emilio, *Sexual Politics*, 121–122; Boyd, *Wide Open Town*, 204–206; Meeker, *Contacts Desired*, 63–66; Howard, *Closet and the Cul de Sac*, 167.

45. "Smooth Sailing on Waterfront," *San Francisco News–Call Bulletin*, November 19, 1959, 2; "Crash Basis for Gateway Project," *San Francisco News–Call Bulletin*, December 17, 1959, 18; Joseph Bodovitz, "1st Golden Gateway Bldg. Sale," *San Francisco Examiner*, December 30, 1959, 1.

46. The *San Francisco Chronicle* coined the term "gayola" in its coverage of the trial beginning in July 1960. "Cops at Bribery Trial: Jury Picked in 'Gayola' Scandals," *San Francisco Chronicle*, July 23, 1960. For coverage of the grand jury investigation and subsequent trials, see Scrapbook Collection (SBC), San Francisco Police Department Records, SFH61, SHC.

47. For a careful analysis of the impact of this scandal on gay community formation, queer publics, gay migration, and police reform, respectively, see John D'Emilio, "Gay Politics, Gay Community: San Francisco's Experience," in *Making Trouble: Essays on Gay History, Politics, and the University*, ed. John D'Emilio (New York: Routledge, 1981), 74–95; Boyd, *Wide Open Town*; Meeker, *Contacts Desired*; Agee, *Streets of San Francisco*.

48. The 1959 Castaways flyer reads: "A special surprise, A rather SPECIAL show, TUESDAY NITE, Nov. 10 [1959] starring MAURICE as BANKHEAD and LA MONTE as DAVIS and . . . GUEST STAR, JOSE of Black Cat fame as COUNTESS BATNICK." Box 16, folder 9, José Sarria Papers (1996–01), GLBTHS.

49. Sarria identified a parody of *Madame Butterfly* with McGinnis at the Black Cat in March 1958 as his first "camp opera." Gorman, *Empress Is a Man*, 210. The oldest dated manuscript in a collection of roughly seventy scripts in the José Sarria Papers is a photocopied version of "Die Lustige Witwe (The Merry Widow)," which he performed for the first time on August 31, 1958. Box 18, folder 1, José Sarria Papers, GLBTHS.

50. In an oral history with San Francisco gay community historian Paul Gabriel, Sarria related that he moved his operas to Castaways because Stoumen refused to allow Black Cat employees to unionize. In another oral history, Sarria recalled that he and McGinnis performed at 90 Market for about month, drawing business away from the Black Cat, until Stoumen lured them back with better wages. See Hector Navarro interviewed by Paul Gabriel, transcript, June 17, 1998, GLBTHS oral history collection, 98–30: GLBT-OHC, GLBTHS, 11–12; Gorman, *Empress Is a Man*, 126.

51. William Thomas, "State Liquor Chief in Reply, S.F. 'Pervert' Charge Denied," *San Francisco Chronicle*, November 10, 1959, 3.

52. "Department of Alcoholic Beverage Control, Northern Coastal Area, Staff Meeting, May 19, 1960, Hearing Room, San Francisco," General Correspondence-Meetings-Area Staff-Northern Coastal (1959–1961) folder, F3718:226, ABCB Records, CSA.

53. Jack Morrison, "Wide Censorship? Court Ruling Held Threat to All Bars," *San Francisco Chronicle*, January 12, 1960. For more on the Vallerga case, see Boyd, *Wide Open Town*, 181–183, 206–207; William N. Eskridge Jr., "Privacy Jurisprudence and the Apartheid of the Closet, 1946–1961," *Florida State University Law Review* 24, no. 4 (1997): 802–803.

54. ABC Director to District Supervisors, memomorandum, "Schedule of Penalties," December 29, 1959, "Subject Files Schedule of Penalties (1958–1960)" folder, F3718:362, ABC Records, CSA.

55. Baron Muller, "State Crackdown on Homosexual Haunts," *San Francisco Call–News*, November 6, 1959.

56. "Homosexual Acts in Bars Alleged," *San Francisco Chronicle*, January 6, 1960. "Veteran Sergeant: Cop Charged with Extortion of Bar in S.F.," *San Francisco Chronicle*, February 27, 1960.

57. Stoumen made his involvement in exposing the payoff system a core argument in his legal fight to keep his liquor license at the Black Cat. In his opening brief appealing a lower court decision to revoke his operating permit, he asserted that he first learned about the payoffs at Castaways and Jack's Waterfront Hangout in February 1960 when the operators of Castaways offered to sell him the business. See pp. 75n3 and 78n2 in Sol M. Stoumen, "Appellant's Opening Brief in the District Court of Appeals, State of California, First Appellate District, Division Two, Sol M. Stoumen, Petitioner and Appellant, vs. Russell S. Munro, Director of the Department of Alcoholic Beverage Control, et al. Respondents," District Court of Appeals Docket no. 1 Civil no. 20,310. Filed on June 1962, the 444-page opening brief was prepared by Stoumen's attorneys, Morris and Juliet Lowenthal, and printed by the Pan-Graphic Press—the printing company operated by the Mattachine Society, Inc. For more on the preparation of this and other briefs in the case, see "Black Cat Appeal Case Goes to the Supreme Court," *Mattachine Newsletter* (San Francisco), October 1963, 4–6.

58. Stoumen described in detail his communications with ABC administrators about protection payments and his participation in an unsuccessful sting operation. He tried to stop the revocation of his liquor licenses, in part, by establishing that state liquor authorities had agreed to show him leniency for his assistance in exposing payola practices by ABC agents. Stoumen, "Appellant's Opening Brief," 68–94 and 167–98.

59. Stoumen, "Appellant's Opening Brief," 168.

60. Stoumen, "Appellant's Opening Brief," 169.

61. Stoumen, "Appellant's Opening Brief," 75n3.

62. Stoumen, "Appellant's Opening Brief," 167.

63. Tullis's participation in the sting operation, as an alternative to Stoumen, was likely an intentional decision on the ABC's part to keep the Black Cat revocation proceedings and Stoumen's connection to 90 Market out of the headlines. Ernest Lenn, "2 S.F. Cops Accused in Bar Bribes, Homosexual Taverns in City Facing Crackdowns," *San Francisco Examiner*, May 4, 1960; "2 S.F. Cops Investigated in Bribery," *San Francisco Chronicle*, May 4, 1960; "3 Cops Quizzed in Bar-Payoff Probe," *San Francisco News–Call Bulletin*, May 4, 1960.

64. "More Cops Involved in Bar Payoff," *San Francisco Examiner*, May 5, 1960; "4 Cops Now Linked to Bar Bribe Case," *San Francisco Chronicle*, May 5, 1960, 1; "Police Sergeant Quizzed in Probe of Bar Payoffs," *San Francisco News–Call Bulletin*, May 5, 1960.

65. "Jury Report Links 2 More Cops to Payoff."

66. "Bar Owners Met during Bribe Probe."

67. "Jury Report Links 2 More Cops to Payoff"; "'Higher-Up' Police in Payoff Probed," *San Francisco News–Call Bulletin*, June 7, 1960; "Bar Bribery Story Tagged 'Lieutenant.'"

68. A third trial resulted in a one-year jail term for a police sergeant who pled guilty to taking payments from the Handlebar, a gay bar on Nob Hill. The scandal was the first to break, in February. "4 Others Freed; 2 May Be, Cop Who Took a Bribe to Serve Year in Jail," *San Francisco Examiner*, September 8, 1960, 6.

69. "Wives Defend 'Gay Bar' Cops," *San Francisco Chronicle*, August 16, 1960; "Police Payoff Trial: L.A. Cop Testifies on S.F. Bar Bribes," *San Francisco Examiner*, August 17, 1960; "'Gayola' Trial Nearly Ready for the Jury," *San Francisco News–Call Bulletin*, August 17, 1960.

70. "All 4 Cops Acquitted in 'Gayola' Trial," *San Francisco Chronicle*, August 20, 1960; "4 Cops Not Guilty in Bar Trial, Jury Takes 3 Ballots," *San Francisco Examiner*, August 20, 1960.

71. "'Immunity' in Bar Bribe?," *San Francisco Examiner*, September 14, 1960, SBC, SFPD, SHC; "Bar Scandal Echoes: Ousted State Aide Asks New License," *San Francisco Examiner*, September 30, 1960.

72. "State Liquor Agent Fined in Bribe Case," *San Francisco News–Call Bulletin*, November 17, 1960.

73. Boyd makes a similar point about media coverage during the gayola trials. Boyd, *Wide Open Town*, 209.

74. One of the earliest references to a "gay bar" in San Francisco newspapers appeared during a 1953 extortion trial involving a magazine publisher. A bartender identified the Silver Rail, where he worked, as a "gay bar" before explaining to the court that it was "a bar where homosexuals go." Jack Loughner, "Tarantino Named Shakedown Artist, Manager of 'Gay' Bar Testifies Defendant Made Personal Call," *San Francisco News*, October 14, 1953, 13. Research for this book indicated that the term "hangout for homosexuals" was commonly used in the 1940s. Coinciding with a major revision of state liquor laws in 1955, however, the statutory term "resort for perverts" became the favored term. During the trials, "homosexual bar" or "gay bar" soon supplanted these older terms. During this shift, it was often used with quotation marks. See, for example "Cops, State Crack Down on 'Gay Bars,'" *San Francisco News–Call Bulletin*, May 6, 1960, 33.

75. D'Emilio, *Sexual Politics*, 183–184.

76. Christopher Agee, "Gayola: Police Professionalization and the Politics of San Francisco Gay Bars, 1950–1968," *Journal of the History of Sexuality* 15, no. 3 (July 2006): 462–489; Christopher Agee, "Gayola: Gay-Bar Politics, Police Corruption, and Sexual Pluralism," in *The Streets of San Francisco: Policing and the Creation of a Modern Liberal Politics, 1950–72* (Chicago, IL: University of Chicago Press, 2014), 73–108.

77. Ernest Lenn, "Income Tax Quiz on Bar Bribe Cops, More Payoffs Hunted, Mayor Orders Full Probe," *San Francisco Examiner*, May 12, 1960, 1.

78. "U.S. Tax Lien against 'Protected' Bar," *San Francisco Chronicle*, June 15, 1960; "Bar Payoff Figure Faces $19,773 Lien," *San Francisco Examiner*, June 14, 1960.

79. Stoumen, "Appellant's Opening Brief," 172–174.

80. Fred D. Prakel, *Appraisal Report of Property Known as 84–98 Market Street*, real estate appraisal, 1961, microfiche, Block 234, Lot 9, ELM drawer, Acquisition Files, SFRAR, 22. Stoumen's testimony in the Black Cat revocation proceedings corroborates

the $39,000 lease liability that he took on with the purchase of the Castaways liquor license for $10,000. Stoumen, "Appellant's Opening Brief," 173.

81. Vend-a-Teria, Inc., "Articles of Incorporation," July 1, 1960, domestic stock corporation number C0399031, Business Entity Records, California Secretary of State, businesssearch.sos.ca.gov.

82. José Sarria interviewed by Paul Gabriel, transcript, September 15, 1996, GLBTHS oral history collection, 02–174: GLBT-OHC, GLBTHS, 1.

83. "Grand Opening, December 1, Talk of the Town and Hi-Lo's," advertisement, *San Francisco Chronicle*, November 30, 1960, 11.

84. The mix of receipts, operating budgets, menu plans, and payroll calculations that Sarria saved in relation to the Vend-a-Teria corporation underscores this assessment. José Sarria Papers.

85. See entries in 1960 and 1960 Polk City Directories for San Francisco.

86. Stoumen, "Appellant's Opening Brief," 78.

87. Stoumen, "Appellant's Opening Brief," 168–170, 174.

88. The details of Stoumen's cooperation come from his testimony in the ABC's revocation proceedings against the Black Cat. Based on his own characterization, he assisted the ABC by convincing other gay bar operators to produce evidence and to testify in court against corrupt officials. During the investigation and trials, Feinberg likely used the promise of leniency to keep Stoumen from testifying about the extent of the payoff racket. In exchange for Stoumen's silence, Feinberg paused license revocations proceedings against the Black Cat and approved Stoumen's expansion of his bar business to 90 Market. Once the trial was over, however, Stoumen lost his leverage. Feinberg denied making any assurance of leniency and moved swiftly to put Stoumen out of business.

89. Stoumen, "Appellant's Opening Brief," 178.

90. Stoumen, "Appellant's Opening Brief," 179–183.

91. See Stoumen, "Appellant's Opening Brief," 185. The text of the letter is reproduced in a footnote.

92. "Black Cat Loses Fight for License," *San Francisco Chronicle*, March 31, 1961.

93. Kirkman, interview, 29.

94. Gorman, *Empress Is a Man*, 204–206.

95. José Sarria, interview, 97–28, 16–17.

96. Boyd, *Wide Open Town*, 210.

97. Queens and trans people of color bore the brunt of harassment, discrimination, and anti-queer violence and were also crucial leaders in efforts to push back. Members of the Gay and Lesbian Historical Society of Northern California, "MTF Transgender Activism in the Tenderloin and Beyond, 1966–1975," in *GLQ: A Journal of Lesbian and Gay Studies* 4, no. 2 (1998): 349–372; Susan Stryker, *Screaming Queens: The Riot at Compton's Cafeteria* (San Francisco, CA: Frameline, 2005), documentary film; Lillian Faderman and Stuart Timmons, *Gay L.A.: A History of Sexual Outlaws, Power Politics, and Lipstick Lesbians* (New York: Basic Books, 2006), 1–2; Retzloff, "Eliding Trans Latino/a Queer Experience"; Jessi Gan, "'Still at the Back of the Bus': Sylvia Rivera's Struggle," *CENTRO* 19, no. 1 (Spring 2007): 140–161.

98. Gorman, *Empress Is a Man*, 162.

99. Declaration of Candidacy, General Municipal Election, November 7, 1961, SF Board of Supervisors Campaign Materials folder, José Sarria Papers.

100. Declaration of Candidacy.

101. For more on the social and cultural significance of Sarria's 1961 campaign, see D'Emilio, *Sexual Politics*, 187–188; Boyd, *Wide Open Town*, 210–212. See also Gorman, *Empress Is a Man*, 203–207.

102. Boyd, *Wide Open Town*, 211; Meeker, *Contacts Desired*, 171.

103. Paul Welch and B. Eppridge, "Homosexuality in America," *Life*, June 26, 1964. By collaborating on the development of this article, homophile leaders and bar operators in San Francisco generated positive publicity about homosexuality and the city's vibrant, relatively open sexual subcultures. See Martin Meeker, "Publicizing the Gay *Life*," in *Contacts Desired*, 151–195.

104. S.F. Board of Supervisors Campaign Materials, 1961, in José Sarria Papers.

105. S.F. Board of Supervisors Campaign Materials.

106. "Final S.F. Vote," *San Francisco Chronicle*, November 8, 1961, 1.

107. "Special Halloween Party and other upcoming events in November at 90 Market," advertisement, *LCE News*, October 16, 1961, 2.

108. The city's two homophile groups, the Mattachine Society and DOB, had grown to national prominence during the 1950s. Each group had built a national network of activists, challenged state-sanctioned discrimination against homosexuals, and promoted positive societal attitudes toward homosexuality. The center of gravity in the Mattachine's network of local chapters shifted from Los Angeles to San Francisco in the mid-1950s, due in large part to its publishing program. For more on the San Francisco Mattachine chapter, see Meeker, *Contacts Desired*, 44, 52–53.

109. José Sarria, interview, 5. During the gayola investigation, police lawyers tried to characterize this circle of bar operators as a nefarious group of conspirators. In 1962, they formed the Tavern Guild, incorporating as a business association of gay bar interests. "Bar Owners Met during Bribe Probe."

110. José Sarria, interview, 5.

111. The San Francisco Mattachine Society always engaged in local issues, acting behind a "mask of respectability" as a social service agency offering job referrals, legal aid, and housing assistance to new arrivals to the city. Martin Meeker, "Behind the Mask of Respectability: Reconsidering the Mattachine Society and Male Homophile Practice, 1950s and 1960s," *Journal of the History of Sexuality* 10, no. 1 (January 2001): 77–116.

112. Elizabeth A. Armstrong, *Forging Gay Identities: Organizing Sexuality in San Francisco, 1950–1994* (Chicago, IL: University of Chicago Press, 2002), 52.

CHAPTER 5: THE DEMISE OF THE QUEER WATERFRONT

1. "No State Shall Deny Equal Protection," *LCE News*, December 10, 1962, 7.

2. On the normative assumptions of whiteness in postwar planning, see George Lipsitz, "The Possessive Investment in Whiteness: Racialized Social Democracy and the 'White' Problem in American Studies," *American Quarterly* 47, no. 3 (1995): 369–387; Eric Avila, *Popular Culture in the Age of White Flight: Fear and Fantasy in Suburban Los Angeles* (Berkeley: University of California Press, 2004). For more on heteronormative and cisgender-biased assumptions of postwar planning, see Michael Frisch, "Planning as a Heterosexist Project," *Journal of Planning Education and Research* 21, no. 3 (2002): 254–266; Dolores Hayden, "What Would a Non-Sexist City Look Like?," in *The City Reader*, ed. Richard T. LeGates and Frederic Stout (New York: Routledge, 2003), 448–463.

3. For more on the racial logics and long-term impacts of urban renewal on communities of color, see June Manning Thomas, *Redevelopment and Race: Planning a Finer City in*

Postwar Detroit (Baltimore, MD: Johns Hopkins University Press, 1997); Mindy Thompson Fullilove, *Root Shock: How Tearing Up City Neighborhoods Hurts America, and What We Can Do about It* (New York: New Village Press, 2004; repr., 2016). For more on how urban renewal sharpened and hardened patterns of residential racial segregation to the detriment of communities of color, see J. F. Bauman, *Public Housing, Race, and Renewal: Urban Planning in Philadelphia, 1920–1974* (Philadelphia, PA: Temple University Press, 1987); Douglas S. Massey and Nancy A. Denton, *American Apartheid: Segregation and the Making of the Underclass* (Cambridge, MA: Harvard University Press, 1993); Arnold R. Hirsch, *Making the Second Ghetto: Race and Housing in Chicago* (Chicago, IL: University of Chicago Press, 1998); Colin Gordon, *Mapping Decline: St. Louis and the Fate of the American City* (Philadelphia: University of Pennsylvania Press, 2008); N. D. B. Connolly, *A World More Concrete: Real Estate and the Remaking of Jim Crow South Florida* (Chicago, IL: University of Chicago Press, 2014).

4. Paul Groth, *Living Downtown: The History of Residential Hotels in the United States* (Berkeley: University of California Press, 1994); Josh Sides, "Excavating the Postwar Sex District in San Francisco," *Journal of Urban History* 32, no. 3 (2006): 355–379; Clayton Howard, *The Closet and the Cul de Sac: The Politics of Sexual Privacy in Northern California* (Philadelphia: University of Pennsylvania Press, 2019).

5. History Project, comps., *Improper Bostonians: Lesbian and Gay History from the Puritans to Playland* (Boston, MA: Beacon Press, 1998), 190–193; Bryant Simon, "New York Avenue: The Life and Death of Gay Spaces in Atlantic City, New Jersey, 1920–1990," *Journal of Urban History* 28, no. 3 (2002): 300–327; Julie A. Podmore, "Queering Discourses of Urban Decline: Representing Montréal's Post–World War II 'Lower Main,'" *Historical Geography*, no. 43 (January 2015): 57–83; Timothy Stewart-Winter, *Queer Clout: Chicago and the Rise of Gay Politics* (Philadelphia: University of Pennsylvania Press, 2016), 57–58; Elsa Devienne, "Urban Renewal by the Sea: Reinventing the Beach for the Suburban Age in Postwar Los Angeles," *Journal of Urban History* 45, no. 1 (2019): 99–125; Clayton Howard, "Policing and Redeveloping the Queer City," in *Closet and the Cul de Sac*, 177. The same heteronormative logics targeted sexual subcultures in the neoliberal city. See Samuel R. Delany, *Times Square Red, Times Square Blue* (New York: New York University Press, 1999).

6. John D'Emilio, *Sexual Politics, Sexual Communities: The Making of a Homosexual Minority in the United States, 1940–1970* (Chicago, IL: University of Chicago Press, 1983); William N. Eskridge Jr., "Privacy Jurisprudence and the Apartheid of the Closet, 1946–1961," *Florida State University Law Review* 24, no. 4 (1997): 703–839; Nan Alamilla Boyd, *Wide Open Town: A History of Queer San Francisco to 1965* (Berkeley: University of California Press, 2003); Christopher Lowen Agee, *The Streets of San Francisco: Policing and the Creation of a Cosmopolitan Liberal Politics, 1950–72* (Chicago, IL: University of Chicago Press, 2014). See also Michael Robert Gorman, *The Empress Is a Man: Stories from the Life of José Sarria* (New York: Harrington Park Press, 1998).

7. Referring to the lesbian bar the Front, historian Clayton Howard noted that the Golden Gateway project "directly forced out at least one gay bar." Two much larger, predominantly male gay bars, the Ensign Café and 90 Market, were also within the project area boundaries, subjecting them to the same SFRA condemnation proceedings. Of them, 90 Market had close social and operational connections to nearby gay bars just outside the Golden Gateway—specifically, the Black Cat, the Headhunters, the Barrel House, the Crossroads, and Jack's. Howard, *Closet and the Cul de Sac*, 177.

8. For more on the history of the LCE, see Boyd, *Wide Open Town*, 221–223.

9. Chester Hartman and Sarah Carnochan, *City for Sale: The Transformation of San*

Francisco, rev. and updated ed. (Berkeley: University of California Press, 2002); Jasper Rubin, *A Negotiated Landscape: The Transformation of San Francisco's Waterfront since 1950* (Chicago, IL: Center for American Places at Columbia College, 2011); Alison Isenberg, *Designing San Francisco: Art, Land, and Urban Renewal in the City by the Bay* (Princeton, NJ: Princeton University Press, 2017).

10. Guy Strait, "Exodus," *LCE News*, April 30, 1962, 1.

11. "Land Sold for Ramps of Freeway," *San Francisco News*, June 15, 1959, NCF, SFRAR.

12. Guy Strait, "Jack's," *LCE News*, May 28, 1962, 1.

13. Strait explained the nickname to out-of-town readers of the *News*: "There is a group of the finest coiffeurs in all of San Francisco who have for years congregated along the Embarcadero at Jack's. They are all close friends when they do not have their knives out and travel very muchly in a pack. So we have a name for them 'Hairburners' or in an abbreviation '"H"Burners.'" Guy Strait, "Roving Report," *LCE News*, November 26, 1962, 6.

14. Mr. Candy Lee may have been the drag name of "Mr. Carlyle," who protested the warning sign posted at the Broken Drum by the SFRA's site manager when the Agency took possession of the building. The same week of the first encounter of the operators of the queer nightlife complex with the Agency, the LCE announced Lee's was moving "right soon."

15. "News and Notes: Impersonator Shows," *Transvestia*, 1961.

16. The *News* announced that "Candy Lee has finally opened a Coffee Shop at 14 Embarcadero. No show, just Coffee and Candy." Strait, "Roving Report," *LCE News*, April 30, 1962, 2.

17. Guy Strait, "Roving Report," *LCE News*, May 14, 1962.

18. Guy Strait, "Roving Report," *LCE News*, June 25, 1962.

19. "3-Alarm Fire at Ferry Building," *San Francisco Chronicle*, July 14, 1962, 1, 8; "Transient Cigarette? Ferry Bldg. Fire Damage $100,000," *San Francisco Chronicle*, July 15, 1962, 2.

20. Guy Strait, "Roving Report," *LCE News*, July 9, 1962, 7.

21. Sol M. Stoumen, "Appellant's Opening Brief in the District Court of Appeals, State of California, First Appellate District, Division Two, Sol M. Stoumen, Petitioner and Appellant, vs. Russell S. Munro, Director of the Department of Alcoholic Beverage Control, et al. Respondents," District Court of Appeals Docket no. 1 Civil no. 20,310, 172–174.

22. "Eddie's 90," *LCE News*, June 11, 1962, 3.

23. "Grandest," *LCE News*, July 23, 1962, 3.

24. "Don's to Close," *LCE News*, December 25, 1961, 6.

25. "Don's to Give L.C.E. Benefit," *LCE News*, December 11, 1961, 4; "Don's to Close."

26. "Police Raiders Arrest Ten in S.F. Night Club," *San Francisco Chronicle*, July 20, 1936; "Singers Jailed 30 Days for Naughty Tunes," *San Francisco Chronicle*, July 22, 1936.

27. "Michelle," *LCE News*, November 26, 1962, 1, 3; "Michelle International," *LCE News*, December 10, 1962, 5.

28. League for Civil Education, "Michelle International Souvenir Program, L.C.E. War Chest Benefit, November 19th and 20th [1962]," booklet, box 99, folder 9, José Sarria Papers, GLBTHS.

29. Guy Strait, "Michelle International," *LCE News*, December 10, 1962, 5.

30. Guy Strait, "Testimony about Jack's," *LCE News*, January 7, 1963, 5–8.

31. Guy Strait, "ABC & LCE," *LCE News*, December 10, 1962, 4; Guy Strait, "What Happened at Jack's?," *LCE News*, December 10, 1962, 1.

32. "What Happened at Jack's?"

33. Guy Strait, "Two Bottles Missing," *LCE News*, January 7, 1963, 1.

34. Guy Strait, "Roving Report," *LCE News*, January 21, 1963, 8.

35. Public mourning over the loss of important bars and social spaces has been a recurring aspect of queer life in San Francisco. See Damon Scott and Trushna Parekh, "Three Recent Scenes in the Affective Life of Gentrification in San Francisco's Polk Gulch," *Cultural Geographies* 28, no. 2 (2021): 301–317. See also Paris Poirier, *Last Call at Maud's* (U.S.A., 1993), documentary film, http://lastcallatmauds.com/.

36. Guy Strait, "Around the City," *LCE News*, April 15, 1963, 5–6.

37. Guy Strait, "Barrel House," *LCE News*, September 17, 1962, 9.

38. "Barrel House," 2.

39. The one-story building was on the same block as the Ensign Café but just outside of the urban renewal project boundaries. Although the San Francisco Parks Department purchased the parcel in early 1964, ostensibly for the park, it was never incorporated into the final design. The site was redeveloped by a boutique hotel chain in the 1990s. Conveyance of Deed (Block 3714, Lot 8), Dennis Carlin and Elizabeth J. Carlin to CCSF, February 3, 1964, digitized microfilm, Book A773, page 486–487, SFOAR.

40. Forty policemen descended on the Chukker Club in the early morning hours. They made fifty-four arrests after checking the identity of two hundred patrons. Lara, "heavily made-up [and] dressed in tight slacks and a V-necked sweater" was among the "23 mascaraed men" arrested for impersonating women. "Biggest Raid on San Francisco Homosexuals," *San Francisco Chronicle*, February 14, 1965, 3; "Night Club Raid Case Continued," *San Francisco Chronicle*, February 16, 1965, 2.

41. "Bunny Breckenridge Arrested as Vagrant," *San Francisco Chronicle*, May 16, 1955, 3; "Vagrancy Charges against 'Bunny' Breckenridge Dropped," *San Francisco Chronicle*, May 27, 1955, 3; "$1818 Tax Lien Filed on Breckenridge," *San Francisco Chronicle*, May 28, 1955, 3.

42. "Owner Says Paper Doll 'Gay' Joint," *San Francisco Chronicle*, December 4, 1956, 22.

43. Guy Strait, "Roving Report," *LCE News*, January 21, 1963, 8; "Notice of Intention to Engage in the Sale of Alcoholic Beverages, 109 Steuart, on Sale Beer and Wine Public Premises, Dorothy Tsunoda and Satoshi Tsunoda," legal notice, *San Francisco Chronicle*, April 26, 1963, 27.

44. "Michelle International," *LCE News*, December 10, 1962, 5.

45. Jack's Waterfront, "Exodus to the Tool Box," advertisement, *LCE News*, January 7, 1963, 7. For more on the Tool Box, see Meeker, "Publicizing the Gay *Life*." For more about the history of the gay male leather community in San Francisco, see Gayle Rubin, "The Valley of the Kings: Leathermen in San Francisco, 1960–1990" (dissertation, University of Michigan, 1994); Gayle Rubin, "Elegy for the Valley of the Kings: AIDS and the Leather Community in San Francisco, 1981–1996," in *In Changing Times: Gay Men and Lesbians Encounter HIV/AIDS*, ed. Martin P. Levine, Peter M. Nardi, and John H. Gagnon (Chicago, IL: University of Chicago Press, 1997), 101–144; Gayle Rubin, "The Miracle Mile: South of Market and Gay Male Leather, 1962–1997," in *Reclaiming San Francisco: History, Politics, Culture*, ed. James Brook, Chris Carlsson, and Nancy Peters (San Francisco, CA: City Lights Books, 1998), 247–272; Gayle Rubin, "Sites,

Settlements, and Urban Sex: Archaeology and the Study of Gay Leathermen in San Francisco, 1955–1995," in *Archaeologies of Sexualities*, ed. Robert A. Schmidt and Barbara L. Voss (New York: Routledge, 2000), 62–88; Gayle Rubin, "Studying Sexual Subcultures: The Ethnography of Gay Communities in Urban North America," in *Out in Theory: The Emergence of Lesbian and Gay Anthropology*, ed. Ellen Lewin and William Leap (Urbana: University of Illinois Press, 2002), 17–68.

46. "New Restaurant," *LCE News*, February 20, 1963, 5; "Original Don's," *LCE News*, April 1, 1963, 2.

47. "Don's to Close."

48. From the beginning, Guy Strait was the president of the LCE and the editor of its newsletter. The name of the publication had minor variations between October 1961 and December 1963, including *The LCE News* and *The News*. After he was ousted as president of the LCE, he renamed the paper the *Citizen's News*, moved to South of Market, and continued publishing the paper for several more years, including as the *Cruise News and World Report*. Boyd, *Wide Open Town*, 222–223. For more on Strait and his role publishing early gay travel guides, see Meeker, *Contacts Desired*, 208–217.

49. "Two Clubs Raided: Cops Find Some Tainted Teapots," *San Francisco Chronicle*, November 22, 1965, 2; "Correction," *San Francisco Chronicle*, November 23, 1965, 3. Police raided and shut down the reconstituted after-hours club in November 1965. The tavern reopened soon afterward as a gentlemen's club with topless waitresses. "Early Hour Topless Show Raid," *San Francisco Chronicle*, January 23, 1966, 3.

50. "Roving Report," *LCE News*, October 26, 1964, 12.

51. Kennedy Hotel, "Business for Sale [226 Embarcadero]," classified advertisement, *San Francisco Chronicle*, March 20, 1965, 22.

52. In October 1903, Frederick A. Hihn and his wife transferred the deed to a newly registered corporation, the Coast Realty Co. "Real Estate Transfers," *San Francisco Chronicle*, October 31, 1903, 8. The Hihns' property manager maintained detailed records of the collection and distribution of rental income from the building, as well as building-related correspondence with banking and government officials. Coast Realty Records (Cowell Estate), Noel Patterson Papers, Collection number: MS 218, University of California Special Collections, Santa Cruz.

53. The officers of Coast Realty elected to dissolve the domestic stock corporation on March 16, 1962. The dissolution was made final later that year in late November. Coast Realty Co., "Certificate of Winding Up and Dissolution," November 11, 1962, Business entity number C0038699, Business Entities Database, California Secretary of State, https://businesssearch.sos.ca.gov/.

54. George H. Thomas, "Appraisal [of] Land and Improvements, Lower Market–Embarcadero Redevelopment Area E, San Francisco, California, as of January 10, 1958 for [the] Redevelopment Agency of the City and County of San Francisco," box RED-01031, Real Estate Division Records, SFRAR; Eling and Hyman, real estate appraisal, 1961, microfiche, Block 3714, Lot 1, ELM drawer, Acquisition Files, SFRAR.

55. Letter from Herman to McCabe, Re: Request for Concurrence in Value, February 14, 1962, "Land and/or Improved Property: Acquisition (#3)" folder, box PAA-00253, Project Administration Division Records, SFRAR.

56. Rental Statement from Coast Realty to SFRA, December 14, 1961, microfilm, Block 3714 Lot 1, ELM drawer, Acquisition Files, SFRAR.

57. G. L. Carter to tenants (Arthur Flores, #3 Market; Jordan and Wooley, 20–22

Embarcadero; Foster and Klein, billboard; Giles Cordero, #1 Market), letter (multiple), April 11, 1962, microfilm, Block 3714, Lot 1, ELM drawer, Acquisition Files, SFRAR.

58. In a memo to her boss, Wortman recounted her conversation with Carter. She documented her interactions with the unauthorized tenants to rationalize her subsequent actions to try to bar them from entering the building. Virginia Wortman to Julia B. Smith, "RE: 10–24 Embarcadero & 1–3 Market Street Acq. No. 3135," memorandum, May 1, 1962, "Property Management—Area E to SEPT/64" folder, box CSR-483, Community Services Division Records, SFRAR.

59. Wortman to Smith, May 1, 1962, memo.

60. The case was referenced in an eviction order request sent from the agency counsel to the sheriff. Morley Goldberg to Sheriff Carberry, "RE: *Redevelopment Agency v. Mike Caldaralla, Opal Waldo, Broken Drum, et al.* Municipal Court No. *472,548*," letter, August 16, 1962, "Property: Mangement, GG, 12–1–59 to 1–14–63" folder, box CRA-137, Central Records and Archives Division, SFRAR.

61. In a July 26 internal memorandum, Smith laid out the specific terms of the agreement for Wortman to oversee. Julia B. Smith to Virginia Wortman, "RE: The Broken Drum—10 Embarcadero Street," letter, July 26, 1962, "Area E—General" folder, box CSR-483, Community Services Division Records, SFRAR.

62. Goldberg to Carberry, August 16, 1962, letter.

63. The first mention of the Broken Drum in the *San Francisco Chronicle* appeared in the nightlife column and a paid advertisement in January 1951, announcing that the newly renamed nightclub would feature the Gene Ortet Orchestra along with Italian dinners, dancing, and cocktails. "Now Broken Drum, #1 Market Street, across from the Ferry Building," advertisement, *San Francisco Chronicle*, January 27, 1951, 2.

64. "Queer Bars and Other Establishments in the San Francisco Bay Area," compiled by Willie Walker, Eric Garber, et al. (Microsoft Word files, last modified 1997), personal collection of the author; "San Francisco LGBTQ Businesses and Organizations," compiled by Elizabeth A. Armstrong (Microsoft Access file, last modified 2001), personal collection of the author; "An Interrupted Breakfast," *San Francisco Chronicle*, May 2, 1963, 44; "Vice Squad Raids 'Club'—47 Arrests," *San Francisco Chronicle*, September 13, 1964, 1A; "Cops Smell Brewing Trouble," *San Francisco Chronicle*, October 4, 1964, 6.

65. "Vice Squad Raids 'Club.'"

66. "Cops Smell Brewing Trouble."

67. Virginia Wortman to Julia B. Smith, "RE: Block 3714," letter, November 9, 1962, "Property Management—Area E to SEPT/64" folder, box CSR-483, Community Services Division Records, SFRAR.

68. "Market Street Cafe, No. 1 Market Street [Block 3714/1, Aquisition No. 3135, Acquisition Date 4/11/1962, Rental Agreement Effective 4/11/62]," annotated accounting register, July 21, 1965 (final entry), microfilm, ELM drawer, Tenant Ledger Records, SFRAR.

69. Hal Schaefer, "The Owl Steps Out," *San Francisco Chronicle*, September 3, 1960, 8.

70. "Ensign Club, Kandyman and His Trio," advertisement, *San Francisco Chronicle*, December 14, 1963, 30.

71. "The New Ensign Club," advertisement, *San Francisco Examiner*, February 29, 1964, 11.

72. "Market Street Cafe."

73. "Relocation Claim, Business, Move from 1 Market St. to Market Street Café [Mr.

M.A. Caldaralla, $3,879.32]," accounting form, August 3, 1965, "Receipts for Outgoing Checks, #24227 (April 1, 1964) to #24620 (Sept 30, 1965)" folder, box FAA-289, Finance and Administration Division Records, SFRAR.

74. "Structure Control Card [Acquisition Number 3135; Block 3714, Lot 1; 1–24 Embarcadero, 1 Market; acquired 11 April 1962]," inventory record of occupants, October 3, 1966 (final entry), microfilm, ELM drawer, Structure Files, SFRAR.

75. Myers to Herman, letter, December 28, 1961, "Golden Gateway, General, (Not Pertaining to Specific Properties)" folder, box RED-1037, Real Estate Division Records, SFRAR.

76. Fred D. Prakel, *Appraisal Report of Property Known As 84–98 Market Street*, real estate appraisal, 1961, microfiche, Block 234, Lot 9, ELM drawer, Acquisition Files, SFRAR.

77. Emerson to Davis, letter, March 2, 1962, "Land and/or Improved Property: Acquisition, 1/2/1962–1/29/65" folder, box PAA-253, Project Administration Division Records, SFRAR.

78. Final Order of Condemnation, *San Francisco Redevelopment Agency v. Ernest Blumenthal, Sadie Blumenthal; Sol M. Stoumen; Cooper Brothers, Inc, a Corporation; M. Jean Pinkerton and Lilian M. Kazerle; City and County of San Francisco; Peter Garajotis and Anna Garajotis; Charles Stavros; Bryan L. Ray; Norman L. Tullis; Charles Liangos; Southern Pacific Company; Plant Bros. Corp*," Case No. 528,383 (Parcel 1), San Francisco Superior Court, November 1, 1963, court filing, File L45128, Book A678, Page 521–522, Record of Deeds, SFOAR.

79. The appraisal identified Charles Liangos and Charles Stavros as the sublessors— the former was a merchant seaman and the latter was the manager of the Talk of the Town nightclub.

80. Obsolescence was a common rationalization for redevelopment during the mid-century turn to modern urban design practices. Daniel M. Abramson, *Obsolescence: An Architectural History* (Chicago, IL: University of Chicago Press, 2016).

81. Prakel, *Appraisal Report*, 21, emphasis added.

82. The auction was held to pay off part of the back taxes owed by the previous owners who operated Castaways. The terms of the sale were detailed in Stoumen's legal filings related to the revocation of his Black Cat liquor license. Stoumen, "Appellant's Opening Brief," 172–174.

83. Justin Herman to McCabe, "Re: Request for Concurrence in Value," letter, February 14, 1962, "Land and/or Improved Property: Acquisition, 1/2/1962–1/29/65" folder, box PAA-253, Project Administration Division Records, SFRAR.

84. While property records and internal correspondence in the SFRA's files repeatedly refer to the condemnation proceedings and final settlement, the details of the negotiated sale are inferred rather than based on a complete record of the case. According to municipal court staff, eminent domain legal cases associated with Area E were either misfiled or destroyed. The names of the litigants are preserved in real estate transfer records maintained by the assessor's office. Final Order of Condemnation, November 1, 1963.

85. George W. Emerson to Henry F. Davis, regarding Golden Gateway Acquisitions, letter, March 2, 1962, box RED-1037, Real Estate Division Records, SFRAR.

86. Final Order of Condemnation, November 1, 1963.

87. Justin Herman to McCabe, "Re: Request for Reconcurrence in Value," letter,

October 10, 1963, "Land and/or Improved Property: Acquisition, Eminent Domain Proceedings" folder, box PAA-253, Project Adminstration Records, SFRAR.

88. Stoumen, "Appellant's Opening Brief," 172–174.

89. The agency's property log included an annotation that "Sol Stoumen" had "MOVED PRIOR TO ACQ." on October 31, 1963, the day before they took possession of the building. Stoumen's commercial space was immediately re-rented to "August Casazza" in an "ON-SITE MOVE." "Structure Control Card [Block 234, Lot 9; 86–98 Market Street; Acquired November 1, 1963; Acquisition Number: 3160]," inventory record of occupants, November 1, 1963, microfilm, ELM drawer, Structure Files, SFRAR.

90. B. Levy and Sons, "Auction Sale, the Last Resort, Modern Fully Equipped Restaurant-Bar-Night Club, 90 Market," classified advertisement, *San Francisco Chronicle*, November 10, 1963, 34.

91. Smith to Maheras, memorandum, June 22, 1964, "Property Management—Area E to Sept 64" folder, box CSR-483, Community Services Division, SFRAR.

92. "New Appeal: The Black Cat Clings to Life," *San Francisco Chronicle*, October 30, 1963, 27.

93. Only Stoumen was among the three directors of Vend-a-Teria in the articles of incorporation. In the 1961 *Polk City Directory*, Sarria was listed as the vice president and Stoumen as treasurer of "Vend-a-Teria, Inc.," located at 90 Market. Vend-a-Teria, Inc., "Articles of Incorporation," July 1, 1960, domestic stock corporation number C0399031, Business Entity Records, California Secretary of State, businesssearch.sos.ca.gov.

94. "Notice of Intention to Engage in the Sale of Alcoholic Beverages, 90 Market, On Sale General, Vend-a-Teria, Inc.," legal notice, *San Francisco Chronicle*, December 10, 1961, Classified 1.

95. "State Refuses Liquor Permits to 2 S.F. Men," *San Francisco Chronicle*, May 11, 1962, 2.

96. "Eddie's 90."

97. Julia B. Smith to Florence T. Conlin, letter with attachment, "Report of Business Concerns Which Have Ceased Operations, Embarcadero–Lower Market E-1, for Six-Month Period Ending June 30, 1964," September 3, 1964, "Area E—Business" folder, box CSR-483, Community Services Division Records, SFRAR.

98. "Report of Business Concerns."

99. None of the coverage of the last call at the Black Cat mentioned Stoumen's simultaneous eviction from 90 Market. See Ernest Lenn, "Hexed . . . So Black Cat Goes on Milk at Last," *San Francisco Examiner*, November 1, 1963, 37; Bill Yarlan, "Black Cat's Dry Halloween," *San Francisco Chronicle*, November 1, 1963, 2; Merla Zellerbach, "Rights, Liberties and the Black Cat Closing," *San Francisco Chronicle*, October 30, 1963, 41. In addition, social and legal histories of the Black Cat emphasize his earlier legal victories while overlooking his economic ruination by state officials. See D'Emilio, *Sexual Politics*; Eskridge, "Privacy Jurisprudence"; Elizabeth A. Armstrong, *Forging Gay Identities: Organizing Sexuality in San Francisco, 1950–1994* (Chicago, IL: University of Chicago Press, 2002); Boyd, *Wide Open Town*; Josh Sides, *Erotic City: Sexual Revolutions and the Making of Modern San Francisco* (New York: Oxford University Press, 2009).

100. "No State Shall Deny Equal Protection."

CONCLUSION: DESTRUCTION AND CREATION

1. The growth of so-called homosexual hangouts for men on the waterfront was mirrored by the growth of lesbian nightspots in North Beach, which Nan Boyd characterized as the city's "first lesbian neighborhood." Between 1949 and 1959, there were always a cluster of four to seven venues frequented by lesbians in the area. For more on the Front, see Nan Alamilla Boyd, *Wide Open Town: A History of Queer San Francisco to 1965* (Berkeley: University of California Press, 2003), 69, 83, and 156–157.

2. In a reassessment of Herman's legacy, this open space was renamed the Embarcadero Plaza in 2017. Adam Brinklow, "City Officially Removes Justin Herman's Name from Plaza," *SF Curbed*, November 17, 2017.

3. Boyd, *Wide Open Town*, 220.

4. Guy Strait, "The Citizens News," *LCE News*, January 13, 1964, 1.

5. Guy Strait, "L.C.E. Is No More," *LCE News*, June 8, 1964, 1; "Campaign by Society for Individual Rights," *Town Talk*, no. 1, July 1964, 2.

6. John D'Emilio, *Sexual Politics, Sexual Communities: The Making of a Homosexual Minority in the United States, 1940–1970* (Chicago, IL: University of Chicago Press, 1983); Susan Stryker and Jim Van Buskirk, *Gay by the Bay: A History of Queer Culture in the San Francisco Bay Area* (San Francisco, CA: Chronicle Books, 1996); Boyd, *Wide Open Town*; Armstrong, *Forging Gay Identities*. Drag was an important and contested aspect of SIR's fundraisers and variety shows. See Betty Luther Hillman, "'The Most Profoundly Revolutionary Act a Homosexual Can Engage In': Drag and the Politics of Gender Presentation in the San Francisco Gay Liberation Movement, 1964–1972," *Journal of the History of Sexuality* 20, no. 1 (January 2011): 153–181.

7. In much larger cities, as early as the 1890s, drag balls were an institutionalized cultural tradition that fostered a sense of collective identity, drew thousands of participants, and knitted together extensive gay social networks. Chauncey, *Gay New York*, 291–298; History Project, *Improper Bostonians*, 110; Heap, *Slumming*, 264–266, 271; Beemyn, *Queer Capital*, 29–32.

8. Meeker, *Contacts Desired*.

9. "Year's Finest Drags Head Up Gala Parade as Beaux Arts Ball," *Town Talk*, December 1965, 1–2.

10. "Manhattanization" became shorthand for the seemingly rapid expansion of the central business district during the skyscraper boom in the 1970s. Its use also carried an implicit critique of the political influence of corporate elites over urban planning and development decisions. The seeds for this scramble to build upward were planted in the 1950s when the leading business and banking executives spearheaded waterfront redevelopment. For more on the cultural politics of height restrictions on new downtown construction projects, see Isenberg, *Designing San Francisco*.

11. A number of popular documentary films, biographies, and television series center on the Castro in the 1970s and the political rise and death of Harvey Milk as the period of greatest historical significance in the growth of San Francisco's LGBTQ community. Randy Shilts, *The Mayor of Castro Street: The Life and Times of Harvey Milk* (New York: St. Martin's Press, 1982); Rob Epstein, *The Times of Harvey Milk* (San Francisco, CA: TC Films, Inc., 1984), documentary film; Gus Van Sant, *Milk* (Los Angeles, CA: Focus Features, 2008), feature film; Lillian Faderman, *Harvey Milk: His Lives and Deaths* (New Haven, CT: Yale University Press, 2018). See also Timothy Stewart-Winter, "The Castro: Origins to the Age of Milk," *Gay and Lesbian Review Worldwide*, no. 16 (2009): 12–15.

12. Bérubé, *My Desire for History*, 306. See also Timmons, *Trouble with Harry Hay*, 68–69; Susan Stryker and Jim Van Buskirk, *Gay by the Bay*, 26.

13. Guy Strait, "Why?," *LCE News*, October 29, 1962, 7.

14. Guy Strait was the first to speculate in print about the size of the gay consumer market in San Francisco. The *San Francisco Chronicle* recognized the significance of the city's "pink economy" in 1977. "A Market Survey . . . 12,000,000 Homosexuals Will Earn and Spend $49,236,000,000 This Year," *LCE News*, August 31, 1964; "Pink Economy," *San Francisco Examiner–Chronicle*, August 28, 1977, 1–2. For a critical assessment of marketing to gay consumers, see Alexandra Chasin, *Selling Out: The Gay and Lesbian Movement Goes to Market* (New York: Palgrave, 2000).

15. Damon Scott, "Before the Creative Class: Blight, Gay Movies, and Family Values in the Haight-Ashbury Neighborhood, 1964," *Journal of Planning History* 14, no. 2 (May 2015): 149–173.

16. Manuel Castells, "Cultural Identity, Sexual Liberation and Urban Structure: The Gay Community in San Francisco," in *The City and the Grassroots: A Cross-Cultural Theory of Urban Social Movements* (Berkeley: University of California Press, 1983), 138–172; Brian Godfrey, *Neighborhoods in Transition: The Making of San Francisco's Ethnic and NonConformist Communities* (Berkeley: University of California Press, 1988). The Haight-Ashbury briefly rivaled the Castro in significance as a proto-gayborhood before the youth counterculture movement of the mid-1960s transformed the character of the neighborhood. See Scott, "Before the Creative Class."

17. For an excellent analysis of the emergence of "queer clout" at the municipal scale in Chicago, see Timothy Stewart-Winter, *Queer Clout: Chicago and the Rise of Gay Politics* (Philadelphia: University of Pennsylvania Press, 2016).

18. Castells, "Cultural Identity, Sexual Liberation and Urban Structure"; Godfrey, *Neighborhoods in Transition*.

19. Richard Florida, *The Rise of the Creative Class: And How It Is Transforming Work, Leisure, Community and Everyday Life* (New York: Basic Books, 2002); Charles J. Brinks, "Gayborhoods: Intersections of Land Use Regulation, Sexual Minorities, and the Creative Class," *Georgia State University Law Review* 28, no. 3 (March 2013): 789–850.

20. Dereka Rushbrook, "Cities, Queer Space, and the Cosmopolitan Tourist," *GLQ: A Journal of Lesbian and Gay Studies* 8, nos. 1–2 (2002): 183–206; Greggor Mattson, "Bar Districts as Subcultural Amenities," *City, Culture and Society*, no. 6 (2015): 1–8.

21. On the demise of gayborhoods, see Amin Ghaziani, *There Goes the Gayborhood* (Princeton, NJ: Princeton University Press, 2015); Petra L. Doan and Harrison Higgins, "The Demise of Queer Space? Resurgent Gentrification and the Assimilation of LGBT Neighborhoods," *Journal of Planning Education and Research* 31, no. 1 (2011): 6–25; Damon Scott and Trushna Parekh, "Three Recent Scenes in the Affective Life of Gentrification in San Francisco's Polk Gulch," *Cultural Geographies* 28, no. 2 (2021): 301–317. On critiques of gay urban entrepreneurialism, see Christina B. Hanhardt, *Safe Space: Gay Neighborhood History and the Politics of Violence* (Durham, NC: Duke University Press, 2013); Juan Miguel Kanai and Kai Kenttamaa Squires, "Remaking South Beach: Metropolitan Gayborhood Trajectories under Homonormative Entrepreneurialism," *Urban Geography* 36, no. 3 (2015): 385–402; Kai Kenttamaa Squires, "Rethinking the Homonormative? Lesbian and Hispanic Pride Events and the Uneven Geographies of Commoditized Identities," *Social and Cultural Geography* 20, no. 3 (2017): 1–20; Rae Rosenberg, "The Whiteness of Gay Urban Belonging: Criminalizing LGBTQ Youth of Color in Queer Spaces of Care," *Urban Geography* 38, no. 1 (2017): 137–148.

INDEX